Readings in AMERICAN RELIGIO[...]

The Latino/a American Religious Experience

Edited by

JON R. STONE ■ CARLOS R. PIAR

— with Contributions by Gabriel Estrada

Kendall Hunt
publishing company

For our former CSULB graduate students both here and abroad, including:

Angelo Anagnos, Jordan Almanzar, Henry Bens, Angela Chompff, Jennifer Dick, Antonio Dillehunt, Jonathan Friedmann, Javier Gonzalez, Heather Mackey, Jennifer Hoddevik, Shafiel Karim, Daniel Majors, Ethan Quillen, Jessica Rehman, Vanessa Soriano, Timothy Vizthum, Nikolas Xiros, and Suzette Zazueta.

Cover image @ Shutterstock, Inc.
Black madonna. Catholic icon in street. Cartagena de Indias. Colombia.

www.kendallhunt.com
Send all inquiries to:
4050 Westmark Drive
Dubuque, IA 52004-1840

ISBN 978-1-4652-7750-3

Printed in the United States of America

Contents

Chapter Sources for Volume Three: The Latino/a American Religious Experience

Chapter 1: Aurelio M. Espinosa and J. Manuel Espinosa (ed.). *The Folklore of Spain in the American Southwest: Traditional Spanish Folk Literature in Northern New Mexico and Southern Colorado*. Norman: University of Oklahoma Press, 1985.

Chapters 2–5: Cleofas M. Jaramillo. *Shadows of the Past*. Santa Fe: Seton Village Press, 1941.

Chapter 6: Donald Demarest and Coley Taylor. *The Dark Virgin: The Book of Our Lady of Guadalupe*. New York: Coley Taylor, Inc., 1956.

Chapter 7: Jeanette Rodriguez. *Our Lady of Guadalupe: Faith and Empowerment among Mexican-American Women*. Austin: University of Texas Press, 1994.

Chapter 8: Richard Rodriguez. *Days of Obligation: An Argument with My Mexican Father*. New York: Penguin Books, 1992.

Chapter 9: César E. Chavez. "The Mexican American and the Church." *Voices: Readings from El Grito*. Berkeley: Quinto Sol Publications, 1971.

Chapter 10: Rudolfo A. Anaya and Francisco A. Lomelí (eds.). *Aztlán: Essays on the Chicano Homeland*. Albuquerque: University of New Mexico Press, 1991.

Chapter 11: Arlene M. Sánchez Walsh. *Latino Pentecostal Identity: Evangelical Faith, Self, and Society*. New York: Columbia University Press, 2003.

Chapters 12–14: Cristina Garcia. *Dreaming in Cuban*. New York: Ballantine Books, 1992.

Chapter 15: Judith Ortiz Cofer. *Silent Dancing: A Partial Remembrance of a Puerto Rican Childhood*. Houston: Arte Publico Press, 1990.

Chapter 16: Timothy Matovina (ed.). *Beyond Borders: Writings of Virgilio Elizondo and Friends*. Maryknoll, NY: Orbis Books, 2000.

Chapter 17: Ada María Isasi-Díaz. *En La Lucha/In the Struggle: A Hispanic Women's Liberation Theology*. Minneapolis: Fortress Press, 1993.

Other Volumes in This Series

THE NATIVE AMERICAN RELIGIOUS EXPERIENCE

1. Coyote Steals the Sun and Moon [Zuni]
2. Coyote, Ikotome, and the Rock [White River Sioux]
3. Coyote and the Origin of Death [Caddo]
4. The Creation of Man (Second Version) [Morris Edward Opler; Jacarilla Apache]
5. The Creation and Loss of the Sun and Moon [Morris Edward Opler; Jacarilla Apache]
6. The Emergence [Morris Edward Opler; Jacarilla Apache]
7. Creation and the Origin of Corn [Frank Hamilton Cushing; Zuni]
8. Red Sky's Scrolls and Origin Lore [Selwyn Dewdney; Southern Ojibway]
9. Other Origin Tales and Scrolls [Selwyn Dewdney; Southern Ojibway]
10. The Creation of the Ocean [Kashaya Pomo; told by Herman James]
11. The Creation of People and the Ocean [Kashaya Pomo; told by Herman James]
12. The Flood [Kashaya Pomo; told by Essie Parrish]
13. Doctoring [Kashaya Pomo; told by Essie Parrish]
14. Indians in Overalls [Jaime de Angulo]
15. Selections from Black Elk Speaks [as told through John G. Neihardt]
16. Fall 1917-Spring 1918: Manigou-geezis Strong Spirit Sun [Louise Erdrich]
17. Ceremony [Leslie Marmon Silko]
18. Missionaries and the Religious Vacuum [Vine Deloria, Jr.]
19. The Presence of Isanaklesh: The Apache Female Deity and the Pollen Path [Inés Talamantez]
20. The Native American Church of Jesus Christ [Emerson Spider, Sr.]
21. Who Can Sit at the Lord's Table?: The Experience of Indigenous Peoples [Rosemary McCombs Maxey]
22. The Native Church: A Search for an Authentic Spirituality [Laverne Jacobs]

THE AFRICAN AMERICAN RELIGIOUS EXPERIENCE

1. A Thanksgiving Sermon 1808 [Absalom Jones]
2. A Dialogue between a Virginian and an African Minister [Daniel Coker]
3. Ethiopian Manifesto [Robert Alexander Young]
4. Appeal to the Colored Citizens of the World [David Walker]
5. Narrative of the Life of Frederick Douglass, an American Slave [Frederick Douglass]
6. Religious Experience and Journal of Mrs. Jarena Lee [Jarena Lee]

7. Religious Instruction [Peter Randolph]
8. Pastor and Flock [from *Lay My Burden Down*]
9. Count the Stars through the Cracks [from *Lay My Burden Down*]
10. The Chanted Sermon [Albert J. Raboteau]
11. Of the Faith of the Fathers [W.E.B. DuBois]
12. Religion in the South [W.E.B. DuBois]
13. Jesus Christ in Georgia [W.E.B. DuBois]
14. Letter from a Birmingham Jail [Martin Luther King, Jr.]
15. Black Man's History [Malcolm X]
16. God in Black Theology [James H. Cone]
17. Womanist Theology: Black Women's Experience as a Source for Doing Theology, with Special Reference to Christology [Jacquelyn Grant]
18. Women in Islam [Aminah Beverly McCloud]

THE ASIAN AMERICAN RELIGIOUS EXPERIENCE

1. The Chinese in San Francisco 1893 [Rev. Ng Poon Chew]
2. The Chinese in America 1909 [Sui Sin Far]
3. Chinese Traditional Religion in North America and Hawaii [L. Eve Armentrout Ma]
4. Preserving Chinese Culture [Fenggang Yang]
5. The Kitchen God's Wife [Amy Tan]
6. Chinese Temples in Honolulu [Sau Chun Wong]
7. Changing Rituals in Chinese Births and Deaths [Anonymous]
8. Some Filipino Traits Transplanted [Roman Cariaga]
9. Japanese Buddhist Temples in Honolulu [Toshimi Yoshinaga]
10. The Second Generation Japanese and the Hongwanji [Katsumi Onishi]
11. Religion in Our Family [Masako Tanaka]
12. Mother and Her Temple [Margaret Miki]
13. My Family [Dorothy Yashima]
14. Religion and Resistance in America's Concentration Camps [Gary Y. Okihiro]
15. The Role of the Buddhist Church in the Ethnic Adjustment of the Japanese American [Tetsuden Kashima]
16. The Adjustments of a Young Immigrant [Joyce Nishimura]
17. Reflections: An Autobiographical Sketch [Andrea Sakai]
18. Selections from *Talking to High Monks in the Snow* [Lydia Yuri Minatoya]
19. North Vietnamese Buddhist Nun [from *Hearts of Sorrow*]
20. Look Tha: A Former Buddhist Monk [Usha Welaratna]

Foreword to the Second Edition of This Series

The need to renew the copyright permissions for most of the selections in these volumes now occasions the publication of a second edition. Since first appearing in 2007, the selections in these four volumes of *Readings in American Religious Diversity* (originally published as one hefty quarto tome!) have been changed only modestly. For the 2012 revised edition, I added only two or three readings to volumes one and two, ones that helped fill-in some of the instructional gaps in the course material. For this second edition, my colleagues and I have decided (reluctantly) to drop several readings—ones that our faculty have tended not to assign—in favor of several newer and fresher ones. In terms of size and substance, the most noticeable additions have been to volumes three and four, which our faculty had deemed a little lean as compared to the first two volumes. And for this second edition, as lead editor, I have also taken this opportunity to revise and reword a number of the discussion questions in each volume as well as update the introductory material in each volume to reflect the changes in content (with thanks to Professors Gabriel Estrada, Bradley Hawkins, Sophia Pandya, and Carlos Piar for contributing helpful suggestions).

As I had noted in the *Foreword* to the first edition, it has become a commonplace to speak of America as a religiously diverse nation. From its origins, dating well before the arrival of European settlers, the American continent contained a great variety of peoples, languages, cultures, and religions. The native groups that came to inhabit this vast and varied landscape were of many types, from pueblo dwelling peoples, to those living in the woodlands, prairie, mountain, and coastal regions. During the period of European exploration and colonial expansion, the Americas soon became home to English, French, Spanish, Portuguese, and Dutch settlers. And, after slavery was introduced into the New World, peoples of African tribal descent added their own cultural and religious expressions to the growing ethnic and racial diversity of the land. From many peoples there emerged one nation; from one nation there arose many religious voices. The long conversation—and the spirited debate—over issues of religious and cultural identity continues to this day. What does it mean to be an American? What does it mean to be part of an ethnic or racial community in America? In what ways have religious beliefs and traditional cultural practices informed that meaning or helped shape that identity?

This four volume series presents to students of American religion a collection of primary source materials that serves to illustrate the ethno-racial dimensions of religion in America beyond its usual European expressions. The ethno-racial religious communities featured in this anthology broadly include Native American, African American, Asian American, and an array of Latino communities. A unique feature of these volumes is that their readings come from within the communities themselves, rather than from researchers commenting upon these communities from the outside. Thus, students reading these selections will come to hear the voices and sense the deeply-felt passion, sorrow, frustration, hope, and joy of those individuals who were or are still part of the important conversations at the heart of these four ethno-racial communities' ongoing dialogue and debates within themselves.

More specifically, these primary-source readings are designed to complement the religious and historical materials of the junior-level interdisciplinary capstone course, "American Religious Diversity," which is offered every semester at California State University, Long Beach. For this course, students are required to read religious literature produced by women and men from within at least two of the four ethno-racial communities mentioned above. While many of our instructors have assigned works of fiction, such as short stories or novels, we have found that fictional literature has tended to give our students only a partial picture of the religious dimensions of these communities and the difficulties these groups have experienced in their attempts to maintain traditional beliefs and practices in a predominantly "white" and Protestant culture. Thus, in addition to works of fiction, we have discovered that the diversity of religious experience as well as responses within these communities to discrimination, social dislocation, and loss of traditional culture could be "read" within other types of literature. These include folktales, sermons, letters, speeches, essays and addresses, autobiographies, oral histories and published interviews, as well as immigrant community histories, scholarly treatises, and ethnic denominational self-studies.

Because the course for which these four volumes are designed is taught each semester by six full-time and part-time faculty members, I do not believe that it has been my role as the lead editor of this anthology to instruct my colleagues in how to use these selections. At the same time, because not all of our faculty work in the area of American religious and ethnic history, I think that it is important to provide an outline of themes that emerge from these readings, especially as they show both the similarities as well as the differences in the experiences of these four ethno-racial communities and the role that religious ideas and practices have played within each. Thus, despite differences in their origins and in their specific experiences in the Americas, the literature produced by persons within the Native American, African American, Asian American, and Latino communities share a number of themes which students and instructors can reflect upon and fruitfully discuss. Among these themes is the experience of being outsiders, of social and cultural "otherness," of dislocation, disorientation, and uprootedness, of turning to tradition and relying upon religious institutions for personal and communal support, of the importance of family and the larger ethnic community, of striving after the recognition of basic rights and of one's human worth, of resistance to assimilation and the struggle against the secularizing influences of modern social and cultural life, and of drawing upon mythologies to strengthen one's sense of self and importance in the world.

Owing to all these difficulties and other personal and social experiences, it is profound that, beyond everything, people have continually turned to religion and to traditional expressions of community life for their remedy. There are those who seek succor within a religious community as well as those who adapt themselves and their traditions to meet the exigencies of life as immigrants, as sojourners or as outsiders, in a world where one's experiences are constantly defined by harassment, discrimination, and unrelenting assaults upon one's dignity. But also, and perhaps more importantly, people's experiences have likewise been defined by family, faith, community, friendship, religious mystery, wonder, thankfulness, laughter, and the renewal of the human spirit in the face of adversity.

Of course, while these themes predominate, one can also discern from these readings many lesser and many more contrasting themes. From this quartet of ethno-racial communities, a *discors concordia* or discordant concord can also be heard. The themes and variations that play throughout the pages of this anthology intersect in grand fugal style, and bear witness to the resilience of the human spirit, the signal significance of community, and the central role that religion plays in defining one's place in the world. Religion has been the tie that has bound individuals to their communities, has strengthened those same communities by renewing members' commitments to long-standing traditions, even as those traditions are transformed by the challenges that these and other like communities have had to face.

With respect to the selections themselves: originally it had been the hope of our faculty to include at least 25 readings per volume. But, due to obvious page limitations and higher than expected copyright costs, we have had to limit the number of selections in each volume to about 17–22. Despite these constraints, but not because of them, we decided that it was important to reprint the selected chapters, speeches, essays, and articles in their entirety, unedited, and as they originally appeared in print—coarse language and all. To understand and appreciate the positions and views being advanced or expressed, students need to read these selections *in toto*—two notable exceptions being the journal of Mrs. Jarena Lee and the lengthy chapter from Leslie Marmon Silko, both of which I felt obliged to condense by some 25–30 original printed pages.

Additionally, because the aim of these volumes is to highlight the various types of religious literature produced by members of these four ethno-racial communities, it is evident that not all communities produce the same varieties of literature, neither in the types nor in the same quantity. This difference is most evident in the volume on the Asian American religious experience, in which, to maintain some balance of material among volumes, I have had to include more scholarly and historical types of literature.

Lastly, while this primary-source anthology is primarily intended to meet the interdisciplinary and human diversity requirements of a specific course at Long Beach State, my colleagues and I are also aware of its potential instructional value outside Southern California. Recognizing that instructors and their students at other colleges and universities throughout the United States might likewise find these selections of interest, the volumes are designed to appeal more generally to faculty teaching similar courses in the fields of history, religious studies, ethnic studies, American studies, rhetoric, and comparative literary studies. To help familiarize readers with the four ethno-racial religious communities that comprise this anthology, I have also provided a brief preface or "foretaste" for each volume, along with several suggested questions to help facilitate class discussion. And so that those using this reader may be encouraged to explore further the histories and literatures of these communities, at the beginning of each volume I have included a list of recommended sources for both instructors and students to consult (with credit to Carlos Piar for Volume 3).

Notwithstanding these limitations, my colleagues and I have sought to create an anthology that allows a variety of voices within these communities to be heard, in many cases for the first time under the same cover. Indeed, this text represents a true celebration of the religious diversity that defines the American nation.

Vox manet—the Voice remains (Ovid).

—Jon R. Stone, Ph.D.
Long Beach, Calif.
May 2015

Sources and Selected General Works in American Religious History

Ahlstrom, Sydney E. *A Religious History of the American People.* New Haven, CT: Yale University Press, 1972.

Albanese, Catherine L. *America: Religions and Religion,* 3rd ed. Belmont, CA: Wadsworth, 1999.

Alba, Richard, Albert J. Raboteau, and Josh DeWind (eds.). *Immigration and Religion in America: Comparative and Historical Perspectives.* New York: New York University Press, 2009.

Barkan, Elliott Robert (ed.). *Immigrants in American History: Arrival, Adaptation, and Integration,* 4 vols. Santa Barbara, CA: ABC-CLIO, 2013.

Becker, Penny, and Nancy Eiesland (eds.). *Contemporary American Religion: An Ethnographic Reader.* Walnut Creek, CA: AltaMira Press, 1997.

Butler, Jon, Grant Wacker, and Randall Balmer. *Religion in American Life: A Short History.* NY: Oxford University Press, 2003.

Carroll, Bret E. *The Routledge Historical Atlas of Religions in America.* New York: Routledge, 2000.

Corrigan, John, and Winthrop S. Hudson. *Religion in America,* 7th ed. Upper Saddle River, NJ: Prentice-Hall, 2004.

Ebaugh, Helen, and Janet Chafetz. *Religion and the New Immigrants: Continuities and Adaptations in Immigrant Congregations.* Walnut Creek, CA: AltaMira Press, 2000.

Eck, Diana L. *A New Religious America.* San Francisco: HarperSanFrancisco, 2002.

Gaustad, Edwin S (ed.). *A Documentary History of Religion in America,* 2 vols. Grand Rapids, MI: Eerdmans, 1982–1983.

______. *A Religious History of America,* rev. ed. San Francisco: Harper & Row, 1990.

Goff, Philip, and Paul Harvey (eds.). *Themes in Religion and American Culture.* Chapel Hill, NC: University of North Carolina Press, 2004.

Hackett, David G. (ed.). *Religion and American Culture: A Reader.* New York: Routledge, 1995.

Handy, Robert T. *A History of the Churches in the United States and Canada.* New York: Oxford University Press, 1977.

Hemeyer, Julia Corbett. *Religion in America,* 5th ed. Upper Saddle River, NJ: Prentice-Hall, 2005.

Lippy, Charles H., Robert Choquette, and Stafford Poole. *Christianity Comes to the Americas, 1492–1776.* New York: Paragon House, 1992.

McDannell, Colleen (ed.). *Religions of the United States in Practice,* 2 vols. Princeton, NJ: Princeton University Press, 2001.

Neusner, Jacob (ed.). *World Religions in America,* 3rd ed. Louisville, KY: Westminster/John Knox Press, 2003.

Porterfield, Amanda (ed.). *American Religious History.* Oxford, UK: Blackwell Publishers, 2002.

Warner, R. Stephen, and Judith G. Wittner (eds.). *Gatherings in Diaspora: Religious Communities and the New Immigration.* Philadelphia: Temple University Press, 1998.

Williams, Peter W. *America's Religions: From Their Origins to the Twenty-first Century,* 3rd ed. Urbana: University of Illinois Press, 2008.

______ (ed.). *Perspectives on American Religion and Culture: A Reader.* Oxford, UK: Blackwell Publishers, 1999.

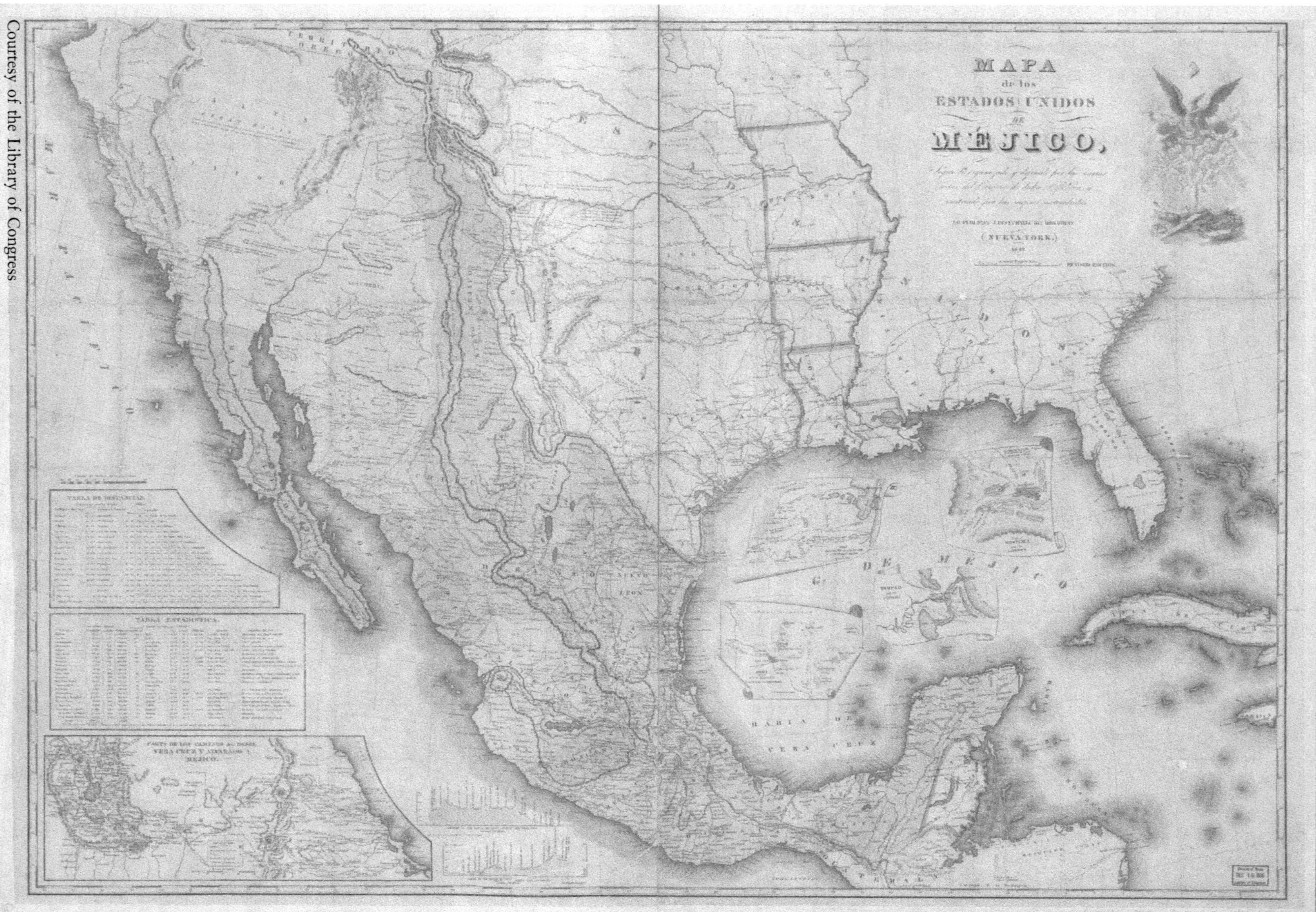
MAPA
de los
ESTADOS UNIDOS
DE
MÉJICO,
(NUEVA YORK.)
TABLA DE DISTANCIAS
TABLA ESTADISTICA
MAR PACIFICO
G. DE MÉJICO
BAHIA DE VERA CRUZ
NUEVO LEON

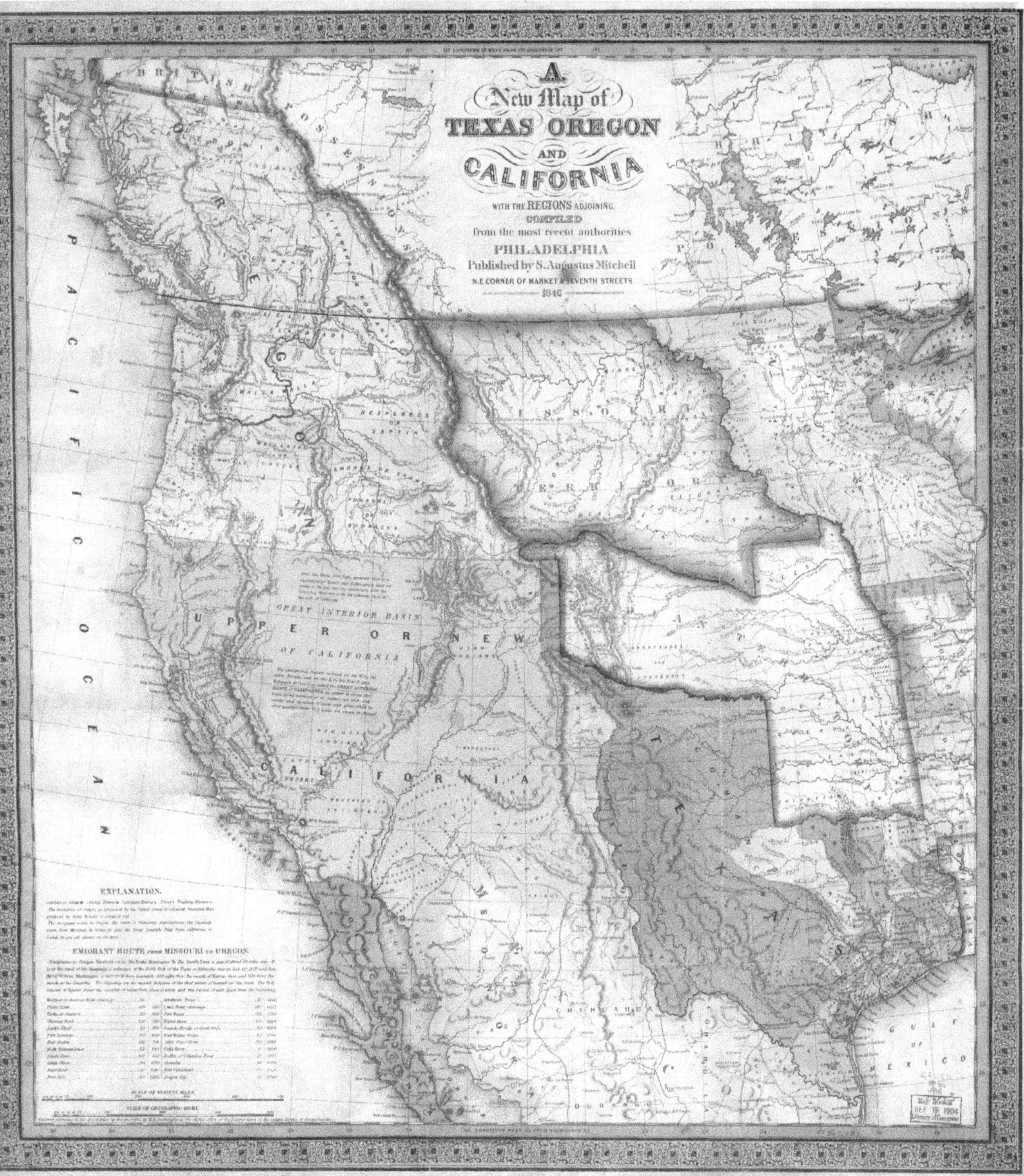

Courtesy of the Library of Congress

Readings in Latino American Religious Traditions: A Foretaste

Latinos constitute one of the largest ethnic groups in America. Recent waves of immigration, especially from Mexico and Central America, have swelled the Latino population even further. This demographic growth has made the rest of America aware that although Latinos share the same language and a common cultural ancestor—Spain—there are significant differences among them, including their religious experiences, due to history and contact with non-European peoples. A Mexican from Oaxaca and an Argentine from Buenos Aires, for example, are as different as an American from Brooklyn and a New Zealander from Whataroa. Immigrants from Latin America and the Caribbean have brought these dissimilar cultural and religious expressions with them to the United States. And they cling to these differences despite the broader culture's misperception of Latinos as culturally and religiously homogeneous.

Religiously, Latinos are still predominantly Roman Catholic. In the last century, however, Protestantism, and especially Pentecostalism, made significant gains in Latin America to the consternation of the Vatican. Latino immigrants to the United States, more than ever before, espouse a variety of religious commitments.

Whether Catholic or Protestant, Latinos have given their particular brand of Christianity their own unique cultural flavor. Latinos, both in Latin America and North America, have adapted the Christianity they received to fit their own needs and cultural style. The readings included here show Latinos' creative adaptations of religion within the new socio-historical context of Anglo-America.

The three largest Latino groups in the United States are Mexican, Puerto Rican, and Cuban. Three historical events are of special importance in accounting for the presence of these particular Latinos: (1) the Mexican-American War of 1846-48, (2) the Spanish-American War of 1898, and (3) the Cuban Revolution of 1959.

With the defeat of Mexico and the signing of the Treaty of Guadalupe Hidalgo, the southwestern lands north of the Rio Grande became part of the United States and the estimated 80,000 Mexican inhabitants already living there became American citizens. These inhabitants saw themselves more as *Californios*, *Nuevo Mexicanos*, and *Tejanos* than *Mexicanos* and became the first significant Spanish-speaking ethnic enclave in the United States. These groups, and the millions of Mexicans who immigrated later (some during the Mexican revolution of 1910 and others in subsequent decades), introduced their own forms of popular religiosity: the devotion to the Virgin of Guadalupe or *Guadalupismo*, *curanderismo*, and the *Penitente* tradition, which were in many ways foreign to institutional American Catholicism.

In 1898, the United States defeated Spain in an expansionist war and acquired Puerto Rico along with several other Spanish colonies (Cuba and the Philippines) as part of the terms of surrender. While the other acquisitions were subsequently given independence, Puerto Rico was kept as a U.S. territory. Later, with the passage of the Jones Act of 1917, Puerto Ricans were granted U.S. citizenship. Subsequently, thousands of Puerto Ricans would eventually immigrate to the mainland in search of better economic opportunities. Protestant missionaries, for their part, would come to the island seeking to both convert and Americanize this new cohort of Spanish-speaking citizens. Because of the Catholic Church's conservatism and its alliance with the government of Spain, by the late nineteenth century many liberal and independence-minded Puerto Ricans had rejected institutional Catholicism for allegedly scientific Kardecism or Spiritism (*Espiritismo Mesa Blanca*). Judith Ortiz Cofer's childhood memories of her spiritist grandfather in "Talking to the Dead" portray the bourgeois sensibility characteristic of Puerto Rican *Espiritismo*.

With the entry of American missionaries in the early twentieth century, many Puerto Ricans embraced Protestantism as a progressive and liberal religious alternative to Catholicism. When, after World War II, Puerto Ricans came to the United States in greater numbers, they brought with them their forms of Catholicism, Protestantism, and Spiritism.

Finally, the Cuban Revolution of 1959, in which Fidel Castro ousted Fulgencio Batista and established a Marxist-Leninist state, resulted in waves of Cuban refugees coming into the United States seeking political asylum. These immigrants brought with them, not only their own Catholic devotion to the patron saint of Cuba, *La Virgen de la Caridad del Cobre* (the Virgin of Charity), but also *Santería* and *Palo Monte Mayombé*, both syncretistic or creolized forms of African religion. The selections from Cristina García's *Dreaming in Cuban* give insight into the multi-layered functions of *Santería* in the construction of racial, ethnic, and religious identity both in Cuba and in the United States.

With the ethnic consciousness-raising that occurred in the 1960s, Latinos began to look at religion more critically. This was especially true within the Chicano movement. *Chicanismo* was a political movement that sought greater civil rights for Mexican Americans and also to infuse a sense of cultural pride. It was analogous to the Black Power movement within the African American community and the Red Power movement among Native Americans. As a movement of radical politics it began to turn a critical eye on the Roman Catholic Church, which in the United States has historically been dominated by Irish and German American clergy. Consequently, various Mexican American leaders, such as Oscar Zeta Acosta and César Chávez (sometimes unaccented), began to give voice to Latinos' sense of alienation from the Catholic Church. Chávez, for example, in his essay "The Mexican-American and the Church," criticizes the Catholic Church for its reluctant, then sluggish, response to the plight of migrant workers. Like Chávez, many felt that the church did not take the concerns of Mexican Americans or other Latinos seriously.

At roughly the same time, less religiously-interested activists, inspired by Latino writers, among them Rudolfo Anaya and Luis Leal, sought to reclaim lost pre-Columbian traditions. The search for *Aztlán*, the original homeland of the Aztecs in the Southwest, became a search for the roots of an ancient Chicano identity (*Chicano de Aztlán*). As with the myth of the Virgin of Guadalupe (*La Morenita*/the Darkling) and its connection to the concept of *mestizaje* (a person of mixed race), the myth of *Aztlán* effectively drew upon similar legendary elements in constructing a new, more ennobling, identity, one that rejected the post-Columbian historical realities of Spanish imperial conquest and American territorial acquisition. Still, despite its apparent masculine appeal, it is yet to be seen whether the utopian vision of *Aztlán* can ever hope to replace the warm motherliness of *La Virgen*. For, after musing on these historical realities in his essay "India" from *Days of Obligation*, Richard Rodriguez concludes that "The image of Our Lady of Guadalupe . . . has become the unofficial, the private flag of Mexicans. Unique possession of her image is a more wonderful election to Mexicans than any political call to Nationhood" (1992:19).

Along with political mythmaking, the concomitant rise of ethnic and gender consciousness in the 1960s came to produce new forms of theological reflection as well. But unlike traditional theology, these new forms took the experiences of marginalization and discrimination as their point of departure. Thus, alongside black theology, feminist theology, and the womanist response, there emerged Hispanic theology and Mujerista theology. Representing these new theologies we have included essays by Virgilio Elizondo and Ada María Isasi-Díaz. Elizondo, the best known of these Hispanic theologians, focuses in his writings on the Mexican American experience of living on the borderlands, both geographically and culturally, and on the reality of the *mestizaje*, which he interprets theologically as symbolizing the overcoming of separateness through "a new creation."

For their part, *Mujerista* theologians, such as Cuban-American Isasi-Díaz, focus on Latinas' experience of double oppression: racism *and* sexism. Latinas confront the sexism of Anglo-American culture, of the institutional Catholic Church which sacralizes the exclusion of women, and of Latino men who have been socialized into the ideology of male dominance and superiority called *machismo*. She rejects as patriarchal, therefore, the eschatological notion of a Kingdom of God, arguing instead for a "*Kin-dom*" in which "the fullness of God becomes a day-to-day reality in the world at large" and where "we will all be sisters and brothers—kin to each other" (1990:304). More generally, *Mujerista* theology seeks to empower Latinas in the struggle (*en la lucha*) against these forms of oppression and exclusion.

The person reading these selections will discover that the Latino religious experience in the United States reflects the diversity that has existed in Latin America since the sixteenth century, when Spanish Catholicism encountered Amerindian and African religions and new forms of religious expression were conceived.

Sources and Selected Works in Latino/a American History, Literature, and Religions

[* indicates works of fiction]

Acosta, Oscar Zeta. *The Revolt of the Cockroach People*. New York: Vintage Books, 1989.

Alexander, Kay. *California Catholicism*. Santa Barbara, CA: Fithian Press, 1993.

*Anaya, Rudolfo. *Bless Me, Ultima*. Berkeley, CA: TQS Publications, 1972.

Aponte, Edwin D. ¡Santo!: *Varieties of Latina/o Spirituality*. Maryknoll, NY: Orbis Books, 2012.

Aquino, Maria Pilar, Daisy L. Machado, and Jeanette Rodriguez (eds.). *A Reader in Latina Feminist Theology: Religion and Justice.* Austin, TX: University of Texas Press, 2002.

Avalos, David T. *Latinos in the United States: The Sacred and the Political.* South Bend, IN: University of Notre Dame Press, 1986.

Avalos, Hector (ed.). *Introduction to the U.S. Latina and Latino Religious Experience.* Boston: Brill Academic Publishers, 2004.

Badillo, David A. *Latinos and the New Immigrant Church.* Baltimore: The Johns Hopkins University Press, 2006.

Beebe, Rose Marie, and Robert M. Senkewicz. *Lands of Promise and Despair: Chronicles of Early California, 1535–1846.* Santa Clara, CA: Santa Clara University Press; Berkeley, CA: Heyday Books, 2001.

Boyer, Richard, and Geoffrey Spurling (eds.). *Colonial Lives: Documents on Latin American History, 1550–1850.* New York: Oxford University Press, 2000.

Brading, D.A. *Mexican Phoenix: Our Lady of Guadalupe: Image and Tradition Across Five Centuries.* Cambridge, UK: Cambridge University Press, 2001.

Camarillo, Albert. *Chicanos in a Changing Society: From Mexican Pueblos to American Barrios in Santa Barbara and Southern California, 1848–1930,* new ed. Cambridge, MA: Harvard University Press, 1996.

Castillo, Ana (ed.). *Goddess of the Americas/La Diosa de las Américas: Writings on the Virgin of Guadalupe.* New York: Riverhead Books, 1996.

Chen, Carolyn, and Russell Jeung (eds.). *Sustaining Faith Traditions: Race, Ethnicity, and Religion among the Latino and Asian American Second Generation.* New York: New York University Press, 2012.

Christensen, Mark Z. *Nahua and Maya Catholicisms: Texts and Religion in Colonial Central Mexico and Yucatan.* Stanford, CA: Stanford University Press, 2013.

Christensen, Mark Z. *Translated Christianities: Nahuatl and Maya Religious Texts.* University Park, PA: Pennsylvania State University Press, 2014.

Cruz, Samuel. *Masked Africanisms: Puerto Rican Pentecostalism.* Dubuque, IA: Kendall/Hunt, 2005.

De La Torre, Miguel A., and Edwin David Aponte. *Introducing Latino/a Theologies.* Maryknoll, NY: Orbis Books, 2001.

De La Torre, Miguel A. *Trails of Hope and Terror: Testimonies on Immigration.* Maryknoll, NY: Orbis Books, 2009.

Deck, Allan Figueroa (ed.). *Frontiers of Hispanic Theology in the United States,* 2nd ed. Maryknoll, NY: Orbis Books, 1992.

Diaz-Stevens, Ana Maria, and Anthony M. Stevens-Arroyo. *Recognizing the Latino Resurgence in U.S. Religion.* Boulder, CO: Westview Press, 1998.

Dolan, Jay P., and Allan Figueroa Deck (eds.). *Hispanic Catholic Culture in the U.S.: Issues and Concerns.* South Bend, IN: University of Notre Dame Press, 1997.

Dolan, Jay P., and Jaime R. Vidal (eds.). *Puerto Rican and Cuban Catholics in the U.S., 1900–1965*. South Bend, IN: University of Notre Dame Press, 1994.

Duany, Jorge. *The Puerto Rican Nation on the Move: Identities on the Island and in the United States*. Chapel Hill, NC: University of North Carolina Press, 2002.

Early, John D. *Maya and Catholic Cultures in Crisis*. Gainesville: University Press of Florida, 2012.

Edmonds, Ennis B. and Gonzalez, Michelle A. *Caribbean Religious History: An Introduction*. NY: New York University Press, 2010.

Espinosa, Gastón, and García, Mario T. *Mexican American Religions: Spirituality, Activism, and Culture*. Durham: Duke University Press, 2008.

Espinosa, Gastón, Virgilio Elizondo, and Jesse Miranda (eds.). *Latino Religions and Civic Activism in the United States*. New York: Oxford University Press, 2005.

Fernandez Olmos, Margarite, and Lizabeth Paravisini-Gebert. *Creole Religions of the Caribbean: An Introduction from Vodou and Santería to Obeah and Espiritismo*. New York: New York University Press, 2003.

Flores, Juan. *Divided Borders: Essays on Puerto Rican Identity*. Houston: University of Houton/ Arte Público Press, 1993.

García, Alma M. (ed.). *Chicana Feminist Thought: The Basic Historical Writings*. New York: Routledge, 1997.

García Canclini, Néstor (Lidia Lozano, trans.). *Transforming Modernity: Popular Culture in Mexico*. Austin, TX: University of Texas Press, 1993.

Gonzalez, Justo. *Harvest of Empire: A History of Latinos in America*. New York: Penguin, 2001.

______. *Voces: Voices from the Hispanic Church*. Nashville, TN: Abingdon Press, 1992.

Griswold del Castillo, Richard, and Arnoldo de León. *North to Aztlán: A History of Mexican Americans in the United States*. New York: Twayne Publishers, 1996.

Gutiérrez, Ramón A. *When Jesus Came, the Corn Mothers Went Away: Marriage, Sexuality, and Power in New Mexico, 1500–1846*. Stanford, CA: Stanford University Press, 1991.

Gutiérrez, Ramón A., and Richard J. Orsi (eds.). *Contested Eden: California Before the Gold Rush*. Berkeley, CA: University of California Press, 1998.

Hernández, Edwin I., et al. (eds.). *Emerging Voices, Urgent Choices: Essays on Latino/a Religious Leadership*. Boston: Brill Academic, 2006.

Hernández Hiraldo, Samiri. *Black Puerto Rican Identity and Religious Experience*. Gainesville: University Press of Florida, 2006.

Hernandez, Jose Angel. *Mexican American Colonization during the Nineteenth Century: A History of the U.S.-Mexico Borderlands*. Cambridge: Cambridge University Press, 2012.

Heyck, Denis Lynn Daly (ed.). *Barrios and Borderlands: Cultures of Latinos and Latinas in the United States*. New York: Routledge, 1994.

Isasi-Diaz, Ada María. *En La Lucha/In the Struggle: An Hispanic Women's Theology*. Minneapolis, MN: Fortress Press, 1993.

______. *"Solidarity: Love of Neighbor in the 1980s."* pp. 31–40 and 303–305 in Lift Every Voice: Constructing Christian Theologies from the Underside, edited by Susan Brooks Thistlethwaite and Mary Potter Engel. San Francisco: Harper and Row, 1990.

Isasi-Diaz, Ada María, and Fernando F. Segovia (eds.). *Hispanic/Latino Theology: Challenge and Promise*. Minneapolis, MN: Fortress Press, 1996.

Isasi-Díaz, Ada María, and Mendieta, Eduardo. *Decolonizing Epistemologies: Latina/o Theology and Philosophy.* NY: Fordham University Press, 2012.

Isasi-Diaz, Ada María, and Yolanda Tarango. *Hispanic Women: Prophetic Voice in the Church*. Minneapolis, MN: Fortress Press, 1992; (bilingual ed.) Scranton, PA: University of Scranton Press, 2006.

Lopez, Tiffany Ann (ed.). *Growing Up Chicano: An Anthology*. New York: Morrow, 1993.

Martell-Otero, Loida I., Maldonado Pérez, Zaida, Conde-Frazier, and Elizabeth Jones, Serene. *Latina Evangélicas: A Theological Survey from the Margins*. Eugene, OR: Cascade Books, 2013.

Martin, Patricia Preciado. *Songs My Mother Sang to Me: An Oral History of Mexican American Women*. Tucson, AZ: University of Arizona Press, 1992.

Martínez-Fernández, Luis. *Protestantism and Political Conflict in the Nineteenth-Century Hispanic Caribbean*. New Brunswick, N.J.: Rutgers University Press, 2002.

Matovina, Timothy. *Guadalupe and Her Faithful: Latino Catholics in San Antonio, from Colonial Origins to the Present*. Baltimore: The Johns Hopkins University Press, 2005.

Matovina, Timothy, and Gerald E. Poyo (eds.). *Presente!: U.S. Latino Catholics from Colonial Origins to the Present*. Maryknoll, NY: Orbis Books, 2000.

Matovina, Timothy, and Gary Riebe-Estrella (eds.). *Horizons of the Sacred: Mexican Traditions in U.S. Catholicism*. Ithaca, New York: Cornell University Press, 2002.

Medina, Nestor. *Mestizaje: Remapping Race, Culture, and Faith in Latina/o Catholicism*. Maryknoll, NY: Orbis Books, 2009.

Moore, Joan W. *Mexican Americans*. Englewood Cliffs, NJ: Prentice Hall, 1976.

Olmos, Margarite Fernández, and Lisbeth Paravisini-Gebert. *Creole Religions of the Caribbean: An Introduction from Vodou and Santería to Obeah and Espiritismo*. New York: New York University Press, 2003.

Rodriguez, Jeanette. *Our Lady of Guadalupe: Faith and Empowerment among Mexican American Women*. Austin, TX: University of Texas Press, 1994.

Rodriguez, Richard. *Days of Obligation*. New York: Penguin Books, 1992.

______. *Hunger of Memory: The Education of Richard Rodriguez*. New York: Bantam Books, 1983.

Román-Odio, Clara. *Sacred Iconographies in Chicana Cultural Productions*. NY: Palgrave, 2013.

Román, Reinaldo L. *Governing Spirits: Religion, Miracles, and Spectacles in Cuba and Puerto Rico*, 1898–1956. Chapel Hill: University of North Carolina Press, 2007.

Romero, C. Gilbert. *Hispanic Devotional Piety: Tracing the Biblical Roots*. Maryknoll, NY: Orbis Books, 1991.

Sandoval, Moises. *On the Move: A History of the Hispanic Church in the United States,* 2nd ed., rev. Maryknoll, NY: Orbis Books, 2006.

Sarat, Leah. *Fire in the Canyon: Religion, Migration, and the Mexican Dream.* NY: New York University Press, 2013.

Stavans, Ilan. *The Hispanic Condition: The Power of a People,* 2nd ed. New York: Harper-Collins, 2001.

Tweed, Thomas A. *Our Lady of the Exile: Diasporic Religion at a Cuban Catholic Shrine in Miami.* New York: Oxford University Press, 1997.

Valdez, Luis, and Stan Steiner (eds.). *Aztlan: An Anthology of Mexican American Literature.* New York: Alfred A. Knopf, 1972.

Whalen, Carmen Teresa, and Víctor Vázquez-Hernández. *The Puerto Rican Diaspora: Historical Perspectives*. Philadelphia: Temple University Press, 2005.

Some Suggested Questions for Discussion

1. Please compare Luis Leal, Jeanette Rodriguez, Richard Rodriguez on the meaning and significance of the myths of the Virgin of Guadalupe and of Aztlán for Mexican-Americans. In what ways have these myths become contemporary expressions of Mexican-American identity? Adding Ada María Isasi-Diaz to the conversation, how might these myths serve either to help or hinder the *Mujerista* historical project (*proyecto histórico*) that she advances?

2. Please discuss how popular religious practices (rather than institutional forms of religion), such as those of the Penitentes of New Mexico and of Cubans living in Miami, serve to maintain a sense of connection to heritage and homeland. Including Holy Week and Saint's Day observances, what types of adjustments or modifications to these practices seem to have taken place in the context of the immigrant experience in America?

3. Please compare the selections from Cristina Garcia's *Dreaming in Cuban* and Virgilio Elizondo's "Mestizaje as a Locus of Theological Reflection." Discuss whether or not Elizondo's understanding of *mestizaje* is an idealization of racial relations among Latinos. Is *mestizaje* an adequate or inadequate locus of theological reflection? Why or why not?

4. Please compare Judith Ortiz Cofer's "Talking to the Dead" in *Silent Dancing* with César Chavez's "The Mexican-American and the Church." From the perspective of these authors, what role does religion play in Latinos' lives? Can similar comparisons be made using the other selections in this volume?

1. Hymns, Prayers, and Other Religious Verses

AURELIO M. ESPINOSA AND J. MANUEL ESPINOSA

Popular Themes: Christ of the Passion, Prayers and Hymns (Alabados) of the Penitentes, the Child Jesus, the Holy Family, the Virgin Mary, the Matins; the Bachelor's Prayer. Special Invocations.

The history of the Catholic Church in Spanish America is the continuation of its history in Spain. Catholicism was transported to America in exactly the same form, with all its doctrines, ceremonies, pomp, and traditions. The Franciscan missionaries who labored in New Mexico for nearly two and one-half centuries established there the same institutions that they had in Spain to keep alive the fires of the faith among the colonizers and their descendants and to Christianize the Indians.

There are popular prayers, ballads, hymns, dramatic representations, legends, and beliefs which keep alive in the hearts and in the memories of the people practically all the scenes of the birth, life, sufferings, and death of Christ, special devotion to the Virgin Mary, and prayers to favorite saints. While many of these ceremonies and practices are inspired directly in the liturgical ceremonies of the Church, many others are of popular origin and have a history as old as the Church itself.

Christ of the Passion

The Christ of the Passion has been ever present in the tradition of Catholic Spain. In New Mexican tradition He has been the special object of adoration and reverence from the days of the *conquistadores* to the present time. When entering New Mexico, the first *conquistador* and colonizer, Juan de Oñate, not only whipped himself in the company of his soldiers in reverence to Christ Crucified on Holy Thursday of the year 1598, but also everywhere and on many occasions erected large wooden crosses before which he prayed for victory that he might succeed in Christianizing the Indians. The complete gospel narrative of the Passion and Death of Christ is commemorated in various forms of Spanish traditions: prayers, hymns, ballads, dramatic compositions, and iconography, a related popular artistic expression of

---

religious sentiment. In New Mexican tradition all these manifestations of Spanish religious tradition are to be found in popular form.

Christian communities in early times gave dramatic forms to some of the scenes of the Passion as they were depicted in the gospels, at first perhaps as ceremonies accessory to the liturgy of the mass during Lent. In the Middle Ages religious worship was always very real, very dramatic. The mass, with its dramatic action and dialogue between the officiating priest and his assistants, the choir, and the people who participated, was in reality drama of the highest form. The elaborations of the liturgy called *tropes* were soon developed, and these may be considered the beginnings of the Passion plays of Christian tradition. The people then developed independent scenes, among them the scene of the Descent from the Cross, and began the truly popular religious drama, often separated from the official ecclesiastical ceremonies.

The so-called Easter plays of mediaeval Catholic tradition were a development of the earlier *tropes*, with the addition of the characters of Pilate, Judas, the Roman soldiers, Mary Magdalen, and so on. From these were developed the Passion plays of the fourteenth and fifteenth centuries. In the fifteenth century the Church authorities took a great interest in the Passion plays, but in the sixteenth century they generally left them to the people. The plays had become too long and complicated, with legendary elements added, and were often a source of mirth and amusement in some respects rather than of sorrow and devotion. From that time on, the Passion play was relegated to the people.

In Spain, however, the scenes of the Passion were not altogether relegated to the people, being continued, in a way, by the *autos sacramentales* produced in the streets of Madrid on carriages, each of which, as it passed along, represented a scene from a secular play in honor of the Eucharist or some scene from the Passion. Moreover, popular religious drama had a greater development in Spain than in any other European country. Nowhere in Europe are the scenes of the Passion and Death of Christ popularized for public devotion as in some cities of Spain: Barcelona, Seville, Toledo, Valencia. The religious orders and confraternities that have represented in one form or another some of the outstanding scenes of the Passion are legion. Holy Week in Seville has produced since the sixteenth century practically every scene that can be dramatized.

The Passion was a popular theme for dramatization in all parts of the Spanish world. Among the scenes of the Passion that have been popularly dramatized in New Mexico there is the popular dramatic representation called *La primera persecutión de Jesús* (The first persecution of Jesus). I know of two manuscript versions from Taos. The older and better version is very short and represents the visit of the three Magi Kings to the Child Jesus at Bethlehem, the Herodian persecution and massacres, and the flight to Egypt. This popular composition, which is still produced in Taos, is not properly speaking a Passion play; it is more fully described in another chapter.

Scenes from the Passion are apparently no longer performed today in New Mexico, although it seems that they were often staged up to the end of the nineteenth century. No texts of any of them have been found, but certain fragments of ballads and other verse narratives that have been preserved may have been parts of such plays. According to authentic information, a Passion play was part of the Church ceremony of Holy Week, following the mass on Good Friday, although some of the preparatory scenes were performed on previous days; Roman soldiers with helmets, the Centurion, and the Cyrenian appeared in them in costume. The play began with the adoration of Christ on the Cross, represented by a large image of Christ crucified on a huge cross. Longinus then appeared with his lance, often on horseback. It is said that at Tomé, Longinus actually entered the Church on a horse to pierce the side of the Savior. All this was accompanied by weeping and by the singing of sacred hymns, perhaps some of those, cited below, now found only in the ritual manuscripts of the Penitentes. Next, the lamentations of the Virgin took place. The lamentations are preserved in one of the most beautiful traditional Spanish ballads now found in New Mexico. The Descent from the Cross followed, and the lamentations continued. The image of Christ was taken down from the cross and delivered into the arms of the Virgin Mary. Finally, there took place the *Santo entierro*, or the burial. This consisted of placing the body of *nuestro padre* Jesús in the sepulchre, a large wooden box, to be venerated in the Church. I myself have witnessed some of the above scenes. None, to my knowledge, are performed today, except in the ceremonies of the Passion that are included in the practices of the Penitentes. The Ecce Homo, or Jesús Nazareno, of which there are still in New Mexico some very realistic iconographic examples, may have appeared also immediately before the scene of the Crucifixion.

Although these traditional scenes of the Passion were performed by the people, the Church officials approved them and took part in them. The scene of the Descent from the Cross, with the lamentations of the Virgin, was especially popular, and at Taos, Santa Fe, and other places it lasted longer than the other scenes, with ecclesiastical sanction and direction. The lamentations of the Virgin are found in several popular versions.

Prayers and Hymns (*Alabados*) of Penitentes

The hermanos penitentes, or Penitent Brothers of the society now called La Sociedad de Nuestro Padre Jesús Nazareno, represent an interesting New Mexican Spanish religious survival. Just when this Catholic religious society of New Mexican flagellants was given its present name we do not know. Up to the turn of the century its members were usually called Los Hermanos Penitentes de Nuestro Padre San Francisco. (The Penitent Brothers of Our Father Saint Francis), and there is much evidence to indicate that the society was a popular development of the Third Order of Saint Francis. The members of this lay religious brotherhood are generally referred to as Penitentes. The Passion of Christ is the central theme of the religious ritual and ceremonies of the Penitentes.

A study of the ritual, with its traditional Spanish prayers, ballads, hymns, and Passion narratives, together with the practices now in vogue, reveal at once the Spanish origin of the society and of practically all its ritual and ceremonies. The same or similar practices were common in mediaeval Europe. In modern Spain most of the ceremonies, including self-flagellation as penance for sin, are still to be found. The religious processions of various parish religious groups during Holy Week, with the carrying of heavy crosses, for example, are still commonplace in Madrid, Toledo, Seville, Valencia, and other cities in Spain. Similar examples can be given from some of the countries of present-day Hispanic America.

The New Mexican Spanish *penitentes* have practiced flagellation since the earliest years of the conquest, attested to by the fact that they did so when Oñate entered New Mexico in 1598, it was described by Father Benavides in the 1630's and religious societies have practiced it to our knowledge until recent years not only in New Mexico (the Penitentes), but also in Mexico, Spain, Italy, and other countries. At Santa Fe, members of the Third Order of Saint Francis, or *terciarios*, who flagellated themselves especially during Holy Week ceremonies, had their Franciscan chaplain and maintained a chapel which in the seventeenth and eighteenth centuries adjoined the Church of San Miguel. Its concession was annulled in 1826.

In the nineteenth century the Penitentes were numerous in northern New Mexico. After the American occupation, they were frequently in conflict with the ecclesiastical authorities, but the society seems to have flourished most when the opposition of the Church was the strongest. New Mexican ecclesiastical authorities of that era sometimes spoke rather harshly about the organization. Very often the conflict between the Penitentes and the Church seems to have been precipitated by overzealous ecclesiastics who attempted to stamp out too abruptly old customs such as these.

The members of the Penitente brotherhood are Catholic men who gather during Lent to perform certain religious rites, consisting of prayers and hymns about the Passion and Death of Christ, and who, in addition, practice flagellation during Holy Week and on other special occasions, such as the night of a vigil held for a deceased member. The march to Calvary from the *morada*, or chapel, on Good Friday is the special occasion for flagellation, and up to the end of the nineteenth century it was the usual custom to simulate a crucifixion: a Penitente was tied to a cross, which was raised for the period of the Agony on the Cross or for such time as the Penitente could endure. The Lenten and other devotions of the organization are not of New Mexican origin but are traditional Spanish prayers, hymns, and Passion ballads—the work, no doubt, of Franciscan missionaries of the seventeenth and eighteenth centuries or versions of Spanish originals printed in Spain in the sixteenth and seventeenth centuries.

The organization of the New Mexican Penitentes is very simple. The local *morada* has an *hermano mayor*, chief brother, as its supreme director, who holds office for four or five years together with as many as eleven other officers: the *pitero cantador*, or leader in singing; the *curandero*, or doctor who looks after the wounds of the members during their religious exercises; and others. The officers are usually selected from those who have finished their flagellation period of four or five years and are not obliged by the rules to whip themselves any more. Until recent years, the various *moradas* of northern New Mexico, some thirty in number, sometimes sent representatives to a general assembly that met usually at Santa Cruz to discuss matters of interest to the society, but there is no well-defined central organization. The local *morada*, with its officers, is an independent unit. It alone decided whether or not to send delegates to the general assemblies at Santa Cruz. Some Penitentes speak of the Santa Cruz chapel as the *morada madre*, or mother chapel, which seems to indicate that the general meetings held there may have been a continuation of meetings that were formerly the regular assemblies of a general and more highly organized society that since the days of Governor Vargas in the last years of the seventeenth century had its center at Santa Cruz. The division of the society into *moradas* of independent rule and organization was probably the result of the ecclesiastical opposition in the first half of the nineteenth century.

The entire ritual and actual ceremonies and practices of the New Mexican Penitentes are a commemoration of the Passion and Death of Christ. Although now continued chiefly by the lower classes in the old Spanish-speaking rural areas, the institution is not of popular origin. The Spanish tradition itself has a mediaeval Catholic origin, monastic in its beginnings. Even in the modern imperfect and garbled versions of the prayers, hymns, and religious ballads that are found in the hand-written *cuadernos*, or hymn books, of the New Mexican Penitentes, recopied and handed down from one generation to another, the learned sources are clearly observable. The existence of this mediaeval Spanish institution, a society of Christian flagellants, with their traditional Spanish ritual in prayers, hymns, ballads, and Passion narratives, is one of the most extraordinary features of Spanish tradition in New Mexico.

Of the various traditional Spanish prayers and Passion ballads that are found in the ritual and prayer manuscripts of the present-day New Mexican Penitentes, none appears to be a modern composition. All are versions of traditional Spanish seventeenth- and eighteenth-century compositions. The ballads *Por el rastro de la sangre, Un ángel triste lloraba*, and some of the traditional forms of the prayer *Bendito y alabado* certainly go back to the sixteenth and seventeenth centuries. The religious ballads preserved by the Penitentes are among the gems of the contribution of northern New Mexico and southern Colorado to Spanish balladry, the *romances tradicionales*.

One of the longest and best of the Passion narratives in verse—one that is chanted or sung at the *morada* on Holy Thursday—consists of 144 octosyllabic quatrains, or 576 verses. It narrates the complete story of the Crucifixion. The first 52 and the last 24 verses of this version are the following:

Con mansedumbre y ternura
y señas de fino amor
les previno a sus discípulos
la última cena el Señor.
Y con mucha caridad,
que en los mortales no ves,
después de haber cenado
les lava humilde los pies.
Luego consagró su sangre
y con cariñoso afán
se les dio muy escogido
en accidente de pan.
Por este medio dispuso
aquel nuevo testamento,
sacrificándose así
para desterrar el viejo,
pues en este sacrificio
era sangre de animales,
y en el nuevo la de Cristo

With meekness and deep affection
and signs of the most pure love,
the Lord for his twelve disciples
provided the Last Supper.
And with the greatest charity,
the charity we never see,
after the supper was over
He humbly washed their feet.
He then consecrated His blood,
and with affectionate zeal
He gave Himself to them
in the accident of bread.
In this way He established
the New Testament and Faith,
thus sacrificing Himself
to do away with the Old;
for in the Old they offered
as a sacrifice animals' blood,
while in the New it is Christ's blood

para redimir mortales.
Y para mayor firmeza
de lo que en él ordenó
les hizo beber su sangre
en el cáliz que les dio.
También quiso que durara
el sacramento en su Iglesia,
y para ello potestades
a sus discípulos deja.
Estos las comunicaron,
del modo que ha de durar,
a sus hijos sacerdotes
hasta que vuelva a juzgar.
Y al mismo tiempo les manda
que al hacer el sacrificio
se acordasen del Señor
por tan grande beneficio.
Concluida que fue la cena
dio gracias al Padre Eterno,
y con tal echó a nosotros
el más saludable ejemplo.
Despidióse de su madre
con gran ternura y dolor;
el de la madre fue grande,
pero el del Hijo mayor.
Después de esta despedida
con sus discípulos fue
desde la ciudad al huerto,
donde había orado otra vez.
En la cena antes les dijo
que habían de experimentar
que aquella misma noche
todos lo habían de dejar.
. . . .
Ya resucita Jesús,
ya el tercer día ha sacado
de allá del seno de Abrán
los justos depositados.
Consigo al cielo los sube,
que se mantuvo cerrado
hasta que sirvió de llave
la sangre que ha derramado.
Con la cual el nuevo Adán

that was shed for the sins of men.
And to confirm their faith
in all the things he commanded,
He gave them in the chalice
His precious blood to drink.
This Sacrament He wished
should abide in His living church,
and for that purpose He gave
to His disciples His powers.
These have then transmitted them
and their powers are thus continued
in all the priests who follow them
until He comes to judge.
He also commanded them
that when offering the sacrifice
they should do it in remembrance
of Him Who did such good.
And when the supper was finished
He gave thanks to the Father,
giving us thus an example
of what we too must do.
He took leave of His Mother
with deep affection and sorrow;
great was the Mother's sorrow,
but greater was that of the Son.
After this sad parting
with His disciples He went
from the city to the garden,
where He had prayed before.
He had told them during the supper
that it would come to pass
that on that very night
all of them would abandon Him.
. . . .
On the third day Jesus has risen,
and has already delivered
from the bosom of Abraham those
just souls that were waiting there.
He took them with Him to heaven,
the heaven that was ever closed
until it was opened at last
by the blood that Christ has shed.
In this manner the New Adam

recuperó aquella tierra
que primero había perdido
causa una serpiente fiera.
Reconozcamos después
a Nuestro Jesús Amado;
nuestros yerros son la causa
que le ponen nuevos clavos.
Acabemos con su muerte
nuestras culpas, sus agravios,
y no le ofendamos más,
que seremos muy ingratos.
Intercédenos, Maria,
se borren nuestros errores,
ya que vuestro Hijo os dejó
por madre de pecadores.

recovered all that paradise
that in ages past he had lost
through the serpent's evil advice.
Les us praise forever and ever
the name of Our Loving Jesus;
our sins alone are to blame
for the nails that pierced his flesh.
He died for us; let us end
our life of sin and His grief
and let us offend Him no more,
for we would be most ungrateful.
Intercede for us, Virgin Mary,
that our sins may be forgiven,
for Your Son has deemed to name you
as the mother of all sinners.

As a sample of part of the ritual of the Penitentes, the complete ceremony, with the password and prayers performed on the arrival of each Penitente at the *morada* after the door has been closed, as found in the Santa Cruz manuscripts, is given below. Most of the language of the ceremony is in octosyllabic verse.

—Dios toca en esta misión
las puertas de su clemencia.
—Penitencia, penitencia,
que quieres tu salvación.
—San Pedro me abra las puertas,
bañado entre clara luz;
soy esclavo de María;
traigo el sello de Jesús.
Pregunto a esta cofradía,
¿Quién a esta casa da luz?
—Jesús.
—¿Quién la llena de alegría?
—María.
—¿Quién la conserva en la fe?
—José.
—Luego bien claro se ve
que siempre habrá contrición
teniendo en el corazón
a Jesús, María y José.
Para entrar a esta misión

"In this mission God unbolts
the gates of His boundless mercy."
"Penance we preach, penance,
for you wish your salvation."
"May Saint Peter open the gates,
for me with brilliant light;
I am the slave of Mary;
I have the seal of Jesus.
I ask this confraternity,
"Who gives light to this house?"
"Jesus."
"Who fills it with joy?"
"Mary."
"Who keeps it in the faith?"
"Joseph."
"It is perfectly clear, then,
that all those will be saved
who hold in their hearts
Jesus, Mary, and Joseph.
In order to enter this mission

el pie derecho pondré,
y alabo a los dulces nombres
de Jesús, María y José.

I will put first my right foot,
and will praise the sweet names
of Jesus, Mary, and Joseph."

The door is opened and the penitent enters, stepping in first with his right foot. He then kneels and on his knees he advances toward the Cross on the altar. In the long prayer that the penitent recites while venerating the Cross, he is often accompanied by all those present. Sometimes the prayer is omitted. After the veneration of the Cross, the penitent recites the following prayer in verse, performing the various acts indicated in the words:

—Señor Mío Jesucristo,
yo soy este pecador
que vengo a hacer mi ejercicio
y cumplir mi devoción.
Besaré este santo velo
para que mi alma suba al cielo;
besaré esta santa mesa,
que es lo que mi alma confiesa;
besaré esta santa cuerda
para que mi alma no se pierda.

My Lord, Jesus Christ,
I come, a grievous sinner,
to perform my exercises
and accomplish my devotions.
I will kiss this holy veil
so that my soul may be saved;
I will kiss this holy altar
for it confirms my faith;
I will kiss this holy cord
that my soul may not be lost.

All those present then pray:

"—Adorámoste, Nuestro Señor Jesucristo y bendecímoste que por tu Santa Cruz redimiste al mundo y a mí pecador también."

"We adore Thee and we bless Thee, Our Lord Jesus Christ, because through Thy Cross Thou hast redeemed the world and also me, a sinner."

The Penitente then withdraws from the altar backwards, always facing the Cross and on his knees. He then kisses the feet of the *hermano mayor* and asks pardon of all those he may have offended, and the others answer him:

"—Perdónenme, hermanos míos, si en algo los he ofendido y escandalizado.
—Que le perdone Dios, que de nosotros ya está perdonado."

"Pardon me, brothers, if in any way I have offended you and scandalized you."
"May God pardon you, because we have already pardoned you."

In most of the *moradas* the above ceremony apparently takes place only at the beginning of the Lenten ceremonies, when the Penitentes first gather at the *morada* for their regular Lenten exercises. Each Penitente enters individually until all have been received.

The Child Jesus

In New Mexico, as in all Spanish-speaking countries, the veneration for the Child Jesus is deeply rooted in popular tradition. Prayers to the Child Jesus are taught to New Mexican children by their parents and relatives as soon as they learn to speak. Among the most beautiful nursery rhymes known by children we find the following:

Dijo el gallo: —¡Cocorocó! ¡Cristo nació!	Said the cock, "Kokoroko! Christ is born!"
Dijo la cabra: —¡Me, me! ¿Donde? ¿Donde?	Said the goat "Ma, Ma! Where? Where?"
Dijo la oveja: —¡Be, be! ¡En Belén!	Said the sheep, "Ba, ba! In Bethlehem!"
Dijo la mula: —¡Vamos a ver!	Said the mule, "Let us go and see!"
Dijo el buey: —¡No es menester!	Said the ox, "It is not necessary!"

This New Mexican Spanish Christmas rhyme is traditional. There are similar versions from Argentina and Chile and from several parts of Spain. The verses are pan-European and are a survival from mediaeval Latin rhymes. In such a well-known book as *Songs of the Nativity* by William Henry Husk we find the following mediaeval Latin version: "The cock croweth, *Christus natus est* [Christ is born]; the raven asketh, *Quando?* [When?}; the cow replieth, *Hac nocte* [This night]; the ox crieth out, *Ubi? Ubi?* [Where? Where?]; the sheep bleateth out, *Bethlehem*."

The Child Jesus born of the Virgin Mary in the stable at Bethlehem and adored by the Magi Kings and by the shepherds is the special object of adoration, love, and pity. No more beautiful lyric poetry has ever been written than some of the verses composed by Lope de Vega for his *Los pastores de Belén* (The shepherds of Bethlehem). The following verses are sung by the Virgin Mary and the shepherds when the Divine Child trembles and weeps from the cold:

No lloréis, mis ojos; Niño Dios, callad, que si llora el cielo, ¿quién podrá cantar?	Do not weep, my love; Child God, do not weep, for if heaven weeps, who will ever sing?

Vuestra madre hermosa,
que cantando está,
llorará también,
si ve que lloráis.

Los ángeles bellos
cantan, que les dais
a los cielos gloria
y a la tierra paz.

De aquestas montañas
descendiendo van
pastores cantando
por daros solaz.

Niño de mis ojos,
ea, no haya más,
que si el cielo llora,
¿quién podrá cantar?

Your beautiful mother,
who is now singing,
will weep also,
if she sees you weeping.

The angels on high
are singing, for you give
joy to heaven and
peace to earth.

From these mountains
the shepherds are coming
singing joyously
to bring you comfort.

Dear Child, my love,
come, weep no more,
for if heaven weeps,
who will ever sing?

There are many prayers, ballads, legends, and dramatic representations that continue the general Spanish cult of the Divine Child, and some are traditional and very old. The popular verses that may be compared to those of Lope de Vega, although not so beautiful, are numerous. Among the most popular are the following, found as separate verses to the Child Jesus or as part of the dramatic compositions called *Los pastores*, discussed in another chapter. In *Los pastores* they are usually put in the mouths of the shepherds.

Duérmete, Niño chiquito,
duérmete, amado mío;
mis pecados fueron causa
que estés temblando de frío.

Duérmete, Niño chiquito,
duérmete, mi Redentor;
duérmete tierno querido
hasta unirme con mi Dios.

Alarrú, Niño chiquito,
alarrú, mi vida mía;
duérmete, Niño chiquito,
que la noche está muy fría.

¡Quién pudiera, Niño lindo,
lograr en esta ocasión
que te sirvieran de cuna
telas de mi corazón!

Go to sleep, little Child,
go to sleep, my love;
it is on account of my sins
that you suffer from the cold.

Go to sleep, little Child,
go to sleep, my Redeemer;
go to sleep, my dear one,
until I meet my God.

Lullaby, little Child,
lullaby, my life;
go to sleep, little Child,
for the night is very cold.

Would, beautiful Child,
that on this occasion
a cradle could be made for you
from the tissues of my heart!

The novenas to the Holy Child (el Santo Niño), especially to the Santo Niño de Atocha, are very popular in New Mexico. The expression "¡Santo Niño de Atocha!" to express surprise or sorrow, asking the help of the Divine Child to avert disaster or suffering, is heard in New Mexico today. There is a popular prayer in verse to the Santo Niño de Atocha that has many variants, the differences being chiefly in their length. The version given below, which is one of the shorter ones, in its Spanish form consists of nine octosyllabic quatrains, each quatrain with the second and fourth verses in assonance:

¡Adiós, Niñito de Atocha,
mi dulzura y mi placer!
Hermosura de la gloria,
¿cuándo te volveré a ver?

Manuelito de mi vida
líbrame de Lucifer.
Hermosura de la gloria,
¿cuándo te volveré a ver?

Jardín lleno de delicias,
y matizado clavel,
delicia de los arcangeles,
¿cuándo te volveré a ver?

Lucerito de mi vida,
de la más linda mujer,
encanto de las virtudes,
¿cuándo te volveré a ver?

Naciste, divino Niño.
en la ciudad de Belén.
Gloria de (de)nominaciones,
¿cuándo te volveré a ver?

Cielo estrellado, divino,
y todo mi menester,
gloria de los principados,
¿cuándo te volveré a ver?

Por tus santísimos padres
y por tu divino ser,
gloria de los mismos tronos,
¿cuándo te volveré a ver?

Por el natal que tomaste
de una peregrina Ester,

Hail, Child of Jesus of Atocha,
my sweetness and my joy!
Heavenly beauty,
when will I see you again?

Manuelito, my life,
save me from Lucifer's wiles.
Heavenly beauty,
when will I see you again?

Garden of all delight,
multiple-hued carnation,
joy of archangels,
when will I see you again?

Morning star of my life,
born of the loveliest of women,
joy of heavenly virtues,
when will I see you again?

You were born, divine Child,
in the city of Bethlehem.
Glory of denominations,
when will I see you again?

Starry heaven, divine,
the end of my desires,
glory of principalities,
when will I see you again?

Through your divine origin
and your divine essence
glory of thrones, I ask,
when will I see you again?

Through your divine birth
from an Esther full of grace,

gloria de los querubines,
¿cuándo te volveré a ver?

Por el suspenso y afán
de mi señor San José,
gloria de los serafines,
¡cuándo te volveré a ver?

I ask, glory of Cherubim,
when will I see you again?

By the suspense and agony
suffered by St. Joseph, I ask,
glory of the seraphim,
when will I see you again?

The lost Christ Child found with the high priests in the temple is sung in New Mexico in traditional Spanish ballads, usually incorporated in the texts of the popular dramatic composition *El Niño Perdido* (The lost Child). A version from Taos, modernized into strophic form in two different meters and with changes in assonance, is the following:

La Virgen buscaba al Niño—por las calles y las plazas,
y a todos los que veía—por su Hijo preguntaba.
—Decid si habéis visto—al sol de los soles,
al que nos alumbra—con sus resplandores.
Dénos, Señora, las señas,—por si acaso lo encontramos.
—Es blanco como la nieve,—y como la aura encarnado.
Tiene unos cabellos—como el sol dorado;
sus labios y boca—son flores del año.
—Por aquí pasó ese Niño,—según las señas que dais
Al templo se encaminó,—id allá y lo hallaréis.
—Dios os pague, hijos,—esa buena nueva.
Ya encontrará alivio,—el alma en su pena.
Partió el Alma Divina,—al templo se encaminó.
Entre todos los doctores,—al Sol de Justicia halló.

The Virgin sought the Child through streets and squares,
and asked all those she met if they had seen her Child,
"Tell me if you have seen the sun of all the suns,
that one who gives us of his divine light."
"Describe him, dear Lady; we may meet him perchance."
"He is as white as snow, and as fair as the dawn.
The locks of his forehead are of a golden hue;
his lips and his mouth are the flowers of the season."
"That child passed by here, to judge from that description.
Go to the temple, lady, and you will find him there."
"The Lord reward you, children, for the good news.
My grieved heart will now find more comfort and peace."
The Blessed Mother to the temple directed her steps.
Among the doctors the sun of all justice she found.

The Holy Family

The Holy Family is a special object of veneration in New Mexico as well as in all Spanish countries. In New Mexican Spanish tradition, popular dramatic compositions, numerous prayers, hymns, nursery rhymes, and a few ballads attest the great popularity of the veneration for the Holy Family. The first prayer that New Mexican Spanish children learned from their mother's lips is the following one, no doubt traditional. It is known by all. As noted earlier, the Penitentes of New Mexico have a version of it in their ritual, and some of its verses are found in other New Mexican prayers.

—¡Bendito y alabado sea el	Blessed and praised be the
Santísimo Sacramento del altar!	Most Holy Sacrament of the altar!
—¡Ave, María Purísima!	Hail, Most Pure Mary!
—¿Quién en esta casa da luz?	"Who gives light to this home?"
—Jesús.	"Jesus."
—¿Quién la llena de alegría?	"Who fills it with joy?"
—María.	"Mary."
—¿Quién la conserva en la fe?	"Who keeps it in the faith?"
—José.	"Joseph."
—Pues bien claro se ve	"It is perfectly clear, then
que siempre habrá contrición,	that all those will be saved
teniendo en el corazón.	who hold in their hearts
a Jesús, María y José.	Jesus, Mary, and Joseph."
¡Salgan los espíritus malignos	May all evil spirits depart
y entre la suma bondad,	and may true virtue enter
y se estampe en mi alma	and may the Most Holy Trinity
la Santísima Trinidad!	take possession of my soul!
Purísima Concepción,	Most Immaculate Conception,
Madre del Verbo Divino,	Mother of the Divine Word,
échame tu bendición	give me your blessing
y guíanos por buen camino,	and show us the right way,
que yo la recibo en el nombre	for I now receive it in the name
del Padre y del Hijo	of the Father, and of the Son,
y del Espíritu Santo, Amén.	and of the Holy Ghost, Amen.

There are shorter versions, but none omits the beautiful verses beginning with "¿Quién en esta casa de luz?" and ending with "a Jesús, María y José," which are mumbled even by infants just learning to speak. In religious processions, such as first-communion processions, children used to sing the complete version given above. These verses are the oldest form of the prayer and are traditional. They probably came from Spain in some form in the seventeenth century. In the *Noche buena, autos al nacimiento del Hijo de Dios,* a seventeenth-century Spanish work by Gómez Tejada de los Reyes, we find in one of the *villancicos*, or Christmas carols, the following version of the above lines, one very close to the New Mexican prayer and probably one of the oldest versions:

—Zagal, ¿dónde está mi bien?	"Youth, where is my greatest treasure?"
—En María, Jesús y José.	"In Mary, Jesus, and Joseph."
—¿Adónde está mi alegría?	"Where is my joy?"
—En Jesús, José y María.	"In Jesus, Joseph, and Mary."
—¿Adónde toda la luz?	"Where is all my light?"
—En María, José y Jesús.	"In Mary, Joseph and Jesus."

In a Chilean version of the widely known Spanish traditional children's prayer that begins with the words "Con Dios me acuesto, con Dios me levanto," (I retire with God, and I rise with God) we find the following version of the verses in question:

—¿Quién es mi luz	"Who is my light?"
—Jesús.	"Jesus."
—¿Quién es mi guía?	"Who is my guide?"
—María.	"Mary."
—¿Quién corona la fe?	"Who sustains the faith?"
—José.	"Joseph."
Con vosotros viviré	With you I will live
lleno de paz y alegría,	in peace and in happiness,
y me serviréis de guía	and you will guide me,
Jesús, María y José,	Jesus, Mary and Joseph,
y el Santo de mi nombre,	and also the saint
Amén.	whose name I bear, Amen.

From the numerous popular hymns dedicated to the Holy Family it is not easy to select a typical example. Comparison of many of them with similar compositions from Spain and Spanish America reveals, as usual, that some are traditional and very old. Many changes have taken place, however; here and there new verses appear and sometimes entirely new strophes have been added. In New Mexican tradition the most popular hymns in honor of the Holy Family are called alabanzas de Jesús, María y José (praises to Jesus, Mary, and Joseph). All are in the well-known traditional Spanish octosyllabic meter, the meter of the Spanish ballads and, in fact, the most popular meter of Spanish poetry generally. The longest hymn of this series contains twenty-eight octosyllabic rhymed quatrains, or 112 verses. Many of these quatrains appear in shorter versions, so the essential differences between the various versions are to be found in the number of quatrains they contain. Below, with translation, are six quatrains from the long version cited above; it appears in a Penitente ritual and hymn manuscript from Peña Blanca:

Daremos gracias con fe
y crecidas esperanzas,
cantando las alabanzas
de Jesús, María y José.
Canten dulces serafines,
que yo les ayudaré,
a cantarles los maitines
a Jesús, María y José.
Los tres reyes del oriente,
por grande dicha se ve,
que adoran en el portal
a Jesús, María y José.
Esta Sagrada Familia
de Dios escogida fue.
Ya saben sus santos nombres
de Jesús, María y José.
En el trance de la muerte,
cuando agonizando esté,
me asistan los santos nombres
de Jesús, María y José.
—¡Misericordia, Señor,
Dios Uno, Trino!—diré,
poniendo de intercesores
a Jesús, María y José.

With faith and great hope
we will give thanks,
by singing the praises
of Jesus, Mary, and Joseph.
Let sweet seraphim sing,
for I will help them,
to sing the matins
to Jesus, Mary, and Joseph.
The three kings from the East,
what a great joy it is!
have come to adore
Jesus, Mary, and Joseph.
This Holy Family
was chosen by God.
Their names you know:
Jesus, Mary, and Joseph.
At the hour of my death,
when I am in my last agony,
may the holy names assist me
of Jesus, Mary, and Joseph.
"Mercy, my Lord, One God,
Triune God!" I will say,
begging for the intercession
of Jesus, Mary, and Joseph.

The Virgin Mary

The cult of the Virgin Mary in New Mexico is universal. Traditional Spanish ballads preserved in New Mexican tradition in which the Virgin Mary plays the chief role are found like many others in the manuscripts of the Penitentes. Not only ballads but also poetic compositions of other types, prayers, invocations, folktales, anecdotes, and miracles about the Virgin Mary abound in New Mexican tradition.

In the *coplas populares*, called simply *versos* in New Mexico, la Virgen de los Dolores, the traditional Spanish Virgin of Sorrows, is the most popular. Of the following two *coplas*, which are very popular in New Mexico, the first one is found in identical form in Spain, and the second one is apparently not only traditional, but also very old, for its syntax—the use of the subjunctive for the imperative in affirmative commands or requests in the second person singular—is that of fourteenth- and fifteenth-century Spanish.

La Virgen de los Dolores
quiere mucho a los Manueles,
porque se llama su hijo
Manolito de los Reyes.

Our Lady of Sorrows
loves all those called Manuel,
because her son's name is
Manolito of the Kings.

Madre mía de los Dolores, Tú has de ser mi intercesora. En la hora de mi muerte Tú me defiendas, Señora.	Dear Mother of Sorrows, intercede for me. In the hour of my death, Blessed Lady, assist me.

The May devotions to the Blessed Virgin are universally observed in New Mexico. Up to within recent years, it was the custom in every home to adorn with flowers of the field and garden a specially constructed altar in honor of the Virgin. Every night, prayers, including the rosary, were recited by all the members of the family, and hymns were sung. The hymns to the Virgin usually sung during the month of May included the well-known "Dulcísima Virgen del cielo delicia" (Most sweet Virgin, joy of Heaven") and "Venid y vamos todos con flores a María" (Come, let us all offer flowers to Mary), both of which are traditional Spanish hymns to the Virgin found in devotional books of Spain and Spanish America.

But the recitation of the rosary was not limited to the month of May. The devotion of the rosary was widespread in all Spanish Catholic families of New Mexico until the end of the nineteenth century. It is only in recent years that the devotion has decreased. The rosary, prayers, and other devotions were usually recited every night of the year, and hymns and ballads appropriate for the feast celebrated or for the season of the year were sung. The special rosaries for the sick and for the dead have always been popular. In saying the rosary for the dying and for the dead, traditional prayers, ejaculations, and verses accompany the *ofrecimientos* or special offerings of each of the mysteries of the rosary.

These *ofrecimientos* are numerous and varied, and most of them are traditional. In the rosary for the dying or for those recently deceased, and for whom a *velorio*, an evening of prayers and hymns for the dead, in this case, is being held, one of the most common forms of the verse offering at each mystery is the following:

Los ángeles en el cielo alaban con alegría, y los hombres en la tierra responden:—¡Ave, María!	The angels in heaven sing joyous praises, and men on earth reply, "Hail, Mary!"

When the rosary is recited for the souls in purgatory, the above formula is also used, but a more common one is the following, a traditional Spanish one to be sure, and one not altogether of popular origin, for there are two Latin verses in the original text:

Por las ánimas benditas que en el purgatorio están ofrezco este misterio. Lux perpetua luceat eas. ¡Requiescant in pace, Amén!	For the blessed souls who are in purgatory I offer this mystery. May perpetual light shine upon them. May they rest in peace, Amen!

A very extraordinary Spanish religious survival still found in New Mexico, although not generally, is the custom of singing matins in bed at the first signs of dawn. These matins are called *oraciones* or *alabanzas del alba* (dawn prayers or praises). The grandfather or eldest person in the family begins the singing, and the other members from their beds, wherever they may be, respond and join in the singing. According to available sources of information, the same custom exists in the country villages of Spain, Chile, and other regions of Spanish America. One of the best versions from New Mexico is the following:

Cantemos el alba;
ya viene el día.
Daremos gracias.
¡Ave, María!
Ángel de mi guarda,
noble compañía,
vélame de noche
y guárdame de día.
Ya nació María
para el consuelo
de pecadores,
y luz del cielo.
Tan bella grandeza
no quiso ver
la sierpe fiera
de Lucifer.
María Divina,
con ser tan pura,
fué celebrada
por su hermosura.
Éstas sí son flores;
éstas sí que son.
Gracias a María;
gracias al Señor.
En suma pobreza
ya parió María,
al Verbo Encarnado,
Nuestro amparo y guía.
Que todos los santos
del cielo nos valgan.
¡Oh, Jesús Divino,
guía nuestras almas!
La mula se espanta
con el resplandor,

Let us sing the matins;
daylight is coming.
We will give thanks,
Hail, Mary!
My Guardian Angel,
most noble company,
watch over me at night,
and protect me during the day.
Mary was born
for the comfort
of sinners,
and to be the light of heaven.
Such magnificence
Lucifer,
the venomous serpent,
did not wish to see.
Mary Immaculate,
although most pure,
was indeed famous
for her beauty.
These indeed are flowers;
indeed they are.
We thank Mary;
We thank the Lord.
In the greatest poverty
Mary gave birth
to the Word Incarnate,
our refuge and guide.
May all the saints
in heaven protect us.
Oh, Divine Jesus,
guide our souls!
The mule is frightened
at such radiance,

y el buey con el vaho
calienta al Señor.
 ¡Viva Jesús!
¡Viva María!
Cantemos todos
en este día.
 Bendito seas,
sol refulgente.
Bendito seas,
sol del oriente.
 Bendita sea
tu claridad.
Bendito sea
quien nos la da.
 Quien el alba canta
muy de mañana
las indulgencias
del cielo gana.

and the ox with his breath
gives warmth to the Lord.
 Hail, Jesus!
Hail, Virgin Mary!
Let us all sing
on this day.
 Blessed be you,
shining sun.
Blessed be you,
sun from the East.
 Blessed be
your light.
Blessed be the one
Who sends it to us.
 Those who sing the matins
early in the morning
obtain the indulgences
granted by God.

Of traditional Spanish prayers and hymns in New Mexico, there seems to be no end. A large number of hymns, not all of them traditional or really popular, were collected and published by Father Rallière in 1877 in his book *Cánticos espirituales*. Another abundant collection of traditional prayers, including the various versions of "El bendito," "El sudario a las ánimas del purgatorio" (the prayer for the souls in Purgatory), traditional versions of the Act of Contrition, the numerous and diverse prayers to the saints, exorcisms, and the like, could be compiled without great difficulty.

The Bachelor's Prayer

Turning to a lighter vein of religious tradition, one finds many examples of the survival of a special prayer, a humorous one, but one which is very common in all Spanish countries: *la oración del soltero* or *de la soltera*, the prayer of the bachelor or maiden who is looking for a wife or husband. The traditional and popular versions from Spain, Chile, and New Mexico that have been published are very similar. One of the best from New Mexico, which has taken on some modern dress, is the following *oración del soltero*:

 Después de tantos quebrantos
yo me quiero desposar,
y pido a todos los santos
que me quieran ayudar.
 Siendo mis pesares tantos
ya me arriesgo al matrimonio,

 After a long string of troubles
I wish to get married,
and I beg all the saints
to come to my assistance.
 My troubles are now so great
that I am brave enough to marry,

y pido a todos los santos
que me libren del demonio.
  Santa Sinforosa,
si yo he de encontrar esposa,
que sea mujer de casa,
cumplida, limpia y virtuosa.
  Santa Gertrudis,
que esté llena de virtudes.
Para guardar tal tesoro,
espero que tú le ayudes.
  Santa Elena,
que sea una mujer buena,
que cumpla con sus deberes,
y que no me tenga en pena.
  Santa Tomasa,
que cuide bien de su casa,
y no quiera averiguar
cuanto se mueve en la plaza.
  Santa Juliana,
que no se esté en la ventana,
mirando a los que pasan
y oyendo palabra vana.
  Santa Miquela,
que no sea de las que velan,
que deben a todos los santos,
y a cada uno su vela.
  Santa Inés,
si sabe hablar inglés,
que sepa decir, "No,"
y cuando debe, decir "Yes."
  Santa Delfina,
que no sea espadachina,
que no sea curandera,
astróloga ni adivina.
  Santa Dorotea,
ni muy linda ni muy fea;
pero no sirva de pena
si el mundo se ríe de ella.
  Santa Margarita,
si por ventura es bonita,
que sepa prenderse bien,
y ser limpia y exquisita.
  Santa Catalina,

and I beg all the saints
to protect me from evil.
  Saint Sinforosa,
if I really find a wife,
may she be a good housekeeper,
dutiful, neat and virtuous.
  Saint Gertrude,
may she be of fine character.
To keep such a treasure,
I hope you will help her.
  Saint Helen,
may she be a good woman,
may she perform all her duties,
and may she bring me no grief.
  Saint Thomasa,
may she take good care of her home,
and may she never worry
about what happens in the plaza.
  Saint Juliana,
may she not stay at the window,
looking at the passers-by
and listening to vain words.
  Saint Miquela,
may she not be one of those
who are always praying to the saints,
offering each a candle.
  Saint Agnes,
if she knows English
let her know when to say, "No,"
and when to say, "Yes."
  Saint Delfina,
I hope she won't be quarrelsome;
may she not be a medicaster,
an astrologer, or soothsayer.
  Saint Dorothy,
neither very beautiful nor very ugly;
but she must not worry me
if everybody laughs at her.
  Saint Margaret,
if perchance she is beautiful,
I hope she will know how to dress,
and be neat and dainty.
  Saint Catherine,

que sepa bien la cocina,
y no quiera pasar los días
en la calle o en la esquina.
  Santa Ana,
que no quiera andar galana,
paseando de casa en casa
bailando la varsuviana.
  Santa Isabel,
que nunca me sea cruel;
que a la tarde y a la mañana
me dé sopitas de miel.
  Santa Rosa,
que no sea muy mugrosa;
que *amás* de bailar *tustepe*
sepa hacer alguna cosa.
  Santa Sofía,
que se esté en casa de día,
y que no le sea costumbre
darme la comida fría.
  Santa Enriqueta,
que no me salga coqueta
y quiera pasar los días
paseando en la bicicleta.
  Santa Damiana,
que no sea tan cristiana,
que abandone sus quehaceres
a la primera campana.
  Santa Rosario,
que cuide bien de mi diario,
y no quiera gastar tanto
cual si fuera millionario.
  Santa Beatriz,
que ella me haga muy feliz;
y que sea mi escogida
una de las de San Luis.

I hope she will be a good cook,
and not wish to spend her time
in the streets or on the corners.
  Saint Anne,
may she not overdress,
and go from house to house
dancing the varsouvienne.
  Saint Elizabeth,
may she always be good to me;
whether it be late or early
may she always give me fine food.
  Saint Rose,
may she not be too unkempt;
and besides dancing the two-step
may she also know how to work.
  Saint Sophie,
may she stay at home during the day,
and may she never have the habit
of giving me cold food.
  Saint Henrietta,
I hope she will not be a flirt
and want to spend all day
riding around on her bicycle.
  Saint Damiana,
may she not be so religious
that she will give up her work
the moment the first bell rings.
  Saint Rosario,
may she be careful with my money,
and not wish to spend freely
as if I were a millionaire.
  Saint Beatrice,
may she make me very happy;
and may my chosen one be
one of the most virtuous.

Special Invocations

The traditional Spanish formula used in exorcising is rare in New Mexico. The prayers and brief invocations to the saints who are believed to be the special patrons of certain phenomena, however, are almost as common as in Spain. A few of the shorter ones, all traditional and in verse, are the following:

Señora Santa Ana,
Señor San Joaquín,
arrullá este niño,
se quiere dormir.

Dear Saint Anne,
Dear Saint Joachim,
lull this baby, please,
he wishes to go to sleep.

San Lorenzo,
barbas de oro,
ruega a Dios
que llueva a chorros.

Saint Lawrence,
you of the golden beard,
pray to our Lord
that it may rain abundantly.

San Isidro,
labrador,
ruega a Dios
que salga el sol.

Saint Isidore,
tiller of the soil,
pray to our Lord
that the sun will come out.

Santa Bárbara bendita,
que en el cielo estás escrita
con papel y agua bendita,
Santa Bárbara doncella,
líbranos del rayo
y de la centella.

Blessed Saint Barbara,
your name is written in heaven
on holy paper with holy water,
Saint Barbara Virgin,
guard us ever against
thunderbolt and lightning.

The following invocation is recited on setting a hen:

Padre mío,
San Amador,
todas pollitas,
y un cantador.

Dear Father,
Saint Amador,
may one be a rooster,
and the rest pullets.

2. The Penitente Brotherhood

Cleofas M. Jaramillo

In my youth, *La Hermandad de los Penitentes* (the penitentes' brotherhood) was still active.

Some years ago, I wrote to Mr. Jose Maria Chavez of Abiquiu, who was very well read in history, asking him to give me the origin of the penitentes. I quote his answer, translated as closely as possible from his original Spanish.

"As to the origin of the marked association *Los Penitentes*, it is a well-established fact in history. Born in the Holy Land, the same throng who demonstrated their joy by singing "Hosanna" while they spread their garments on the ground before Jesus, as he entered Jerusalem, afterwards cried out, "Crucify Him," which brought his death. On hearing of His resurrection, some of them tried to choke themselves by tying handkerchiefs around their throats. Others covered their heads and ran distracted. A few gashed their flesh and let their blood flow, trying in this manner to atone for the Innocent's bloodshed.

"Here you have the *penitentes;* later on, the *flagelantes*, their actions modified but not in the form of penance. From Egypt the practice spread to Germany, from there to Spain, and from Spain to New Spain. There is nothing wrong in its object, but it seems rather barbarous and scandalous before modern society."

However, the beginning of the sect is lost to history and different opinions exist as to its origin. St. Justin says that it first appeared in Perugia, and soon spread through Italy, across the Alps, into Switzerland and Germany.

During the sixteenth century, the *flagelantes* were found in Spain and all southern Europe. Some opinion prevails that there is a connection between the New Mexico *Penitentes* and the European *flagelantes*. Others believe that they are a survival of the Third Order of St. Francis and that the sect was brought here from Old Mexico by the Franciscan monks, gradually spreading through New Mexico and southern Colorado.

The first Christian to flog himself voluntarily seems to have been St. Pardulf, a Benedictine monk. The sect spread even among Protestants. In 1535, there was a group called Anabaptists, who whipped themselves.

Among the rules of the Order, most of which still hold good today, is one which states that associates must be members of the Catholic Church and of good repute. The *Hermano Mayor* is the elected head. Newly-initiated members are branded by three gashes cut lengthwise on their backs with a sharp *pedernal* (flint). Members must renounce all evil practices and abandon all feuds with their neighbors. Ill-gotten goods must be restored or atoned for by penance. They believe that pain and penance endured here on earth lessens suffering in the hereafter.

Due credit is given to the English writers who come to New Mexico and write such interesting books from second-hand information, but I wish here to contradict some of their statements.

One author starts his article on the *penitentes:* "Are they lunatics or murderers?" They are neither. The members that live according to the brotherhood's rules are the best, most sincere religious people.

My parents, who lived in Taos and Rio Arriba counties, two strongholds of the *Hermandad* penitente brotherhood, never heard of a penitente being crucified alive and left on the cross to die. In some of the most remote places, like Penasco, Mora and Las Truchas, penitentes have been tied to the cross, and there may have been an instance where a *penitente* died on the cross from exhaustion, from the long fast, loss or blood, or from the flogging which he had been practicing.

As to the statement that some of them have been buried alive, in punishment for the betrayal of secrets of the order, this is another exaggeration. I have heard of their being punished in various ways. One penitente was made to walk with chains, tying his feet together, while he carried a cross on each shoulder. Another was forced to walk blindfolded, his arms extended, holding in each hand a sword with its points resting on his loins. It was alleged that this brother met his death, when he stumbled and fell, the two swords crossing through his sides. A few days later, his clothes, tied in a bundle, were sent to his family, with word that the boy had left for the Holy Land.

One form of punishment was the criss-cross gashing of their backs, laying them on the floor and switching them with a knotted rope until they fainted.

A penitente sometimes requested, before his death, that he be buried bare-foot or without a coffin, as a penance. His request was always carried out.

The *disciplinas* (palm whips) were usually dipped in Romero decoction, to soothe the cuts and to keep them from becoming inflamed with the cold, and not to add more sting, as some writers say.

Penitentes never walked into a church or chapel carrying their crosses. They slipped from under them covered with their blanket, and each pair left their two crosses standing outside, interlocked in some way.

The Catholic Church has condemned the Order for years, excommunicating the members of the *moradas* who insisted upon going out and scourging themselves. This strict order of the Church, together with the weight of opinion among the younger members who are becoming educated, will in a few years put an end to the sect.

3. Holy Week at Arroyo Hondo

Cleofas M. Jaramillo

In this hidden nook, isolated from the outside world and still untouched by modern progress, people were contented to live their simple lives. Still holding to ceremonies carried on from the medieval age of faith and religious traditions, during Lent every year they reenacted with sincere religious fervor the Sorrows of the Passion Play. The *penitente* brotherhood took charge of the religious ceremonies, inasmuch as there was no resident priest in the town in my time.

On Monday and Tuesday of Holy Week the conical adobe ovens were seen smoking throughout the three villages, while the week's supply of bread and *panocha* was being baked. The mud ovens must be blessed before using them, or they won't bake the bread right; it will come out heavy and soggy. To bless the oven, a cross is laid on the floor of the oven, salt is sprinkled on the cross and prayers recited.

At the *penitentes' morada* where half the male population congregated on Wednesday, one *mayordomo* (sometimes two) was chosen for each day to supply the food for the brothers who fasted each day from Wednesday morning until Saturday noon, when the *mayordomos*

Penítente Morada

vied with each other in treating the *hermanos* to the nicest repast. Four or five of the *acompañadores* (brethren of light) were seen coming out of the *mayordomo's* house carrying four copper kettles hanging on a stick. These kettles contained *torrejas con chile* (egg fritters in chile sauce), *rueditas* (fried dried squash), and *sopa de fideos* (home-made spaghetti). They carried in an earthen bowl bread pudding, with cheese and raisins. All meat was forbidden during the four Holy days. Recipes for these lenten dishes will be found in my cook book of Spanish recipes.

There was a great deal of exchanging done of *charolitas*—dishes—at noon on both Holy Thursday and Good Friday. Neighbors and friends were seen carrying back and forth small bowls filled with *panocha, capirotada, torejas*, or whatever other nice dish they had prepared. This exchange of special dishes went on in every small village during Holy Week.

The *morada* stood across the river a few yards below the town. On each side of the door, resting against the wall, was a pile of century-old crosses, which were kept inside the secret room from year to year.

With a field glass my family had a very good view of the *penitentes* as they came out of the *morada*. The members were told that with this field glass we could distinguish their faces through the black masks. After this, for fear of being detected, the brethren of light stood in line outside the front of the door, holding up outspread blankets, thus screening the *penitentes* while they came out. They took up their crosses, over which a blanket was thrown, leaving only their heads and feet exposed. Followed by the *hermanos de disciplina* (flagelantes), they dragged their heavy crosses around to the back of the *morada* and proceeded on their painful way up the rocky trail to *el calvario* (Calvary Cross on the hill).

* * * * *

On *Viernes de Dolores*, the Friday before Good Friday, my grandmother carried out her votive promise of giving an alm and a dinner to the poorest family in the village.

She had brought from Old Mexico her favorite painting of *Nuestra Señora de Los Dolores* (Our Lady of Sorrows). The beautiful madonna face, with a tear like a pearl rolling down her pink cheek—her white hands clasping tightly the handle of the sword piercing her breast under her blue mantle—was tinted in soft shades on a tin sheet and framed in a fancy tin frame. Throughout the year every dime or nickel that the grandchildren could save was pasted around the picture inside the glass covering it.

The daughters and their children were invited also to the dinner. At the end of the meal, the tin frame with the painting was brought down; the nickels and dimes were taken off and together with a crown made from coffee cake dough baked very nice and brown, the hollow center filled with *melcochas*—candies, was given to the poor family as the promised alm.

The *Tenebrae*. On Wednesday evening, *Las Tinieblas* were held at the *morada*. The name *Tinieblas* was given this office because towards its close all the lights were extinguished to represent the darkness that shrouded the face of the earth at the time Christ expired on the cross, as well as to express the profound mourning of the Church at that time.

Fifteen candles were placed on a triangular wooden stand. Those at the sides were snuffed out successively, beginning with the lowest one, at the end of each of the eleven Penitential Psalms, representing the flight of the eleven apostles; the other three candles represented the three Marys.

When the central light, representing Christ, was the only one left, it was removed by the *rezador* to the back of the altar, where they continued their chant. Between chants, one of the *rezadores* stepped out to the front of the altar, and striking a match he whirled it around saying, "*Salgan vivos y difúntos, que aquí estamos todos juntos.*" The flash of light from the match represented the lightning. In the dim light the bent, huddled figures of the *penitentes*, their bodies bare to the waist, filed in through the low door. With their masked faces and long white trousers they looked ghostly. The air in the small oratorio room, already packed with men and women kneeling on the floor, became stifling. Above the roar of the wooden *matraca*, the rumbling of chains, the wail of the reed *pito*, groans and prayers, was heard the thud-thud of the *penitentes*' blood-matted whips.

The removal of the central light and its sudden reappearance represented Christ's death and resurrection.

At the close of the ceremony, all but one of the *penitentes* filed out to their secret room across the hall. The one who remained stretched himself across the floor at the door, and the brethren of light who accompanied him told the people that the brother requested in the name of God that every one step on him on their way out. I heard of a cruel woman who more than complied with the request by grinding her heel into the flesh of the *penitente's* bare back. Another one, more kind-hearted, begged the *hermano* to excuse her from complying with his request.

Moved by curiosity to see the inside of the *morada*, I once asked a *penitente's* wife, who was going to pay a votive debt to the *santos* at the *morada*, if I might accompany her. We climbed the hill on which the *morada* stood in the upper town and were admitted to the chapel. On the wall of the hall dividing the chapel from the secret room hung a row of whips. The woman crawled on her knees from one statue to another, placing lighted candles before each. I was left kneeling before the statue of the Crucifixion. Paralyzed with fear, I could not move, for there before me on the mud altar table stood the statue of *La Muerte*, Death, staring at me with one glass eye, the other eye shut, aiming at me with her drawn bow and arrow. Behind me I heard the *hermanos* going in and out of the room. I did not dare turn around for fear of seeing a *penitente* standing in back of me. This visit satisfied my curiosity.

For a couple of years during Holy Week a flagellant *penitente* with his *acompañador* came to our private chapel and asked permission to go in and make a visit. While the brother of light recited the prayers, the brother lay prostrated with arms extended on the floor before the altar. He got up and stood by the door while flogging himself, leaving the bloody marks of his *disciplina* on the white-washed walls. Then he left, still flogging himself as he passed in front of our store on the way back to the *morada*. My family persisted in believing that this was the man who had helped himself to one of the fat lambs from our corral and had come to atone for it. The oft-repeated verse of "*Penitente pecador, porque te andas azotando? Porque me comí un carnero gordo y ahora lo ando desquitando,*" applied in this case.

On one occasion, hearing the doleful notes of the penitentes' flute, I ran out to the front porch in time to see three *penitentes de madero* passing on their way to visit the lower town *morada*. My uncle, sitting on the porch step, teasingly grabbed me by both hands and swung me out towards them. My breath caught with fright as I thought that one of them had stretched out his hand from under his blanket to grab my feet.

Anyone wishing to see a *penitente* now must stay up quite late at night, and then he may get only a glimpse, as they come out only one or two at a time and are very carefully guarded and screened-in by the *acompañadores*.

Holy Week

On Maundy Thursday at two o'clock in the afternoon, the *Emprendimiento* (Seizure of Christ) took place. The men carrying the statue of *Nuestro Padre Jesus*, a life-sized statue of Jesus of Nazareth, crowned with thorns and dressed in a long red tunic, led the procession out of the Church. The *rezador*, reading the seizure and trial of Christ, walked behind the statue, followed by the throng of women.

From *la morada* on the opposite side of the town two files of brethren of light, representing the Jews, started out. These men had red handkerchiefs tied over their heads with a knot on top representing a helmet. They were preceded by a man dressed like a centurion. The Jews carried long, iron chains and *matracas*, or rattlers. On meeting the procession coming from the Church, they stopped before the statue and asked "Who art Thou?" The men carrying the statue answered, "*Jesus de Nazareno.* (Jesus of Nazareth.") The Jews then seized the statue, tied the statue's hands with a white cord, while their leader read the arrest sentence. The other Jews stood, loudly clanging the chains and rattling the *matracas*. They led the procession back to the *morada*, carrying with them the statue.

El Encuentro. The next morning—Good Friday—the same two groups took part in the ceremony. This time the group that left the Church carried the statue of *Nuestra Señora de la Soledad* (The Sorrowful Mary), dressed in black; a black mantle covering her head, over which a silver halo shone. The procession of men representing the Jews came from the *morada* carrying the statue of Christ. The two groups met half way around the town, representing the meeting of Christ and His Mother. One of the women took a white cloth from her head, and approaching on her knees wiped the face of the statue, while the grieving Marys wept real tears aloud. The *rezador* read the passage of the meeting of Christ and His Mother as the procession walked back to the Church.

About half an hour later, *La Procesión de Sangre* (The bloody procession) of all the *penitentes* combined, in the long double file of flagellants, was seen winding its way up the rocky trail to the *calvario*, then back again to the *morada*. Special self-imposed penances were practiced between one and three o'clock in the afternoon. A lone penitente sometimes staggered up the trail surrounded by brethren of light. He dragged his feet tied with a heavy iron chain. On his back a bunch of sharp cactus needles pricked his flesh at every step.

Good Friday. Las Tres Caídas (Three Falls). The largest and heaviest cross was picked out and laid upon the shoulder of the *hermano* who chose to represent the crucified Christ. A crown of thorns was placed on his head, and a bunch of prickly cactus was hung on his back. Laboriously, the *penitente* dragged the scraping cross up the rocky trail. Two brethren of light walked on each side of him, one reading the three falls in the Stations of the Cross from an open book in his hand. The other, acting the part of Simon Cyrene, helped the *hermano* lift the weighty cross when he stumbled and fell under its weight. A group of brethren of light had already dug a pit and gathered a pile of rocks by Calvary Cross. They stood around the *calvario*, awaiting the arrival of the *Cristo* brother, who on reaching the hill was stretched upon his cross and tied with ropes. The cross was raised and placed in the pit surrounded by the pile of rocks to hold it upright.

The *hermanos* knelt with bowed heads around the cross, praying and reciting the Seven Last Words of the crucified Savior. The voice of the man upon the cross grew more and more faint, as he repeated the words, until his body hung limp, and he was taken down and carried on a blanket, too weak to carry his cross back to the *morada*.

Las Estaciones. At three o'clock the people gathered at the Church for the Stations of the Cross. The procession of *penitentes*, some carrying crosses and others switching their lacerated backs, came first. Between the two files walked a masked *penitente* pulling a small cart in which stood the statue of Death. "Comadre Sebastiana" death was called. The *acompañador*, walking behind the cart, now and then picked up a large stone and dropped it into the cart to make it heavier to pull. The men carrying the statue of *Nuestro Padre Jesus*, another man with a crucifix, and the reader walked in the center of the procession. As the *rezador* read each Station of the Cross, the people knelt on the ground, then arose and walked singing a verse of the *alabado de las columnas*.

Én una columna atádo	Onto a pillar,
Estaba El Réy del Cielo.	The King of Heaven was tied.
Chorus	
Herído y ensangrentádo	Wounded and bloody,
Y arrastrádo por los suélos.	He was dragged on the ground.

A few days after the close of Holy Week, some of the young men would appear at the store looking pale and haggard. My brother, curious to find out if a certain young man were a *penitente*, gave him a friendly slap on the back. Taken unawares, the man betrayed his secret by a painful shrug and expression of agony on his face.

Sabado de Gloria closed the Holy Week with joy and cheer, for Lent ended at noon on Holy Saturday, and a big *baile* was given that night.

In most of the old Spanish mansions a *sala* (long living room) was always included. In this room the private invitation dances were given. To these dances only the exclusive Spanish society was invited. For the private dances of *carestrolendas*, egg shells filled with confetti

"Comadre Sebastiana" (Statue of Death)

or cologne water, were taken to the dance. These were playfully broken on the heads of the dancers, providing much merriment. Refreshments of wine, *biscochitos*, cakes and candies were passed to all the guests. This custom was attacked by the towns' parish priests in their sermons, but in the remote villages, which the priest visited only once a month, the people followed their own rules and customs.

* * * * *

On the first of August, the *penitentes* celebrated the wake of *La Porsiuncula*, the most important event, excepting Holy Week. The two *moradas* combined for this wake. The gloomy interior of the old church was illuminated by tallow candles placed on tin sconces hung on the side walls and stuck on the mud floor before the statues of *La Sangre de Cristo* (Christ on the Cross) and *Nuestra Señora de Los Angeles* (Our Lady of the Angels), which were brought down from their niches and set before the sanctuary steps.

The weird strains of the flute announced the approach of the *penitente* procession which stopped outside. The women and men kneeling on the mud floor moved to the sides, men to the left, women to the right, opening an aisle for the *penitente* chief and the brethren of light, who passed in, chanting hymns accompanied by the lonesome notes of the flute.

With arms crossed, they knelt in prayer before the statues, while the *mayordomo del velorio*, chief of the wake, distributed to each person a lantern. The lantern was made from a beer bottle, the bottom of which had been taken off by tying a string saturated in kerosene around it, and then burning off the string. Through the open bottom, candles were set in the neck of the bottle and lighted.

The *penitentes*, numbering about thirty, led the procession. First, walked the *flagelantes*, their bare backs streaming with blood. In unison, their whips were raised first over one shoulder and then over the other. They took two or three steps, paused, and then swung the palm whips over their shoulders again. Following the flagellants were those carrying crosses, each guarded by an *acompañador*, walking by his side. The brethren of light and the men carrying burning pitch-wood torches came next. In the middle of the procession walked the men with the statues; behind them came the *rezador* and the singer, Hemerejildo, reciting with great fervor the rosary on large blue and white glass beads hung around his neck. The women followed. The two lines of candle light circled the town, and the outline of the square could be seen from the top of the hill.

Each decade of the rosary was offered in song:

Jesús mi dulce dueño,	Todo cristiano procura,
Desagraviarte queremos,	Llorar un paso tan tierno,
Recíbe Padre amoroso,	Libra Virgen del infierno
Las flores de este mistério.	Quien rezara su rosario.

The lonesome lament of the flute and the wailful chant, punctuated by the painful slap of the palm whip, lingered in the echo of the hill after the procession had gone back into the *morada*.

4. Noche Buena and Religious Dramas

CLEOFAS M. JARAMILLO

"Let the luminarias leap high
As the night grows long,
And the shadows dance
To the caroler's song."

On the twenty-fourth of December the snow lay heavily on the deep valley, half burying the silent little villages nestling among the white hills. As the last rays of the setting sun turned the highest snow-capped peaks into gold and rose, the men and boys of the three villages busied themselves clearing the snow from the front yards in every house. They were preparing the ground for the *luminarias*, which later in the evening they built of *ocote*—pitch wood sticks, placed by fours in log cabin fashion. Rows of these *luminarias* outlined the towns and *cordilleras*.

As the deepening shadows of night spread over the valley, the brown adobe houses were brightened with the red glow of their fire, which warmed the groups of men and boys standing around them. The fires built in front of my house were kept burning brightly until midnight by an occasional addition of an empty kerosene barrel, which had been saved in the store for that purpose.

Inside the house there was great activity in the kitchen. The children warmed the *piñones* and shelled them by rubbing them between two boards. These nuts were used in the mince meat for the *empanaditas* (little fried pies). An extra hired woman beat the white corn dough until it was so light that a small piece dropped into a cup of water floated on top. It was then ready for the *tamales*, which were made and steamed, to be served with hot coffee after the midnight chapel services. Lupe and her helpers were kept busy until almost midnight, frying the *empanaditas* and *buñuelos* for the *Oremos* boys, who came to the door singing:

Orémos, Orémos,	Oration, Oration,
Del cielo venímos,	From heaven we come,
Angelitos somos,	Angels we are,
Si no nos dán Orémos,	If you won't give us gifts,
Ya no volverémos.	Alas, we won't return.
A las señoras caseras,	From the housekeepers,
Aguinaldos pedímos,	New Year's gifts we ask.
Con mucha alegría,	With great joy,
Con mucho contento,	With great contentment,

Vamos celebrando, Este nacimiento. Dénos aquí, si nos han de dar, La noche es larga, Y hay mucho que andar.	Let's celebrate this birth. Give us here, if you will give, For the night is long, And we have lots to walk.

A large pan of fried dainties was passed to these *Oremos* boys at the kitchen door, and they ate them, sitting around the bonfires.

Santa Claus was still unknown in those days. The *abuelo* (bug-a-boo man) took his place, although he was a stern old man dreaded by the children. Dressed in an old, shabby, patched suit and shabby hat, the *abuelo* went around the *luminarias* cracking his long whip, sending the boys home on the run. He followed some of them into their homes and made them kneel down and say their prayers. If they did not know their prayers, he gave them a good scolding and told them to stay home and learn them, but no sooner was the *abuelo* out of sight than the boys were out again, hopping, running and jumping over the bonfires, for the Spirit of the Christ Child filled their innocent hearts and fear could not remain long in them.

Down in the village the group that was to take part in the performance of the play of *Los Pastores* was going from house to house making *Las Posadas*. They represented Mary and Joseph going through the streets of Bethlehem seeking shelter for the night.

In earlier times, for nine days before Christmas groups of children led by a couple representing Mary and Joseph went through the village to nine houses. The group was refused entrance until they came to the ninth house, where they were admitted and refreshments passed to them. Here the hermit held up his cross at the door, trying to prevent *el diablo* from entering, but the shrewd evil one watched his chance and entered while the hermit was busy eating the refreshments spread before them. Satan played his pranks, helped himself to anything he liked, rattled his long nails, wrote in his book the names of the girls and women who smiled at him when he asked them if they wanted to come with him.

At the end of the village the group came to the chapel where the wake of *el Santo Niño* was taking place. Here the group gave the play of *Los Pastores*, the religious drama of the shepherds.

When making *Las Posadas*, Joseph knocked at the door of each house singing:

¿Quién le da posada A estos peregrinos, Que vienen cansados De andar los caminos?	Who will give lodging To these travelers Who come weary From traveling long roads?

A voice from within answered:

¿Quién da golpes a la puerta, Que de imprudente hace alarde, Sin reflejar que ya es tarde Y a los de casa despierta?	Who bangs at the door? The imprudent makes a commotion, Without noticing that it's late, And the household he awakes.

Joseph:

Señor os imploro Que en vuestra caridad, Le des posada a ésta dama.	O Lord, I implore Thee, That in Thy mercy Thou wilt give shelter to this damsel.

Voice from within:

Para el que tiene dinero Mi casa está lista, Para el que no tiene, Dios lo asista.	For him who has money, My house is ready, For him who has nothing, May God assist him.

Into a stable door they retired, where an ox and a mule were their only companions.

A BRIEF SYNOPSIS OF THE DRAMA "LOS PASTORES." There were twelve shepherds in the original play of *Los Pastores*, but at the time of which I write only six took part:

Characters

Shepherds—Tubal	Gila
Belicio	San Miguel
Lipido	El Ermitaño
Bato	La Estrella Oriental
Lizardo	Bartolo
Tebano	El Diablo

In earlier reproductions of this play, there was another female character—Dora, wife of Barto, one of the shepherds.

A shrine had been arranged with white sheets and a table at the head of the *oratorio* chapel. A double row of pine trees formed an aisle from the shrine to the middle of the room, through which the shepherds marched in double file, carrying flowery staffs with dingling little bells. A bundle slung over one shoulder suggested the bedding of the shepherds.

Ahead of them walked Hila, a serious-looking little girl, dressed in white, wearing over the veil on her head a tinfoil covered crown. She carried a small baby statue in a basket filled with snow.

Bartolo, the lazy shepherd, walked behind the other shepherds, carrying a sheepskin, which he spread under a tree and then lay upon.

The shepherds tramped up and down the aisle singing verses about the heavy snow and their flocks sleeping down in the valley.

Shepherd Song

Cielos soberanos, Tenednos piedad Que ya no sufrimos,	Que copas de nieve, Caen sobre el ganado, Aunque entre el monte

La Nieve que cae.

Suspende tus íras
Y tanto quebranto,
Que ya están poblados,
De Nieve los campos.

Las estrellas brillan,
Y luego se apagan
Absortas se quedan
De ver tal nevada.

The stars shine brightly,
Then get dim
Amazed to see
Such a heavy snow.

Está reclinado.

Sovereign heavens,
Have pity on us
For we cannot longer endure
The snow that falls.

Suspend Thy rage
So many damages,
For the valleys
Are already covered with snow.

What large snow flakes
Fall over the flock,
Although resting
Under the forest.

Belicio suggested stopping a while, to let the flocks rest, saying:

Pues hermanos míos,
Ya que el cielo nos ha permitido,
Traernos con grán dicha,
A estos valles dé Egipto,
Si les parecíere bien,
Parémos aquí un poquíto,
Que descansen los ganádos.

Well, my brethren,
Since heaven has permitted
Bringing us with great happiness
To this valley of Egypt,
If it seems right to you,
Let's stop here a while
To rest the flocks.

The rest of this drama will be found in my book of translated Spanish dramas.

El Día de Los Inocentes (Holy Innocents Day)

I do not know why this day was celebrated on the twenty-eighth of December instead of after the Kings' visit to the Manger, for it commemorates the day on which King Herod put the children of Judea to death by the sword. On this day one had to be very careful about lending things; and if you loaned something, you must not forget to say, "*Se la empresto, pero no por inocente.*" Anyone who forgot to say this had to pay a penalty.

On one occasion my aunt, who lived close by, sent her maid to ask my mother to let her have my baby brother for a little while. My mother, forgetting the day, let the girl take the baby. A few minutes later the maid returned with a tiny broom made of a few straws tied with red floss and wrapped in a little note with the words, "*Barrete la inocencia paga la pena.*" Mother at once set to work baking a cake which she sent to my aunt to *desempeñar* (redeem) the baby; he was sent back with the same cake bearer.

Dia de Año Nuevo (New Year's Day). Instead of the birthday, the Spanish celebrate the Saint's name day. New Year's day is the day of los Manueles, and the women and men called by this name were serenaded on this day.

One year my brother, who was visiting at my home during the holidays, thought he would play a joke on my husband. He slipped quietly out of the house at four o'clock in the morning and rounded up the musicians who were going around the town *dando los dias a los Manueles* (serenading).

We awakened with the sound of music and singing at our front door; my husband in bathrobe and bedroom slippers opened the door and was greeted by the usual verse:

"Por aquí caigo, por aquí levanto,
A darle los buenos días,
Pues hoy es día de su santo."

He politely invited the serenaders to enter; and they made themselves at home, while he ransacked my pantry for refreshments. My brother sat among them, with a broad smile, quite pleased with the success of his joke.

My husband's grandmother's name was Manuelita; and not wishing to disturb her so early in the morning, my brother had them come to our house to give the serenade in her honor.

* * * * *

Gifts were exchanged on the sixth of January, celebrating the arrival of the Three Kings at the Manger in Bethlehem to offer their gifts to the newborn Babe.

On New Year's day Grandma Melita started counting "*Las Cabañuelas*" for twelve days. Each day of the month represented one of the months of the year, and as the weather showed on each day so would the month be fair, stormy or cold. If January the second was fair and mild, so would the month of February be. The third was counted as March, and so on through each succeeding month. On the thirteenth, *Las Cabañuelas* were reversed and counted backwards, beginning with the month of December. This count was said to come out more true. The definition given for the word "*cabañuelas*" is "*Festival of the Jews of Toledo*," so this custom must be originally from Spain.

This marked the end of the Christmas ceremonies.

Religious Dramas

As the dramatization of Bible stories was an old Spanish type of entertainment, it has been assumed that the Spanish *conquistadores* brought the religious drama to Mexico, and that from there the Spanish missionaries introduced it into New Mexico in their efforts to convert the Indians to Christianity. There are four Christmas plays that come in a cycle—in this order: *El Coloquio de San José; El Auto del Niño Dios*, or *Pastorela*, now called *Los Pastores* with several versions; *Los Reyes Magos*; and *El Auto del Niño Perdido*.

El Coloquio de San José begins with a summons from Simeon to all the males to appear at the temple with a reed in hand, for the purpose of choosing a husband for Mary, one of the Virgins in the Temple.

When Feliciano, the herald, comes to Joseph, he voices the wishes of his master, saying:

Vós patriarca escuchad.	Patriarch, thou listen.
Pues ya sabeis que Simeón,	Well thou knowest that Simeon,
Cabéza de éstas comarcas,	Head of this territory,
Manda púes que los patriarcas	Commands that all the patriarchs
En su real generación,	In his royal generation,
Hoy al templo soberano	Today at the sacred temple
Sean obligados a Ilevar,	Are obliged to appear
Una vara en su mano	With a reed in their hand,
Y de parte de Simeón	And I, for Simeon,
He venido a tí avisar.	Have come to inform you.

Joseph, because of his poverty, is reluctant to go into the temple, and he sits in the portico. Suddenly his reed sprouts forth a lily, and he is chosen to espouse Mary.

After the Annunciation, several months elapse; and Joseph and Mary are on their way to Bethlehem. On reaching the town, they go from house to house seeking lodging for the night. This part of the action is represented by *Los Posadas*, which is an introduction to the play of *El Niño Dios*, or *Los Pastores*, the second drama of the cycle.

Then comes the third drama, *Los Reyes Magos*. The three kings, noticing the new star in the East, decide to go to Bethlehem and offer gifts to the Christ Child. They stop at the palace of King Herod, who gives them welcome and asks them to stop again on their return. The kings reach the manger and present their gifts. After they leave, an angel appears and bids Joseph to take Mary and the Infant and flee into Egypt. On the way the Holy Family meets a number of shepherds, who recognize them.

The fourth drama of the series is called *El Niño Perdido*. Christ, being separated from His parents comes, in his wanderings, to a rich man's palace. The rich man is seated at a banquet table when the Child arrives. He tries to confuse the Child with his questions, but is given wise answers. At the end, the Child arrives at the temple, and the Doctors of the temple gather around to question Him, while Mary and Joseph are looking for Him. The script of this play is given in my book of Spanish dramas.

* * * * *

Besides the Christmas cycle, there is an earlier one of more simple folk plays, some of which are still enacted in remote mountain villages. This cycle is composed of three plays: *Adán y Eva, Caín y Abel* or *El Primer Pecado*, and *Lucifer y San Miguel*. It is claimed that "Adam and Eve" is the oldest play written. It opens with a song by Adam and Eve, as they are sitting on a bed of boughs underneath the Tree of Knowledge:

Song

Guerra es la vida del hombre
En la estación de sú império,
De morir en la campaña, irrevocable el decreto.

Lucifer calls all his helpers to dethrone man from the position to which God has elevated him. "Appetite" volunteers to tempt Eve, in the form of a serpent. Eve snatches an apple from the forbidden tree, and passes it to Adam, who is eating it when God, in a thundering voice, reproves them for their disobedience. Shamefacedly, they try to cover their nudity with branches of leaves. God orders them out of the garden. "Mercy" intercedes and begs that the penalty be waived. God promises man redemption through the birth of Christ. Eve laments their fall in a long recitation. The angels then foretell the coming of Christ, and the play ends with the song:

Gloria a Dios en las alturas,	*Glory to God in the highest,*
Y paz al hombre en la tierra.	*And peace to man on earth.*

The first drama presented in New Mexico, was The Moors and The Christians, given at San Juan de los Caballeros, during the dedication of the first church built by the Oñate expedition. When first enacted these dramas were held out in the open; afterwards they were given in *salas* (dance halls).

During the past thirty years the Spanish religious dramas have been discontinued. A few years ago a new legend of Our Lady of Lourdes was presented at Chamita, and in recent years Los Pastores have been revived, and the legend of Our Lady of Guadalupe, but these few presentations given, are not acted with the same vim, nor in the natural setting and costumes, and they have lost much of their attractiveness.

The legend of Our Lady of Guadalupe, which originated in Mexico over four hundred years ago, tells the story of a shepherd:

Juan Diego, the Indian shepherd, while tending his sheep on the hills near the city of Mexico, sees a vision. The Virgin, surrounded by a radiant light, appears to him, saying: "Juan, go to the Bishop and tell him to build a shrine in my honor here on this spot." Juan delivers the message, but the Bishop refuses to believe his story, until after the fourth apparition, when he brings a proof in the form of fresh roses which the Virgin commands him to pick on top of the mountain and to take to the Bishop. This is taken as a miracle, being in the month of November when the country was barren of flowers.

Upon being admitted, Juan kneels before his superior and relates the episode of the roses. As he opens his blanket, the fragrant roses tumble out at the Bishop's feet. On the blanket was stamped the image of the radiant Lady, just as the Indian boy had seen her in the apparitions on the hill. In robes of blue and rose, rays of light surrounding her, she was poised on a crescent moon, born up by a cherub's wings. The astonished Bishop is now convinced and orders the shrine of Our Lady of Guadalupe built on Tepeyac hill. The miraculous blanket was hung in a gold frame over the altar.

A new shrine, noted for its riches, now stands at the foot of the hill. The rail enclosing the sanctuary and the stairways leading to it contain many tons of solid silver. Twelve massive, solid silver candelabras hang from the ceiling, and a dozen silver candlesticks adorn the altar.

I visited the *santuario* during the holidays, which start a week before the celebration of the feast of Our Lady of Guadalupe.

Crowds of pilgrims visited the church. Some of them holding lighted candles crawled on their knees from the door to the rail before the altar. Others sat in the yard eating their lunch, or at the booths where hot lunches were being served. Many climbed the hill to the spring, on the site of the old shrine, and filled bottles with the miraculous water to carry home. Faith still gives it the power to perform miracles and to cure.

5. Saints' Holy Days

Cleofas M. Jaramillo

Día de San Juan (St. John's Day)

Icy winter glided into spring. April showers gave life to the gray valley and turned meadows and fields into verdant seas. In warm, sunny May, rivers and arroyos filled with water that came from the mountain's melting snow. The overflowing *acequias* wound their way through freshly ploughed and planted fields.

School closed late in June, and on the twenty-third my father awaited me in the convent parlor. After bidding goodbye to my teachers and to Sr. Rosana, the principal, who was one of the pioneer sisters brought by Bishop Lamy, I joined him and climbed in the high seat of our buggy, of a make now forgotten. We rode along, inhaling the delicious fragrance of the newly-awakened sage and gray-green rabbit brush, which later in the summer would be covered with yellow blossoms. The desert plain seemed a fairyland. Here and there the road dropped into a verdant little valley, the sparkling river fringed with fresh green trees and drooping willows. From the edge of the highest ridge one looked down into the Arroyo Hondo, sunken valley, which in its rich verdure seemed to lie asleep, the deep silence enveloping the valley—broken only by the rattling of our buggy wheels or the distant barking of a dog.

I arrived home in time for the feast of the beloved disciple St. John. The women of the village were up early on the twenty-fourth of June. At six o'clock they were bathing in the river or in the *acequias*. Later in the morning the small children were seen also in the river and ditches, splashing cold water at each other, for on this day the waters in the streams were believed to be holy. Better health awaited those who rose early to bathe at least their faces and feet in the holy water. For was it not St. John who baptized Jesus in the river Jordan and blessed the waters?

The day was kept at Arroyo Hondo as a Rogation Day. By eight o'clock in the morning a procession started from the Church in the upper town. Standing on a wooden platform, the statue of *Nuestra Señora del Rosario,* dressed in a gala blue silk dress, and the statue of *San Juan,* carried in the arms of one of his devotees, were taken on a tour through the fields, along the foot of the second ridge of hills to the lower village—a distance of three miles. On arriving at the village, the procession visited each house. A boy beating a drum went ahead announcing the approach of the procession, which halted about ten feet from the door of the house. The lady of the house came out to meet the *santos,* with an *escudilla* full of live coals, over which aromatic incense had been sprinkled. She incensed the statues and helped carry them into the *sala,* where they were placed on an improvised altar decorated with wild flowers and tree branches.

Around the altar the crowd of people knelt while the lady of the house recited prayers, sang a hymn, and pinned a flower or jewel on Our Lady's veil or dress. Then the people arose and proceeded to the next house. Having visited every house in the lower village, the procession walked to the middle town, then up the *Cordillera* to the upper town, reaching the Church at dusk, where a wake in honor of the saints was held. Sometimes the wake was held at the house in which the procession stopped just before dusk.

* * * * *

On the Fourth of May was celebrated *El Día de La Santa Cruz* (Feast of the Holy Cross). At the chapel or at thc home of a devotee an altar was erected in tiers. On the top tier a wooden, decorated cross was placed. From here it was brought down and rested on each step, while a prayer or hymn was sung or recited. Then the cross was taken out in procession to the next village, where a wake was held in honor of the Holy Cross.

* * * * *

Día de Santiago

The feast of *Santiago,* the national patron saint of Spain, was and still is celebrated in some of the northern towns, on the twenty-fifth of July. After the morning services at the Church, the statue of Saint James, the patron saint of *los caballeros* (horsemen), was carried in procession through the town. Two files of gallant horsemen, *socios de Santiago,* with their horses' bridles decorated with flowers and flags, rode ahead of the procession. A few yards from the procession they halted, turned, and rode back through the center of the procession in pairs to meet the statue. The two files crossed and galloped ahead. Again they whirled and galloped back to the statue, repeating this during the whole procession.

The *gallo* race, held years ago, has been replaced by horse races and modern sports. The rooster race of old was similar to the rooster race the Indians have at San Juan Pueblo, except that the Mexicans, instead of hanging the rooster as the Indians do, bury it in the ground, leaving its head exposed.

At Arroyo Hondo a group of *galleros* gathered at one end of the street, about fifty feet from the buried cock. One by one, they raced past the rooster, back and forth at full speed, leaning over the side of their saddles to grapple at the fowl, until one of them succeeded in grabbing its head and unearthing it. Swinging it by the legs over his head, with a triumphant shout he spurred his horse and raced ahead, the whole pack of horsemen yelling and racing after him. Up the *cordillera* they chased to the upper town. When finally one of the *galleros* overtook him, he turned and hit the man with the rooster. The challenged horseman grabbed away the trophy and raced on ahead, hotly pursued by the others. The rooster changed hands in this way several times during the race. Back they came like an avalanche, lashing their horses, yelling and racing down the hill to the lower town, where they crowded around the leader. A hot skirmish ensued. The *gallero* defended himself by striking in all directions with the rooster, until the cock was torn to pieces.

After several roosters met this fate, the crowd scattered, and a wagon was hitched, in which the *convite* for the *baile* started out. A fiddler, a guitarist, and a singer climbed into the wagon and rode around the three towns, playing and singing, finally coming back to the hall where the dance was to be held. This was the public invitation to the dance.

Early in the evening the hall was packed. Gray-haired *abuelitas* cuddling the *nietos* lined the back row around the hall. The young women who took part in the dances sat in front. All classes mingled in these public dances, from the silk-gowned *patrona* to the calico-dressed Indian maid. The elite left the dance early, before the men became too gay with drink. Sometimes a drunkard forced his way into the hall, causing great excitement when the *bastonero* tried to push him out.

Jealous husbands and lovers sometimes took advantage of the commotion to get even with their rivals, and a fist fight took place in the middle of the hall. The women—screaming and jumping over seats, dragging by the hand children that were half asleep—pushed their way out. When finally the *bastonero,* with the aid of the sheriff or sober men, restored order, the dance went on.

Through the clouds of smoke from the home-grown *punche* tobacco cigarettes, the bent heads and crouching shoulders of the *musicos* were seen. There was languor and softness in the wire strings, then recklessness and madness, as the dance wore on and *tragitos* from the musicians' pocket flasks went to their heads.

Día de Santa Ana

The next day was *Santa Ana's* day. Every woman fortunate enough to own a riding horse and side saddle brought them out. And with a white sheet thrown over the saddle and tied underneath to keep the long flowing skirts from soiling, she rode off, dressed in all her finery, to join the other lady riders. When tired of riding, they dismounted at the dance, which continued through the hot afternoon into the night.

These Holy days were always gala occasions eagerly awaited and long remembered.

6. The Felicity of Mexico in the Wonderful Apparition of the Virgin Mary, Our Lady of Guadalupe

Luis Becerra Tanco (1675)

Tradition of the Miracle

The year was that of the birth of Our Lord Christ 1531, and the tenth year and almost four months of the dominion of the Spanish in this City of Mexico and the Province of New Spain, the war being over, and the Holy Gospel then beginning to flourish in this Kingdom. On a Saturday, very early in the morning, before the dawn began to break, an Indian, humble, poor and honest, one of the recent converts to our Holy Catholic Faith, who in Holy Baptism was named Juan, surnamed Diego—and who was a native, according to all that is known, of the town of Quatítlan, distant four leagues from this city to the north, a man of the Mexican nation, and married to an Indian who was named María Lucía, of the same station in life—was on his way from the town in which he was living (said to have been Tolpetlac, which was near by) to the church of Santiago el Mayor, Patron of Spain, which was under the rule of the religious of St. Francis, to hear the Mass of the Virgin Mary.

As dawn was breaking he arrived at the foot of a small mount which was called Tepeyacac, which means the extremity or sharp summit of the hills, because it rises above the other mountains which surround the valley and lake[1] in which the City of Mexico lies, and it is the greatest of them; it is the one now called that of Our Lady of Guadalupe, because of the events now to be described.

From the top of a hill, on the summit of rocks which rises above the level plain at the edge of the lake, the Indian heard sweet and harmonious singing which, as he said, seemed to him like that of a multitude and variety of birds who were singing together with delicacy and harmony, the choirs responding one to another in singular concert, with echoes resounding and reechoing, being repeated from the high hill above the little peak where he was, and as he raised his eyes to look at the place where he thought the singing was created, he saw there a white and resplendent cloud, and around and within it a rainbow of many colors, which was formed by rays of light of exceeding clarity which shone forth from within the cloud. The Indian stood entranced, and as if outside himself in a gentle state of ecstasy,

[1] Mexico was originally built on many islands in a large lake, which during the centuries has been filled in.

without fear, or perplexity of any sort, feeling within his heart a joy and gaiety inexplicable, so strong that he said to himself:

> *What is this that I hear and see? Or to what place have I been spirited away? Or where shall I look to find the world? Perhaps I have been taken to the paradise of delights which our forefathers call the origin of our flesh, the flower garden, or celestial land, hidden from the eyes of man?*

While in this state of suspension and rapture, when the singing stopped, he heard himself being called by name, *Juan,* in a woman's voice, sweet and delicate, which came from the splendors of the cloud, and which asked him to draw near; so he climbed the slope in all haste, and came close by.

The First Apparition

He saw in the center of that brightness a most beautiful Lady, very similar to that of the blessed Image today, described by the Indian in words before ever the Image was created or anyone else had seen Her, whose robe, he said, *shone so brightly that its glory shone around over the rough rocks on the hilltop, and the stones appeared to be precious gems and transparent, and the leaves of the thorns and cactuses, which grow very small there, and meanly, because of the dryness of the place, appeared to be clusters of fine emeralds, their twigs and stems and thorns of burnished gold and shining; and even the ground of the little level plain which was there on the summit appeared like jasper with many colors blended together.*

And the Lady began to speak to him with a serene countenance and in endearing tones, in the Mexican language, saying: *Juan Diego, my son, whom I love tenderly, like a little and delicate child* (this is the sense in the Mexican language), *where are you going?*

The Indian answered: *Noble mistress, and my Lady, I am going to Mexico, to the village of Tlatelolco to hear the Mass which the Ministers of God, His substitutes, offer for us.*

Having heard this, the Virgin Mary said to him: *My very dear son, you must know that I am the eternal Virgin Mary, Mother of the True God, Author of Life, Creator of all, and Lord of the Heavens and of the Earth, Who is present everywhere, and it is my desire that a church be built here in this place for me, where, as your most merciful Mother and that of all your people, I may show my loving clemency, and the compassion that I bear to the Indians, and to those who love me and seek me and to all those who seek my protection, and call upon me in their travail and afflictions, and where I may hear their sorrows and prayers and give them consolation and help. And so that my will may be accomplished, you must go to the City of Mexico, to the palace of the Bishop who lives there, to whom you will say that I have sent you, and that it is my pleasure that he build me a church in this place; and tell him all that you have seen and heard; and you may be sure that I will thank you for all that you do for me in this that I put in your care, and you will be noted and exalted by doing this. Now, my son, you have heard my wish; go in peace and be sure that I will repay you for the work and diligence you employ, so spare no effort in doing this.*

The Indian, prostrating himself on the ground before Her, made answer, and said: *I go, most noble Lady, and my Mistress, to carry out your command as your humble servant: wait a little while for me.*

The Indian then took his leave with profound reverence and set out along the dike which leads to the City, below the slope of the hill, facing the west. In doing as he had promised, Juan Diego went straight to Mexico, which was a league distant from that place and hill, and entered into the palace of the Lord Bishop, who was the most illustrious Don Fray Juan de Zumárraga, the first Bishop of Mexico. When the Indian entered the Lord Bishop's palace, he asked the servants to ask the Bishop to see him and talk to him, but they did not go to tell him then, whether it was too early in the morning, or because they saw that he [Juan Diego] was poor and humble; they kept him waiting a long time, until, moved by his patience, they gave him entrance.

When he came into the presence of his lordship, he fell upon his knees and delivered his message, saying that *the Mother of God sent him, Whom he had seen and talked with that day at dawn,* and he related all that he had seen and heard, just as it has been given above.

The Bishop heard with amazement and wonder what the Indian told him, pondering much over a case so astonishing; he did not value the message very highly that he brought, nor did he give him real belief and credence, judging that it was all the Indian's imagination, or dream, or fearing that it might be an illusion of the devil, since the Mexicans were recent converts to our Sacred Religion: and although he raised many questions about what he had related, and found him consistent, yet he dismissed him, saying that he should come back again in a few days because he wanted to inquire into the matter on which he had come very thoroughly, and that he would devote much time later on, in order (it is clear) to inform himself of the quality of the messenger and to have time for deliberation.

The Indian left the house of the Lord Bishop very sad and disconsolate, as much because he knew he was not entirely believed as because he had not been able to bring about the doing of the will of the Holy Virgin Mary, Whose messenger he was.

Juan Diego returned that same day rather late, towards sunset, to the town where he lived, which, so far as we can know from all reports, was the place called Tolpetlac, which lay on the other side of the tallest peak, at a league's distance to the northeast. Tolpetlac means "the place for mats of cat-tail reeds," because in that time it was the sole occupation of the Indians of this pueblo to weave mattings of the leaves of this plant.

The Second Apparition

When the Indian had reached the top of the hill where that morning he had seen the Virgin Mary, he found Her waiting there for the reply to her message; and as soon as he saw Her, he knelt in obeisance and said to Her: *My very dear Daughter, my Queen, my Lady Most High, I did what You asked, and although I was not given entrance right away to see and talk with the Bishop, after a long time I did see him, and gave him your message in the way You commanded: he heard me quietly and with attention, but from what I saw in him, and from the questions he put to me, I do not think he believed me, because he told me to come back again, so that he could inquire of me at greater length about the business on which I came, and examine it to the roots. He presumed that the church which You ask to be built is a fiction of mine, or a fancy of mine, and not your will: and so I pray You, that You send some noble and chief person for this purpose, one worthy of respect and to whom credence will be given; because You see, my Mistress, that I am a poor country man, a humble villager, and this matter on which You send me is not for me: pardon me, my Queen, for my boldness, if in anything I have exceeded what is fitting and owing to your greatness; I do not wish to fall under your indignation or to have displeased You with my reply.*

This colloquy, in the form which is given, is contained in the historic writing of the Indians, and does not have in it anything of mine, but is the translation of the Mexican idiom into our Castilian language, phrase for phrase.

The Blessed Virgin Mary heard the Indian's reply with graciousness, and when he had finished, She said to him: *Listen, my well-beloved son, be assured that I do not lack for servants or people to command, for I have many whom I could send if I wished who would do that which I ask them; but it is very fitting that you attend to this matter, and I ask it of you, and through your intervention my will shall be accomplished, and my desire: and so I pray you, my son, and command you, to return tomorrow to see and to talk with the Bishop and tell him to build me the church that I ask of him; and that She who sends you is the Virgin Mary, Mother of Very God.*

And Juan Diego replied: *Do not be displeased, my Queen and my Lady, with what I said, because I will go with a very good will, and with all my heart, to obey your command, and to take your message; I did not want to excuse myself from it, nor did I consider the road a task, but it was only that perhaps I would not be accepted nor well heard, or if the Bishop did hear me, he would not give me credence. I will do all that You command me; wait for me, Lady, tomorrow in this place, at the setting of the sun, and I will bring back to You the reply which he will make, and so I leave You in peace, my exalted Daughter, and God keep You.*

The Indian took his leave in profound humility, and went to his town and his house. It is not known whether he told his wife[2] or any person what had happened to him, because history does not tell anything about it; but since he was perplexed and ashamed over not having been believed, he likely did not want to say anything until seeing the end of this matter.

On the following day, Sunday, the 10th of December, Juan went to the Church of Santiago Tlatelolco to hear Mass and attend Christian Doctrine; and when the sermon was over which the missionary ministers preached for the native parishioners in each jurisdiction (that at Santiago of Tlatelolco was then one only and very large; it later was divided into others, when there were enough priests), the Indian went again to the palace of the Lord Bishop, in obedience to the command of the Virgin Mary.

And although the Lord Bishop's people delayed a long time in giving notice of him that he might be heard, when he entered, he knelt in the Bishop's presence and told him with tears and lamentation *how for the second time he had seen the Mother of God in the same place where he had first seen Her; that She was waiting there for the answer which the Bishop had given him before; and that She had commanded him anew to return to him and to tell him to build Her a church in that place where he had seen Her and talked with Her; and to assure him that it was the Mother of Jesus Christ who sent him, the eternal Virgin Mary.*

---

[2] His wife had died two years earlier, according to all other chroniclers.

The Lord Bishop heard him with great attention, and began to be moved to give him credence; and to assure himself more about the matter, he asked him various questions, and questioned him over again about what he had said, advising Juan Diego that he looked with favor upon what he was telling him, and he could now tell from the signs that it was Our Lady who sent him, but although he recognized by these that it could not have been a dream, nor a fiction of the Indian's, to better ascertain the obligation of this matter, and so that there would be no levity in giving credence to a simple tale told by a poor and plain Indian, he told him *that it was not enough, this that he had told him, to start to undertake what he asked him to do; and that he should tell the Lady who sent him to give him some signs by which it could be made clear that it was the Mother of God who sent him, and that it was Her will that a church be built there.*

The Indian responded *that he should see whatever sign that he should choose; that he would ask it of Her.*

The Lord Bishop parried this, for he had not expected that the Indian would ask for a sign, or would question him concerning it, until, without any confusion at all, he asked him to choose the sign that he wanted. He called two people, those most in his confidence of his household, and speaking to them in Castilian, which the Indian did not understand, he commanded them to identify him very carefully and to make themselves ready to follow after Juan Diego when he left, and not to lose him from their sight, nor to let him suspect that he was being followed, but to keep behind him until he came to the place he had talked about, and where he said he had seen the Virgin Mary; and he told them to take notice of any with whom he spoke, and to report carefully on all that they might see or hear; and this was done as the Lord Bishop commanded.

When the Indian took leave of his Lordship's presence, the servants followed after him without his noticing them, and they kept him always in sight. But when Juan Diego came to the bridge under which flows the river which at that place, and almost at the foot of the hill, empties into the lake on the east of the City, the Indian disappeared from the sight of the Bishop's servants who were following, and although they searched for him with great care, looking all over the mountain, they did not find him; and taking him for an impostor, and liar, and wizard, they returned indignant over him; and, having informed the Lord Bishop of all this, they besought him not to believe in him, and to let him be punished for the deception, if he should return.

The Third Apparition

As soon as Juan (who had passed out of sight of the Lord Bishop's servants) reached the summit of the hill, he found the Blessed Virgin Mary there, waiting a second time for the answer to her message. Kneeling in Her presence, the Indian told Her *how, in fulfilling her commandment, he had returned to the Bishop's palace, and had given him her message; and that after various questions, and being questioned over again on the same matters, the Bishop had told him that his simple story was not enough upon which to take action in a matter so grave, and that he asks You, Lady, for a sure sign by which he can know that You sent me, and that it was Your will that he build You a church in this place.*

The Blessed Virgin Mary thanked him for his care and diligence most pleasantly, and told him to come back the following day to this same place, and that here She would give him a sure sign by which the Bishop would believe him; and the Indian took his leave of Her courteously and promised obedience.

The next day, Monday, the eleventh of December passed with Juan Diego being unable to carry out what She had asked him to do because, when he had arrived at his town, he had found his uncle, Juan Bernardino, whom he loved very dearly, and revered as a father, to be very ill of a sudden and malignant fever which the Indians call *Cocoliztli* [typhus], and he took compassion on him and spent the greater part of the day in seeking out a doctor among his people, so that some remedy might be applied; and when he had brought the doctor to where the sick man was, he gave him some medicines, but the illness grew much worse. And that night, the sick man, feeling very weak, besought his nephew to go, early in the morning before it grew light, to the monastery of Santiago Tlatelolco to ask one of the religious there to come to administer the Holy Sacraments of penance and extreme unction, because he believed that his illness was mortal.

The Fourth Apparition

When it was nearly dawn on Tuesday, the 12th of December, Juan Diego set out with all haste to call one of the priests and to return there in company with him as his guide; and so, as the day was about to break, he reached the place where he began to climb up the slope of the hill, when it crossed his mind that he had not come back the day before to carry out the will of the Virgin Mary as he had promised. And it seemed to him that if he continued to the place where he had seen Her, She would censure him for not having come back as She had commanded; and in his innocence he thought that by taking another path which went around the foot and lower slopes of the hill, She would not see him nor be able to detain him. Because the errand he was on was most urgent; once free of this duty, he could return to ask for the sign to take to the Bishop; this is what he started to do, and just as he passed by the place where now there is a spring of bitter alum water, right at the turn of the hill, he encountered the Virgin Mary.

The Indian saw Her as She came down from the top of the hill, surrounded by the white cloud and the brilliant light as when he had first seen Her. And She said to him: *Where are you going, my son? And what road is this you are taking?*

The Indian stood there perplexed and frightened and ashamed, and then, having fallen to his knees, he answered Her in confusion:

> *My beloved Daughter, and my Lady, God keep You. How did You waken? In good health? Do not be angry with what I have to say. Hear me, my Lady, and know that a servant of yours, my uncle, is dangerously ill of a sudden sickness and mortal; and because he is very weak, I am hurrying to the church of Tlatelolco in the City, to call a priest to come and confess him and give him unction, as we are all born subject to death. And after I have done this duty, I will come back here to this place to obey your command. Forgive me, I pray You, my Lady, and have a little sufferance, as I am not trying to avoid doing what You have commanded your servant, nor am I making any false excuse. Tomorrow I will return without fail.*

The Blessed Virgin Mary listened to the Indian's apology with a serene expression, and then spoke to him in this manner: *Listen, my son, to what I tell you now. Do not be troubled, nor disturbed by anything; do not fear illness, nor any grievous happening, nor pain. Are you not under my shadow, my protection? And am I not life and health? Are you not in my favor, and do you not go on my errand? Do you need anything else? Do not be troubled, or take thought of your uncle's illness, for he will not die of this seizure, and is well even now.* (And it was so, as he learned later on, according as She had said.)

Now when Juan Diego heard these things, he was so consoled and persuaded that he said: *Then send me, my Lady, to see the Bishop, and give me the sign, as You said, so that he will give me credence.*

The Virgin Mary then said to him: *My very dear and tender son, climb up to the top of the hill where you have seen me and talked with me, and cut the roses that you will find there, and collect them together in the skirt of your cape, and bring them here to me in my presence, and I will tell you what you have to do and to say.*

The Indian obeyed, without making answer, although he knew of a certainty that there were no flowers there in that place, since it was all rocks, and nothing grew there.

When he reached the summit, he found there a beautiful garden of roses of Castile, fresh, fragrant, and with dew upon them; and, holding his mantle, or *tilma,* in the way Indians are accustomed to do, he cut as many roses as he could hold in it, and took them into the presence of the Virgin Mary, who was waiting for him at the foot of a tree of the kind the Indians call *Quançahualt,* which is the same as the spider-web tree, or tree of prayer, which does not produce any fruit, and is a forest tree, and produces only white blossoms in its season. And, considering the site, I judge that it is its ancient trunk which still exists there[3] on the lower slope of the hill, towards the east, with the alum-water spring in front of it. And here was the place, without doubt, where the miraculous painting of the blessed Image took place; because the Indian, kneeling in the presence of the Virgin Mary, showed Her the roses he had cut, and Our Lady, gathering them all into Her hands, put them back again into the Indian's mantle and said to him:

> *Here you see the sign which you have to take to the Bishop, and tell him that with these roses as the signs, he is to do what I have commanded; and listen carefully, my son, to what I tell you: Do not show what you are carrying to anyone on the road, nor open your cape, except in the presence of the Bishop; and tell him what I have just now commanded you to do; and with this you will give him the courage to build my Church.*

The Apparition of the Image

And with this, the Virgin Mary said farewell. The Indian was very happy with the sign, for now he understood that he would have a good outcome and succeed in his mission, and, carrying the roses with great gentleness, without dropping one, he looked at them from time to time, enjoying their fragrance and beauty.

[3] That is, it was standing in 1666, when Becerra Tanco presented his narration in the official Proceedings.

Juan Diego arrived with his last message at the Episcopal Palace, and although he asked various servants of the Lord Bishop to tell him he was there, he did not succeed in this for a long time, until they, being vexed by his importunings, noticed that he had something wrapped in his cloak. They tried to find out what it was, and although he resisted their rudeness as well as he could, they managed by their hardiness to discover what it was that he carried. Finding that he had roses, they tried to take some, seeing how beautiful they were. And when they had tried three times to touch them with their hands, it appeared that the roses were not real, but painted, or woven with art into the cloak. The servants then gave news of all this to the Bishop, and when the Indian entered into his presence and gave him his message, he added that he brought with him the signs which he had commanded him to ask of the Lady who sent him, and, opening his cloak, the roses fell out of it to the floor and, painted upon the cloak, there was the Image of the Blessed Virgin Mary, just as one sees it to this day.

The Lord Bishop gazed with wonder at the marvel of fresh roses, fragrant and with dew upon them, just recently cut, since it was then the most rigorous weather of the winter season in this climate, and (a greater wonder still) the Holy Image, which appeared painted on the cloak. When he had worshipped before it as a Heavenly thing, and all of his household who were present also, he untied the knot of the Indian's cloak—at the back of his head—and took it to his Oratory, and having placed the Image befittingly, he gave thanks to Our Lord and to His glorious Mother.

All that day the Lord Bishop detained Juan Diego in his palace, doing him honor; and the next day he gave order that he go in his company and point out the place where the Blessed Virgin Mary commanded that Her church be built.

When they arrived at the place, he pointed out the site, and the places where he had seen Her and spoken the four times with the Mother of God. And then he asked permission to go to see his uncle Juan Bernardino, whom he had left very ill, and when he had obtained this, the Lord Bishop sent some of his party with him, commanding them that if they found the sick man well, to bring him back with them into his presence.

The Fifth Apparition

When Juan Bernardino saw his nephew accompanied by Spaniards, and the honor in which they held him, and when they had arrived at his house, he asked the reason for that new state of things. Juan Diego then told him the whole relation of his messages to the Lord Bishop, and how the Blessed Virgin had assured him of his uncle's healing. And when Juan Bernardino asked him the hour and moment in which he had been told that he was freed from the fever, he then said that it was in that very same hour and moment that he had seen that same Lady, just as Juan Diego now described her, and that She had given him complete health, and that She had said *that it was Her pleasure that a church be built at the place where his nephew had seen Her, and likewise that Her Image should be called Santa María de Guadalupe.* She did not say why.

And when the servants of the Lord Bishop understood this, they brought both Indians into his presence, and when Juan Bernardino had been questioned about his illness, and the way he had recovered his health, and the form in which the Lady had appeared, which She had given herself, and being satisfied that this was true, the Lord Bishop took both of the Indians to his palace in the City of Mexico.

Already the fame of the miracle had spread all around, and the people of the City were running to the Bishop's Palace to marvel and pay their respects to the Image. Whereupon the Lord Bishop, seeing the great concourse of people, took the Holy Image to the Great Church and put it on the Altar, where all could rejoice in it, and where it remained while the Hermitage was being built in the place which the Indian had showed them, in which later it was installed, after a procession and very solemn *fiesta*.

This is all the plain tradition, and without ornament of words; and this relation is to such a degree certain that if other details were added, whatever they might be, they would be, if not absolutely false, at least apocryphal, because the form in which it is told agrees very closely with the precision, brevity, and fidelity with which the reliable Indians and historians of that century wrote, painted, and related the memorable events.

The reason which the Virgin had for calling Her Image that of Guadalupe, She did not give, and so it will not be known until God will be served by disclosing this mystery.

7. Theological Significance

JEANETTE RODRIGUEZ

Within the Roman Catholic Church, devotion to Guadalupe's image and message has been used to discuss the significance and role of Mary (Mariology). While this is a very rich dimension in the faith life of Roman Catholics, I believe it is not the only or the best utilization of the story and image. There are three areas in which the understanding and application of the Guadalupe event may offer some theological insights to the larger church: (1) popular religiosity, (2) Guadalupe as symbol of God's unconditional love, and (3) the need for "feminine" metaphors for a more comprehensive understanding of the divine.

Guadalupe: "Of the People"

To appreciate the significance of Our Lady of Guadalupe it is crucial to understand the context in which she is recognized: popular religiosity. Popular religiosity—that is, how religion is lived and experienced by a majority of people (Schreiter 1985:122)—contributes to our understanding of Our Lady of Guadalupe. The adjective "popular" literally means "of the people." Although there is no comprehensive theory of popular religiosity, I offer a number of considerations that may assist in understanding this dynamic force.

One of the major elements of life among Hispanics in general and among Mexican-Americans in the United States is a system of folk customs and faith expressions termed popular religiosity or *religiosidad popular* (see Rodriguez 1990), which can be defined as the complexity of spontaneous expressions of faith which have been celebrated by the people over a considerable period of time (Elizondo, personal communication). They are spontaneous in that the people celebrate because they want to and not because they have been mandated by the official hierarchy, in this case the Roman Catholic tradition. When I speak of Catholicism in relationship to the Mexican-American culture, I am not referring to the institutionalized version of Catholicism, but to popular Catholicism, handed down through generations by the laity more than by the recognized and/or ordained clergy. There is a distinction between popular religiosity and what is called official religiosity (the institutional church). Although Hispanic popular religiosity has its historical roots in sixteenth-century Catholicism, it has evolved a life of its own that captures the identity and values and inspirations of the people in a way that I believe official religiosity has ignored. This way of being Catholic has always thought of itself as being the true faith of Christians, as being as "equally Catholic" as the clergy's version (Espín and García 1989:70–90).

From the point of view of the institutional church, popular religiosity has not been seen as equally Catholic, but as primitive and backward, perhaps even childlike. But popular religiosity is a hybrid with a life of its own: it continues to exist because for the poor and marginalized it is a source of power, dignity, and acceptance not found in the institutional church. Popular religiosity is not celebrated by a few, but by the majority of the people. It is an expression of faith which has survived over a considerable period with roots in the historical beginnings of Hispanic culture. Above all, popular religiosity is active, dynamic, lived, and has as its object to move its practitioners, the believers, to live their beliefs. That is, the people's own history, both personal and cultural, their own possibility for being saved in history, is expressed. Popular religiosity not only narrates a people's own history, but also acts it out and represents it. The life of the people is life as a human-divine drama in which the natural and supernatural claims are intimately intertwined. It is the humanization of God and the divinization of humanity. Humanity's cause (the poor) is the cause of God; God's actions for the cause of the poor are the actions that humanity must realize (Siller-Acuña 1981c).

In the example of the story and context of Our Lady of Guadalupe, she is God's action on the side of the poor, as is Juan Diego. In his encounter with the religious powers of the time, he is the protagonist, representing all who are marginalized. Similarly, Mexican-American women are the poor; Guadalupe comes and stands among them to reflect who they are—mother, woman, *morena,* mestiza—and gives them a place in a world that negates them.

Some of the documents of the church support this notion of popular religiosity. One of the fruits of the Latin American Church Conference at Medellín in 1968 was the serious discussion about popular religiosity. In *Pastoral Care of the Masses,* the Medellín Conference confirmed that in our evaluation of popular religion we may not take as our frame of reference the Westernized cultural interpretation (Second General Conference of Latin American Bishops 1973) and reaffirmed the vision of Vatican II that the Christian community should be so formed that it can provide its own necessities. (See Chapter 2, on the Nahuatl interpretation of the story and symbology.) This congregation of the faithful, endowed with the riches of its own culture, should be deeply rooted in the people. ("Decree on the Church's Missionary Activity, Vatican II," article 15, in Flannery 1975). The church attempts to discover and respect the presence of God in the concrete expressions of a particular culture. One such concrete expression has been revealed in the apparition of Our Lady of Guadalupe.

Popular religiosity is not only a vehicle for evangelization of many disparate Hispanic communities, but also functions as a form of resistance to assimilation. At the CTSA (Catholic Theological Society of America) Conference of 1989, Doctors Espín and García pointed out that popular religiosity is an important guardian of culture, history, and identity; without popular religiosity we (Hispanics in general and Mexican-Americans in particular) would not be the people we are. "Our identity as an integral part of the Catholic Church would not have survived the frequent clashes with the non-Hispanic—and often, anti-Hispanic—ways of the church in America" (Espín and García 1989:71).

When "we who are church" begin to theologize, we must be conscious that our theological methods are colored by who we are as individuals and which culture we are interpreting from. I express my ecclesiology with the expression "we who are church" to indicate ownership and identity as opposed to handing over of a church that is something outside of ourselves and a nonevolving institution. Because Our Lady of Guadalupe lives and breathes within this realm of popular religiosity, our theologizing must come from within, in this case, Mexican Americans' popular religiosity. There are many living Gospel values and metaphors of who and what God is that are expressed through Mexican-American culture. Through popular religiosity, Our Lady of Guadalupe's presence and message has been able to empower her people as they interact with the society of the United States. The emphasis on family values, the notion of enduring suffering, the ability to hope against all hope, a spontaneous feeling of connection and relationality, the unquestioned sense of God's providence as it is delivered through Our Lady of Guadalupe, the warm conversational sense of the presence of God, respect and love for all beings—all of these are found in the image of Our Lady of Guadalupe, as expressed by the women of the study in Chapter 6. Other popular faith expressions are pilgrimages, to the basilica for example; or sacred moments like Good Friday, Las Posadas (a reenactment of Mary and Joseph seeking lodging), and the making of *mandas* (promises). For Mexican Americans, the liturgical year begins with the Marian feast of Our Lady of Guadalupe.

These faith expressions of popular religiosity are readily accessible to anyone without exception and no one is excluded from participating in them. They provide a deep sense of unity and joy, while providing a forum for shared suffering. They are participatory and everyone takes an active role in them. The faith expressions, while serious, are not overly organized. The challenge, I believe, is not to eliminate them or simply to reduce them to a devotional celebration but to bring them into constant dialogue with the Word of God as contained in Scripture, tradition, and everyday revelation.

Some principal characteristics of popular religiosity (as set forth by Schreiter 1985, Galilea 1981, and Marzal 1973) are the assertion that God exists and everything is controlled by God; that God is rarely approached directly—hence the importance of powerful mediators such as Jesus and Mary (Schreiter 1985:158); and involvement and participation of the whole community (Schreiter 1985:129). There is, however, a private dimension to popular religiosity which we saw in the interviews with the women of my study. This private dimension is built upon the seeking of favors. The world is seen as interconnected and controlled, which is to say that the concerns of the inhabitants are concrete and requests are directed as immediate needs. Prescriptions for religious activity of the official religion are usually not observed in popular religiosity. For example, attending mass is not considered as important as visiting the basilica (Schreiter 1985:130).

The work of José Luis Gonzàlez (1983) is helpful in expanding our understanding of popular religiosity. He asserts that it operates out of a principle of participation that integrates the world in such a way that everything is perceived as interdependent or relational. For example, I am who I am because I am somehow related to you. Members of community-oriented communities that live and breathe within the realm of popular religiosity refer to each other as *hermana o hermano* (sister or brother).

If God is immediately involved in all worldly affairs, then any event that happens, good or evil (that is, physical, natural evil as opposed to moral evil), can be attributed to God's decision. Even in daily conversation members of the Mexican-American community use the phrase *si Dios quiere* (if God wants).

Vital relationships with nature and nature's integration of positive and negative forces are part of the religious experience in popular religiosity. The world is seen as an interconnected and controlled place and this perception is confirmed by the forces of nature leaving little room for human maneuvering. For example, the earthquake in Mexico in 1985 was attributed to God's disfavor with the people.

Our Lady of Guadalupe's clear connection to nature is seen both in her image and in the fiestas that celebrate her. She is surrounded by the sun, the stars, the moon, and nature. In her fiestas all children carry roses to her image, indicating that a proper celebration of a divine event must contain beautiful elements of nature. In the celebration of Guadalupe, sacred space and time are particularly important. There is a specific day, December 12, designated to celebrate the feast and a specific time, dawn. The people rise at daybreak, the time of new beginnings and the rebirth of the sun, to sing *Las Mañanitas* (a dawn song) to her.

For those who participate in the realm of popular religiosity, religious experience permeates all space and time. There are spaces and times of special strength and power that are part of the religious experience. Some examples of these phenomena are home altars, shrines, processions, and grave sites. Our Lady of Guadalupe clearly represents a familial and relational component in Mexican-American life. She identifies herself as their mother and they are all brothers and sisters to each other. The notion of the sacred being immersed in history is seen as Our Lady of Guadalupe takes a central role regarding the vital necessities of life—food, shelter, safety, and concern for family. She is petitioned for everything from health to the protection of a family-owned business. Her image is found in many homes and businesses in the form of pictures, statues, and altars and is worn on people's bodies in the form of necklaces and even tattoos.

All of these examples are significant to the people and their religious life, but they are not institutionalized, that is, they are not formally structured with rigid rules and procedures.

It is crucial to understand that popular religiosity is rooted in marginality and oppression. Official religiosity usually rejects religious symbols that express the people's marginality, and in doing so also rejects the people. For example, a newly assigned pastor removed the Hispanic people's statue of Jesus, which graphically depicted his suffering. The people, who identified closely with the statue, were outraged and exclaimed, "If you do not want our Jesus then you do not want us either."

In the story of Our Lady of Guadalupe, as in the present, she is still not accepted by some officials of the church. Many parishes with large Hispanic populations still refuse to place an image of our Lady of Guadalupe in their churches. She is, however, recognized and welcome among the people, with whom she shares the experience of rejection.

In the realm of popular religiosity there is a longing to critique and alter our reality and understanding of the sacred. Values and beliefs expressed through liberation theology, such as the value of justice in which all people are co-creators of the reign of God, are part of this longing. I define liberation theology in the terms of Gustavo Gutiérrez (1973): it is a theology of the people whose focus is the struggle of the poor to overcome oppression. It is not a theology created by the intelligentsia, the affluent, or the powerful, but by the poor and oppressed. It is a theology that believes in a God of history, that believes that God is active and present in the world, and that it is not enough that the hearts and minds of women and men be converted, but that the very structures that perpetuate systems of injustice must enter a similar conversion process. This is of course to suggest a radical change in the current social and political situation and overturning the established order. In the same way that Exodus and the Gospels function as a source for theology of liberation, so too has Our Lady of Guadalupe been the driving force behind many struggles for justice among Mexicans and Mexican Americans. We need only look at the Mexican Revolution, the plight of the farm workers, and the emergence of the basic Christian community. When Father Hidalgo called out for the Mexican Revolution in 1821, he rallied the people under the banner of Our Lady of Guadalupe, as did César Chávez and Dolores Huerta in rallying the *campesinos* (farm workers) to fight for their rights as laborers. However, I caution against reducing Our Lady of Guadalupe to a political cause or ideology as the Christian God has been used. Liberation theology may also serve as a challenge to the popular religious notion of ethical and economic evil as being God's will.

Within popular religiosity social organization is predominantly horizontal, with temporal responsibilities which do not separate persons or give unequal weight to functions. In preparation for Las Posadas, Holy Week, Día de los Muertos, or All Souls' Day, everyone plays a role of equal importance, whether their task is to make the tortillas or proclaim the Word. In celebrating Our Lady of Guadalupe, social organization is present in a paramount way. No role is of higher status than any other. All are essential to the celebration, all are valued and affirmed. The presence of clergy, although desired, is not required and the fiesta could easily take place without them.

Guadalupe: Symbol of God's Unconditional Love

As seen in the practices of popular devotion, presence and immediate contact are vital in the world of symbols. The image of Our Lady of Guadalupe in the churches must be accessible and within reach, so that devotees may touch it or rub their hands across the frame or touch the candle before the picture. It is not enough to recognize a symbol; it must be held, experienced, and received. The symbols that emerge from the Guadalupe event are concrete: flowers, music, the sun. Not only does she come in her full presence adorned with cultural symbols that the people recognize, but she enters into their history. Through her affirmation and acceptance of her people, she gives them a reason to hope and to live.

The symbol of Our Lady of Guadalupe manifests the creating energy and creative power which is God. She is nothing less than God's self-giving, or grace. I understand grace in relational terms: not so much God as a person I love or God as a person who loves us, but God as love itself. God is love and the way of experiencing that love is within the dynamic of a relationship. Divine nature is relational and self-sacrificial: to share in the life of God, for God to give God's whole self to us, means that we live in some kind of relationship. How do we know we are living in that kind of relationship? We need to look at the relationships in our life to answer this question: Are they life-giving? Are they hopeful, affirming? Do they inspire growth? In Mexican-American women's relationship with her, Our Lady of Guadalupe comforts and renews their spirit.

God's grace is universally and unconditionally offered; it is God's self-giving. Our Lady of Guadalupe becomes a symbol and a manifestation of God's love, compassion, help, and defense of the poor. She restores her people's dignity and hope and gives them a place in the world and in salvific history. The first manifestation of God's creative energy and creative power is creation—to give life, to bring something forth. To this extent, I believe that Guadalupe may be a symbol of that grace of God. It is the dynamic giving of oneself to another, Guadalupe offering herself to the people in a life-giving and transforming way that is full of grace. One of the first things we say about the historical Mary is that she is filled with grace.

One of the stations of this grace, or God's self-giving, is experienced through the women's relationship with Our Lady of Guadalupe. Presence should be first among our pastoral tasks because of the high value Mexican-Americans place on relationality and interdependence. Within a pastoral context, then, presence is understood as visibility, accessibility, active listening, and sustained dialogue with Our Lady of Guadalupe. These factors are evident in the women's stories as they relate their relationship and their understanding of what and who Our Lady of Guadalupe is.

There is a danger of mistaking the *symbol* for the reality. Our Lady of Guadalupe is not God; she is a metaphor for God. All the qualities attributed to her (loving, comforting, present, maternal) are qualities of God. Her image is as a nurturing woman and mother, but God has what have been stereotypically designated as female as well as male qualities. Thus, the symbol of Our Lady of Guadalupe is a matrix of meaning: she tells us something about who we are (in the Mexican-American women's case, that they are female, mother, *morena,* marginalized), and she tells us something about who God is: God is the source of all life, maternal, compassionate, and present, and protects the poor and marginalized.

At the heart of any assumptive world for an individual or an overarching culture, there is always some ultimate symbol which ties everything together and which people can give themselves to. As anthropologists would say, an ultimate symbol should be capable of containing within itself the highest aspirations and desires of the people. In Julia's words, Our Lady of Guadalupe does this: "Our Lady of Guadalupe represents to me everything we as a people should strive to be: strong yet humble, warm and compassionate, yet courageous enough to stand up for what we believe in, no matter how tense the pressure. Above all, obedient to God's will." As a universal symbol Our Lady of Guadalupe bridges cultures: for Mexican-American women she affirms them because she looks like them and is a woman and a mother, and she affirms their Anglo-educated side, challenging sexism.

Although she may be more appealing to darker-skinned people than to light-skinned people, her message affirms the darker-skinned but also transcends ethnicity. She is grounded in Mexican history, but functions as a symbol of God's love, not only for Mexicans but for everyone.

Certain symbols may not be effective for an individual or for a group. For example, the symbol of God the Father may not work for the Mexican-American community, so the symbol of Our Lady of Guadalupe may speak more to them about the nature of God or about how God relates than do many of the classical symbols of God. Mexican-Americans may experience the Divine working through Our Lady of Guadalupe in symbols that are not the standard ones of official religiosity.

The understanding of where Guadalupe manifests herself is of utmost importance. Within the context of popular religiosity, that is, a context where the people are, a context and source of people's identity and values—this is where Our Lady of Guadalupe engages the people. The things for pastoral ministers and theologians to watch most closely are the ultimate questions her devotees ask, the places God is present in their lives, and how they celebrate and bring that to expression. These things I believe are revelatory.

Guadalupe: The Feminine Face of God

The significance of Our Lady of Guadalupe in popular religiosity must assume a dialectic posture with contemporary Catholic theology, and so we look at the insights that feminist theology has given us in terms of the maternal or feminine face of God.

Hispanic colonial evangelization taught that the Christian God was more powerful than the indigenous gods. The proof was that those who fought under the banner of the Christian God became successful conquerors. The Christian God was, more likely than not, imaged by those in power to reflect themselves. There is thus a metaphor and a constellation of images surrounding the God brought by the conquistadors.

Christianity preached forgiveness, mercy, compassion, and reconciliation. The symbol used by the dominant Spanish culture to communicate these values was the Virgin Mary. Representing Christianity to the newly conquered, the missionaries did not connect these fundamental Christian elements with God in their catechisms; they did connect them with Mary. These traits at the time were held to be maternal and also may have reflected the way the Spanish might have wanted the Indians to feel toward their oppressors. All of these "maternal" qualities were attributed to God by the missionaries, but in the conquered population's mind the association of God with the powerful and victorious was primary. Mary, however, was presented as loving. comforting, and accepting; she was clearly the faithful and solidarious one (Espín 1991:99).

Even in the early history of Hispanic Christianity, there is a dichotomy of attributes: those that are powerful but somewhat alienating were attributed to the male white European Christian God, and the more affective, maternal reconciling ones to the Virgin Mary. Dr. Espín (1991:98) asks, "How do Hispanics experience God as faithfully solidarious with them?" He suggests that perhaps we need to remove from the word "God" all the dominant, conquering demons it evokes.

If, instead of looking for the explicit use of the term "God" or other God-related activities, we look at instances when Mexican Americans seem to be relating explicitly or implicitly to a divinity closer to the Gospel's real God, we will discover a very clear presence of faithful solidarity in their operative definition of that God. The surprise is that this faithfully solidarious one is Mary, the Virgin, says Espín (1991:100). There is historical evidence that these stereotypical attributes of the feminine have been presented through Marian symbols and thus have traditionally been ascribed to Mary as Our Lady of Guadalupe. It is easy to perceive Our Lady of Guadalupe as the maternal or female face of God, because she evokes an unconditional love, solidarity, and a never-failing presence at the affective level. But in doing so, we inaccurately remove these attributes from where they rightly belong: to God.

I myself struggle with this concept, because naturally I am drawn to the caring and nurturing presence of Our Lady of Guadalupe, but I am committed to retrieving the basic meaning of her message and placing it within a new context. I am in a relationship with her; when a relationship is expressed, it reveals something about both the person and (in my case) that person's relationship with God through Our Lady of Guadalupe. What does the metaphor of Our Lady of Guadalupe tell us about who God is?

A tremendous amount of scholarly work has been done on Mariology, less on Our Lady of Guadalupe. Because Our Lady of Guadalupe is a Marian image, Mariology can contribute to an understanding of the image of Our Lady of Guadalupe and the truth about God which she expresses. In this section I rely heavily upon the insightful scholarship of Elizabeth Johnson.

The Marian phenomenon throughout history has been powerful precisely because it is a female representation of the divine, bearing attributes otherwise excluded from mainline Christian perceptions of God as Father, Son, and Spirit. In official religiosity, the feminine face of God has been suppressed and excluded, and female images of God have migrated to the figure of Mary. Now some Catholics feel what Johnson calls a theological necessity: to express the mystery of a Christian God adequately, God must be envisioned in ways inclusive of the reality of women and other marginalized groups. Those elements in the Marian symbol which properly belong to divine reality must be retrieved (Johnson 1989:500–501).

Toward a more gender-inclusive theology of God, the Marian tradition offers its powerful maternal and other female images of the Divine. Through this process of integration, the figure of Mary no longer has to bear the burden of keeping alive female imagery of the Divine, and the figure of God becomes our loving Mother to whom we entrust our needs. Again, for some, it may be difficult to image the male face of God as a loving provider, but the Marian image is not meant to replace but to enhance the personhood of God.

There are many incidents of the split of divine attributes traditional in Christianity. In an influential work, theologian Edward Schillebeeckx (1964:101–128) argued that God's love is both paternal and maternal but that the mother aspect of God cannot be expressed through the historical figure of Jesus as a male. God selected Mary so that the "tender, mild, simple, generous, gentle and sweet" aspects of divine love could be made manifest: "Mary is the translation and effective expression in maternal terms of God's mercy, grace and redeeming love which manifested itself to us in a visible and tangible form in the person of Christ, our Redeemer."

Feminist theologian Elisabeth Schussler Fiorenza (1979) explains the split by a long process of patriarchalization, as a result of which the divine image became more remote and judgmental, while Mary became the beloved "other face" of God. Intellectually a distinction was maintained between adoration of God and veneration of Mary, but on the affective, imaginative level people experienced the love of God and the saving mystery of divine reality in the figure of Mary (Johnson 1989:513; Schussler Fiorenza 1983:130–140).

What accounts for Hispanics' massive and persistent devotion to Mary? Latin American and U.S. Hispanic theologians view Marian images from a liberationist theology point of view: Mary's cult appeals strongly to the oppressed because she gives dignity to downtrodden people and thus renews their energy to resist assimilation into the dominant culture. Further, as Virgil Elizondo points out, the cult not only liberates downtrodden peoples but also liberates us from a restrictive idea of God (Johnson 1989:514; Elizondo 1977:25–33, 1983b).

Within the Roman Catholic tradition Our Lady of Guadalupe is a Marian image, and within the Hispanic culture she is a mestiza, a mixture of both Spanish and Indian blood. The event and figure of Our Lady of Guadalupe combined the Nahuatl female expression of God with the Spanish male expression of God which had been incomprehensible to the Indians' duality—their belief that everything perfect has a male and female component. Each understanding of God was expanded by the other, yielding a new mestizo expression which enriches the understanding of the selfhood of God (Johnson 1989:515). "The results of the new expressions of God and the Mother of God are an amazing enrichment to the very understanding of the self-hood of God. There is no longer the European expression of God-Nahuatl, but a new mestizo expression which is mutually interpreted and enriching" (Elizondo 1983b:61).

"Even for those who do not find Mary a personally viable religious symbol, she nonetheless does represent the psychologically ultimate validity of the feminine, insuring a religious valuation of bodiliness, sensitivity, relationality, and nurturing qualities. . . . The symbol of Mary as feminine principle balances the masculine principle in the deity, which expresses itself in rationality, assertiveness, and independence" (Johnson 1989:517).

Within the Roman Catholic tradition Marian devotion and the study of Mary are sources of understanding the divinity in female language and symbols. Johnson identifies five female images for God: mother, divine compassion, divine power and might, divine presence (immanence), and a source of recreative energy. I take the same five images and apply them to Our Lady of Guadalupe.

Our Lady of Guadalupe manifests God as mother: Our Lady of Guadalupe identifies herself as Our Loving Mother and people see her as a mother, a maternal presence, consoling, nurturing, offering unconditional love, comforting—qualities which tell us that mother is an appropriate metaphor for God. "Transferring this maternal language back to God enables us to see that God has a maternal countenance. All that is creative and generative of life, all that nourishes and nurtures, all that is benign, cherishes, and sustains, all that is solicitous and sympathetic originates in God/Her" (Johnson 1989:520).

Madonna Kolbenschlag's work *Lost in the Land of Oz* (1988:9) addresses the importance and necessity of the maternal. She identifies orphanhood metaphorically as "the deepest, most fundamental reality: experiences of attachment and abandonment, of expectation and deprivation, of loss and failure, and of loneliness." What message does Our Lady of Guadalupe offer to the spiritual orphans of the twentieth century through the metaphor of mother? That we are lovable and capable, that we belong, that we can grow and be transformed, and that there is a reason to live and a reason to hope.

Our Lady of Guadalupe manifests God's compassion: Our Lady of Guadalupe came to show forth her love, compassion, help, defense, and her presence among the people. "Returning this language to God, to whom it properly belongs, enables us to name the holy mystery as essentially and unfathomably merciful. God is the Mother of mercy who has compassionate womb-love for all God's children. We need not be afraid to approach. She is brimming over with gentleness, loving kindness, and forgiveness" (Johnson 1989:521). In the interviews with the women in my study, we have seen how they take their troubles to Our Lady of Guadalupe because they experience her as being compassionate and responsive to their needs, in a way which, if present, nevertheless has not been identified in their relationship to God. She will understand them better than the male face of God because she too is female and a mother.

Our Lady of Guadalupe manifests divine power and might: The word "power" comes from the Latin *posse,* meaning to be able, yet often when we think of power it is in terms of having power *over* someone or something, rather than having power *with*. Again and again, the women in my study found that in encountering and being in the presence of Our Lady of Guadalupe they regained their sense of self in an accepting and empowering relationship.

Our Lady of Guadalupe images power *with,* in a dynamism centered around mutuality, trust, participation, and regard. The power accessed by these women in their dialogue with Our Lady of Guadalupe is the power of memory, which she continues to stand for, justice, solidarity with the oppressed, belonging, unconditional love, the power of expressed feelings and sharing (women come to her and share their immediate needs and they feel heard). The power of commitment, the power to endure suffering, the power of caring, the power of risk ("As long as she is beside me, I'm going to keep trying"), the power of naming their fears, the power of knowing that the way things are is not the way things are meant to be, and with her help they are encouraged and given hope. She gives them not the will to suffer under injustice, but the will to continue *la lucha* (the struggle).

Our Lady of Guadalupe manifests, symbolizes, and activates the power of the people, in this case the power of the poor people. In the *Nican Mopohua,* it is the poor Indian Juan Diego who evangelizes the bishop, whose conversion enables him to work with the poor, the marginalized, and the indigenous. Siller emphasizes the Nahuatl image of *yollo* (the heart), which moves us to action; if a devotion to Our Lady of Guadalupe does not bring us closer to action and to solidarity with the cause of the poor, then the devotion is not authentically Guadalupana. This heart, love, relationship, and consciousness emerging from the poor call us to act on behalf of the poor.

Our Lady of Guadalupe manifests the presence of God: I have addressed this in the previous section about Our Lady of Guadalupe as a symbol of God's unconditional love.

Our Lady of Guadalupe manifests God as a source of recreating energy: "Attributing this imagery of plenty and new beginnings directly to God allows us to affirm that it is God's own self that is the source of transforming energy among all creatures. She initiates novelty, instigates change, transforms what is dead" (Johnson 1989:524). This is clearly seen in the timing of the apparition of Our Lady of Guadalupe. As argued in Chapter 2, she came at a time when the people were spiritually dead, abandoned by their gods, with no reason to live. Our Lady of Guadalupe's coming restored the people's reason to live and to hope. She identified herself using the familiar Nahuatl expressions of God, which showed the people that she came from the region of the gods.

In the Nahuatl culture the one supreme god, Ometeotl, was the god of duality, with both masculine and feminine principles. Because Ometeotl was invisible, there was no physical representation of this god, who was known by the titles of the Most True God, the God Who Gives Us Life, the Inventor and Creator of People, the Owner of What Is around Us and Very Close to Us, and the Owner and Lord of the Earth (Siller-Acuña 1989:48).

The Nahuatl names for God are not just dimensions but ultimate metaphors for who God is. And because they contain that which gave life to the people, those metaphors become a source of recreating energy.

8. India

Richard Rodriguez

At sunrise the next day, the time the Indians appointed, they came according to their promise, and brought us a large quantity of fish with certain roots. . . . They sent their women and children to look at us. . . .

—Álvar Núñez Cabeza de Vaca

I used to stare at the Indian in the mirror. The wide nostrils, the thick lips. Starring Paul Muni as Benito Juárez. Such a long face—such a long nose—sculpted by indifferent, blunt thumbs, and of such common clay. No one in my family had a face as dark or as Indian as mine. My face could not portray the ambition I brought to it. What could the United States of America say to me? I remember reading the ponderous conclusion of the Kerner Report in the sixties: two Americas, one white, one black—the prophecy of an eclipse too simple to account for the complexity of my face.

Mestizo in Mexican Spanish means mixed, confused. Clotted with Indian, thinned by Spanish spume.

What could Mexico say to me?

Mexican philosophers powwow in their tony journals about Indian "fatalism" and "Whither Mexico?" *El fatalismo del indio* is an important Mexican philosophical theme; the phrase is trusted to conjure the quality of Indian passivity as well as to initiate debate about Mexico's reluctant progress toward modernization. Mexicans imagine their Indian part as deadweight: the Indian stunned by modernity; so overwhelmed by the loss of what is genuine to him—his language, his religion—that he sits weeping like a medieval lady at the crossroads; or else he resorts to occult powers and superstitions, choosing to consort with death because the purpose of the world has passed him by.

One night in Mexico City I ventured from my hotel to a distant *colonia* to visit my aunt, my father's only sister. But she was not there. She had moved. For the past several years she has moved, this woman of eighty-odd years, from one of her children to another. She takes with her only her papers and books—she is a poetess—and an upright piano painted blue. My aunt writes love poems to her dead husband, Juan—keeping Juan up to date, while rewatering her loss. Last year she sent me her *obras completas*, an inch-thick block of bound onionskin. And with her poems she sent me a list of names, a genealogy braiding two centuries, two continents, to a common origin: eighteenth-century Salamanca. No explanation is attached to the list. Its implication is nonetheless clear. We are—my father's family is (despite the evidence of my face)—of Europe. We are not Indian.

On the other hand, a Berkeley undergraduate approached me one day, creeping up as if I were a stone totem to say, "God, it must be cool to be related to Aztecs."

* * * * *

I sat down next to the journalist from Pakistan—the guest of honor. He had been making a tour of the United States under the auspices of the U.S. State Department. Nearing the end of his journey now, he was having dinner with several of us, American journalists, at a Chinese restaurant in San Francisco. He said he'd seen pretty much all he wanted to see in America. His wife, however, had asked him to bring back some American Indian handicrafts. Blankets. Beaded stuff. He'd looked everywhere.

The table was momentarily captured by the novelty of his dilemma. You can't touch the stuff nowadays, somebody said. So rare, so expensive. Somebody else knew of a shop up on Sacramento Street that sells authentic Santa Fe. Several others remembered a store in Chinatown where moccasins, belts—"the works"—were to be found. All manufactured in Taiwan.

The Pakistani journalist looked incredulous. His dream of America had been shaped by American export-Westerns. Cowboys and Indians are yin and yang of America. He had seen men dressed like cowboys on this trip. But (turning to me): Where are the Indians?

(Two Indians staring at one another. One asks where are all the Indians, the other shrugs.)

* * * * *

I grew up in Sacramento thinking of Indians as people who had disappeared. I was a Mexican in California; I would no more have thought of myself as an Aztec in California than you might imagine yourself a Viking or a Bantu. Mrs. Ferrucci up the block used to call my family "Spanish." We knew she intended to ennoble us by that designation. We also knew she was ignorant.

I was ignorant.

In America the Indian is relegated to the obligatory first chapter—the "Once Great Nation" chapter—after which the Indian is cleared away as easily as brush, using a very sharp rhetorical tool called an "alas." Thereafter, the Indian reappears only as a stunned remnant—Ishi, or the hundred-year-old hag blowing out her birthday candle at a rest home in Tucson; or the teenager drunk on his ass in Plaza Park.

Here they come down Broadway in the Fourth of July parades of my childhood—middle-aged men wearing glasses, beating their tom-toms; Hey-ya-ya-yah; Hey-ya-ya-yah. They wore Bermuda shorts under their loincloths. High-school kids could never refrain from the answering Woo-woo-woo, stopping their mouths with the palms of their hands.

In the 1960s, Indians began to name themselves Native Americans, recalling themselves to life. That self-designation underestimated the ruthless idea Puritans had superimposed upon the landscape. America is an idea to which natives are inimical. The Indian represented permanence and continuity to Americans who were determined to call this country new. Indians must be ghosts.

I collected conflicting evidence concerning Mexico, it's true, but I never felt myself the remnant of anything. Mexican magazines arrived in our mailbox from Mexico City; showed pedestrians strolling wide ocher boulevards beneath trees with lime-green leaves. My past was at least this coherent: Mexico was a real place with plenty of people walking around in it. My parents had come from somewhere that went on without them.

When I was a graduate student at Berkeley, teaching remedial English, there were a few American Indians in my classroom. They were unlike any other "minority students" in the classes I taught. The Indians drifted in and out. When I summoned them to my office, they came and sat while I did all the talking.

I remember one tall man particularly, a near-somnambulist, beautiful in an off-putting way, but interesting, too, because I never saw him without the current issue of *The New York Review of Books* under his arm, which I took as an advertisement of ambition. He eschewed my class for weeks at a time. Then one morning I saw him in a café on Telegraph Avenue, across from Cody's. I did not fancy myself Sidney Poitier, but I was interested in this moody brave's lack of interest in me, for one, and then *The New York Review.*

Do you mind if I sit here?

Nothing.

Blah, Blah, Blah . . . *N. Y. R. B.?*—entirely on my part—until, when I got up to leave:

"You're not Indian, you're Mexican," he said. "You wouldn't understand."

He meant I was cut. Diluted.

Understand what?

He meant I was not an Indian in America. He meant he was an enemy of the history that had otherwise created me. And he was right, I didn't understand. I took his diffidence for chauvinism. I read his chauvinism as arrogance. He didn't see the Indian in my face? I saw his face—his refusal to consort with the living—as the face of a dead man.

As the landscape goes, so goes the Indian? In the public-service TV commercial, the Indian sheds a tear at the sight of an America polluted beyond his recognition. Indian memory has become the measure against which America gauges corrupting history when it suits us. Gitchigoomeism—the habit of placing the Indian outside history—is a white sentimentality that relegates the Indian to death.

An obituary from *The New York Times* (September 1989—dateline Alaska): An oil freighter has spilled its load along the Alaskan coast. There is a billion-dollar cleanup, bringing jobs and dollars to Indian villages.

> *The modern world has been closing in on English Bay . . . with glacial slowness. The oil spill and the resulting sea of money have accelerated the process, so that English Bay now seems caught on the cusp of history.*

The omniscient reporter from *The New York Times* takes it upon himself to regret history on behalf of the Indians.

Instead of hanging salmon to dry this month, as Aleut natives have done for centuries . . . John Kvasnikoff was putting up a three thousand dollar television satellite dish on the bluff next to his home above the sea.

The reporter from *The New York Times* knows the price modernity will exact from an Indian who wants to plug himself in. Mind you, the reporter is confident of his own role in history, his freedom to lug a word processor to some remote Alaskan village. About the reporter's journey, *The New York Times* is not censorious. But let the Indian drop one bead from custom, or let his son straddle a snowmobile—as he does in the photo accompanying the article—and *The New York Times* cries Boo-hoo-hoo yah-yah-yah.

Thus does the Indian become the mascot of an international ecology movement. The industrial countries of the world romanticize the Indian who no longer exists, ignoring the Indian who does—the Indian who is poised to chop down his rain forest, for example. Or the Indian who reads *The New York Times.*

Once more in San Francisco: I flattered myself that the woman staring at me all evening "knew my work." I considered myself an active agent, in other words. But, after several passes around the buffet, the woman cornered me to say she recognized me as an "ancient soul."

Do I lure or am I just minding my own business?

Is it the nature of Indians—not verifiable in nature, of course, but in the European description of Indians—that we wait around to be "discovered"?

Europe discovers. India beckons. Isn't that so? India sits atop her lily pad through centuries, lost in contemplation of the horizon. And, from time to time, India is discovered.

In the fifteenth century, sailing Spaniards were acting according to scientific conjecture as to the nature and as to the shape of the world. Most thinking men in Europe at the time of Columbus believed the world to be round. The voyage of Columbus was the test of a theory believed to be true. Brave, yes, but pedantic therefore.

The Indian is forever implicated in the roundness of the world. America was the false India, the mistaken India, and yet veritable India, for all that—India—the clasp, the coupling mystery at the end of quest.

This is as true today as of yore. Where do the Beatles go when the world is too much with them? Where does Jerry Brown seek the fat farm of his soul? India, man, India!

India waits.

India has all the answers beneath her passive face or behind her veil or between her legs. The European has only questions, questions that are assertions turned inside out, questions that can only be answered by sailing toward the abysmal horizon.

The lusty Europeans wanted the shortest answers. They knew what they wanted. They wanted spices, pagodas, gold.

Had the world been flat, had the European sought the unknown, then the European would have been as great a victor over history as he has portrayed himself to be. The European would have outdistanced history—even theology—if he could have arrived at the shore of some prelapsarian state. If the world had been flat, then the European could have traveled outward toward innocence.

But the world was round. The entrance into the Indies was a reunion of peoples. The Indian awaited the long-separated European, the inevitable European, as the approaching horizon.

Though perhaps, too, there was some demiurge felt by the human race of the fifteenth century to heal itself, to make itself whole? Certainly, in retrospect, there was some inevitability to the Catholic venture. If the world was round, continuous, then so, too, were peoples?

According to the European version—the stag version—of the pageant of the New World, the Indian must play a passive role. Europe has been accustomed to play the swaggart in history—Europe striding through the Americas, overturning temples, spilling language, spilling seed, spilling blood.

And wasn't the Indian the female, the passive, the waiting aspect to the theorem—lewd and promiscuous in her embrace as she is indolent betimes?

Charles Macomb Flandrau, a native of St. Paul, Minnesota, wrote a book called *Viva Mexico!* in 1908, wherein he described the Mexican Indian as "incorrigibly plump. One never ceases to marvel at the superhuman strength existing beneath the pretty and effeminate modeling of their arms and legs and backs. . . . The legs of an American 'strong man' look usually like an anatomical chart, but the legs of the most powerful Totonac Indian—and the power of many of them is beyond belief—would serve admirably as one of those idealized extremities on which women's hosiery is displayed in shop windows."

In Western Civilization histories, the little honeymoon joke Europe tells on itself is of mistaking America for the extremities of India. But India was perhaps not so much a misnomer as was "discoverer" or "conquistador."

Earliest snapshots of Indians brought back to Europe were of naked little woodcuts, arms akimbo, resembling Erasmus, or of grandees in capes and feathered tiaras, courtiers of an Egyptified palace of nature. In European museums, she is idle, recumbent at the base of a silver pineapple tree or the pedestal of the Dresden urn or the Sèvres tureen—the muse of European adventure, at once wanderlust and bounty.

Many tribes of Indians were prescient enough, preserved memory enough, or were lonesome enough to predict the coming of a pale stranger from across the sea, a messianic twin of completing memory or skill.

None of this could the watery Europeans have known as they marveled at the sight of approaching land. Filled with the arrogance of discovery, the Europeans were not predisposed to imagine that they were being watched, awaited.

* * * * *

That friend of mine at Oxford loses patience whenever I describe my face as mestizo. Look at my face. What do you see?

An Indian, he says.

Mestizo, I correct.

Mestizo, mestizo, he says.

Listen, he says. I went back to my mother's village in Mexico last summer and there was nothing mestizo about it. Dust, dogs, and Indians. People there don't even speak Spanish.

So I ask my friend at Oxford what it means to him to be an Indian.

He hesitates. My friend has recently been taken up as amusing by a bunch of rich Pakistanis in London. But, facing me, he is vexed and in earnest. He describes a lonely search among his family for evidence of Indian-ness. He thinks he has found it in his mother; watching his mother in her garden.

Does she plant corn by the light of the moon?

She seems to have some relationship with the earth, he says quietly.

So there it is. The mystical tie to nature. How else to think of the Indian except in terms of some druidical green thumb? No one says of an English matron in her rose garden that she is behaving like a Celt. Because the Indian has no history—that is, because history books are the province of the descendants of Europeans—the Indian seems only to belong to the party of the first part, the first chapter. So that is where the son expects to find his mother, Daughter of the Moon.

Let's talk about something else. Let's talk about London. The last time I was in London, I was walking toward an early evening at the Queen's Theatre when I passed that Christopher Wren church near Fortnum & Mason. The church was lit; I decided to stop, to savor the spectacle of what I expected would be a few Pymish men and women rolled into balls of fur at evensong. Imagine my surprise that the congregation was young—dressed in army fatigues and Laura Ashley. Within the chancel, cross-legged on a dais, was a South American shaman.

Now, who is the truer Indian in this picture? Me . . . me on my way to the Queen's Theatre? Or that guy on the altar with a Ph.D. in death?

* * * * *

We have hurled—like starlings, like Goths—through the castle of European memory. Our reflections have glanced upon the golden coach that carried the Emperor Maximilian through the streets of Mexico City, thence onward through the sludge of a hundred varnished paintings.

I have come at last to Mexico, the country of my parents' birth. I do not expect to find anything that pertains to me.

We have strained the rouge cordon at the thresholds of imperial apartments; seen chairs low enough for dwarfs, commodious enough for angels.

We have imagined the Empress Carlota standing in the shadows of an afternoon; we have followed her gaze down the Paseo de la Reforma toward the distant city. The Paseo was a nostalgic allusion to the Champs-Elysées, we learn, which Maximilian recreated for his tempestuous, crowlike bride.

Come this way, please. . . .

European memory is not to be the point of our excursion. Señor Fuentes, our tour director, is already beginning to descend the hill from Chapultepec Castle. What the American credit-card company calls our "orientation tour" of Mexico City had started late and so Señor Fuentes has been forced, regrettably,

". . . This way, please . . ."

to rush. Señor Fuentes is consumed with contrition for time wasted this morning. He intends to uphold his schedule, as a way of upholding Mexico, against our expectation.

We had gathered at the appointed time at the limousine entrance to our hotel, beneath the banner welcoming contestants to the Señorita Mexico pageant. We—Japanese, Germans, Americans—were waiting promptly at nine. There was no bus. And as we waited, the Señorita Mexico contestants arrived. Drivers leaned into their cabs to pull out long-legged señoritas. The drivers then balanced the señoritas onto stiletto heels (the driveway was cobbled) before they passed the señoritas, *en pointe*, to the waiting arms of officials.

Mexican men, meanwhile—doormen, bellhops, window washers, hotel guests—stopped dead in their tracks, wounded by the scent and spectacle of so many blond señoritas. The Mexican men assumed fierce expressions, nostrils flared, brows knit. Such expressions are masks—the men intend to convey their adoration of prey—as thoroughly ritualized as the smiles of beauty queens.

By now we can see the point of our excursion beyond the parched trees of Chapultepec Park—the Museo Nacional de Antropología—which is an air-conditioned repository for the artifacts of the Indian civilizations of Meso-America, the finest anthropological museum in the world.

"There will not be time to see everything," Señor Fuentes warns as he ushers us into the grand salon, our first experience of the suffocating debris of The Ancients. Señor Fuentes wants us in and out of here by noon.

Whereas the United States traditionally has rejoiced at the delivery of its landscape from "savagery," Mexico has taken its national identity only from the Indian, the mother. Mexico measures all cultural bastardy against the Indian; equates civilization with India—Indian kingdoms of a golden age; cities as fabulous as Alexandria or Benares or Constantinople; a court as hairless, as subtle as the Pekingese. Mexico equates barbarism with Europe—beardedness—with Spain.

It is curious, therefore, that both modern nations should similarly apostrophize the Indian, relegate the Indian to the past.

Come this way, please. Mrs. . . . Ah . . . this way, please.

Señor Fuentes wears an avocado-green sports coat with gold buttons. He is short. He is rather elegant, with a fine small head, small hands, small feet; with his two rows of fine small teeth like a nutcracker's teeth, with which he curtails consonants as cleanly as bitten thread. Señor Fuentes is brittle, he is watchful, he is ironic, he is metropolitan; his wit is quotational, literary, wasted on Mrs. Ah.

He is not our equal. His demeanor says he is not our equal. We mistake his condescension for humility. He will not eat when we eat. He will not spend when we shop. He will not have done with Mexico when we have done with Mexico.

Señor Fuentes is impatient with us, for we have paused momentarily outside the museum to consider the misfortune of an adolescent mother who holds her crying baby out to us. Several of us confer among ourselves in an attempt to place a peso value on the woman's situation. We do not ask for the advice of Señor Fuentes.

For we, in turn, are impatient with Señor Fuentes. We are in a bad mood. The air conditioning on our "fully air-conditioned coach" is nonexistent. We have a headache. Nor is the city air any relief, but it is brown, fungal, farted.

Señor Fuentes is a mystery to us, for there is no American equivalent to him; for there is no American equivalent to the subtleties he is paid to describe to us.

Mexico will not raise a public monument to Hernán Cortés, for example, the father of Mexico—the rapist. In the Diego Rivera murals in the presidential palace, the Aztec city of Tenochtitlán is rendered—its blood temples and blood canals—as haughty as Troy, as vulnerable as Pompeii. Any suggestion of the complicity of other tribes of Indians in overthrowing the Aztec empire is painted over. Spaniards appear on the horizons of Arcadia as syphilitic brigands and demon-eyed priests.

The Spaniard entered the Indian by entering her city—the floating city—first as a suitor, ceremoniously; later by force. How should Mexico honor the rape?

In New England the European and the Indian drew apart to regard each other with suspicion over centuries. Miscegenation was a sin against Protestant individualism. In Mexico the European and the Indian consorted. The ravishment of fabulous Tenochtitlán ended in a marriage of blood—a "cosmic race," the Mexican philosopher José Vasconcelos has called it.

Mexico's tragedy is that she has no political idea of herself as rich as her blood.

The rhetoric of Señor Fuentes, like the murals of Diego Rivera, resorts often to the dream of India—to Tenochtitlán, the capital of the world before conquest. "Preconquest" in the Mexican political lexicon is tantamount to "prelapsarian" in the Judeo-Christian scheme, and hearkens to a time Mexico feels herself to have been whole, a time before the Indian was separated from India by the serpent Spain.

Three centuries after Cortés, Mexico declared herself independent of Spain. If Mexico would have no yoke, then Mexico would have no crown, then Mexico would have no father. The denial of Spain has persisted into our century.

The priest and the landowner yet serve Señor Fuentes as symbols of the hated Spanish order. Though, in private, Mexico is Catholic; Mexican mothers may wish for light-skinned children. Touch blond hair and good luck will be yours.

In private, in Mexican Spanish, *indio* is a seller of Chiclets, a sidewalk squatter. *Indio* means backward or lazy or lower-class. In the eyes of the world, Mexico raises a magnificent museum of anthropology—the finest in the world—to honor the Indian mother.

In the nave of the National Cathedral, we notice the floor slopes dramatically. "The cathedral is sinking," Señor Fuentes explains as a hooded figure approaches our group from behind a column. She is an Indian woman; she wears a blue stole; her hands are cupped, beseeching; tear marks ream her cheeks. In Spanish, Señor Fuentes forbids this apparition: "Go ask *padrecito* to pry some gold off the altar for you."

"Mexico City is built upon swamp," Señor Fuentes resumes in English. "Therefore, the cathedral is sinking." But it is clear that Señor Fuentes believes the sinkage is due to the oppressive weight of Spanish Catholicism, its masses of gold, its volumes of deluded suspiration.

Mexican political life can only seem Panglossian when you consider an anti-Catholic government of an overwhelmingly Catholic population. Mexico is famous for politicians descended from Masonic fathers and Catholic mothers. Señor Fuentes himself is less a Spaniard, less an Indian, perhaps, than an embittered eighteenth-century man, clinging to the witty knees of Voltaire against the chaos of twentieth-century Mexico.

Mexico blamed the ruin of the nineteenth century on the foreigner, and with reason. Once emptied of Spain, the palace of Mexico became the dollhouse of France. Mexico was overrun by imperial armies. The greed of Europe met the Manifest Destiny of the United States in Mexico. Austria sent an archduke to marry Mexico with full panoply of candles and bishops. The U.S. reached under Mexico's skirt every chance he got.

"Poor Mexico, so far from God, so close to the United States."

Señor Fuentes dutifully attributes the mot to Porfirio Díaz, the Mexican president who sold more of Mexico to foreign interests than any other president. It was against the regime of Porfirio Díaz that Mexicans rebelled in the early decades of this century. Mexico prefers to call its civil war a "revolution."

Mexico for Mexicans!

The Revolution did not accomplish a union of Mexicans. The Revolution did not accomplish a restoration of Mexicans to their landscape. The dust of the Revolution parted to reveal—not India—but Marx *ex machina*, the Institutional Revolutionary Party, the PRI—a political machine appropriate to the age of steam. The Institutional Revolutionary Party, as its name implies, was designed to reconcile institutional pragmatism with revolutionary rhetoric. And the PRI worked for a time, because it gave Mexico what Mexico most needed, the stability of compromise.

The PRI appears everywhere in Mexico—a slogan on the wall, the politician impersonating a journalist on the evening news, the professor at his podium. The PRI is in its way as much a Mexican institution as the Virgin of Guadalupe.

Now Mexicans speak of the government as something imposed upon them, and they are the victims of it. But the political failure of Mexico must be counted a failure of Mexicans. Whom now shall Señor Fuentes blame for a twentieth century that has become synonymous with corruption?

Well, as long as you stay out of the way of the police no one will bother you, is conventional Mexican wisdom, and Mexico continues to live her daily life. In the capital, the air is the color of the buildings of Siena. Telephone connections are an aspect of the will of God. Mexicans drive on the sidewalks. A man on the street corner seizes the opportunity of stalled traffic to earn his living as a fire-eater. His ten children pass among the cars and among the honking horns to collect small coins.

Thank you. Thank you very much. A pleasure, Mrs. . . . Ah. Thank you very much.

Señor Fuentes bids each farewell. He accepts tips within a handshake. He bows slightly. We have no complaint with Señor Fuentes, after all. The bus was not his fault. Mexico City is not his fault. And Señor Fuentes will return to his unimaginable Mexico and we will return to our rooms to take aspirin and to initiate long-distance telephone calls. Señor Fuentes will remove his avocado-green coat and, having divested, Señor Fuentes will in some fashion partake of what he has successfully kept from us all day, which is the life and the drinking water of Mexico.

* * * * *

The Virgin of Guadalupe symbolizes the entire coherence of Mexico, body and soul. You will not find the story of the Virgin within hidebound secular histories of Mexico—nor indeed within the credulous repertoire of Señor Fuentes—and the omission renders the history of Mexico incomprehensible.

One recent afternoon, within the winy bell jar of a very late lunch, I told the story of the Virgin of Guadalupe to Lynn, a sophisticated twentieth-century woman. The history of Mexico, I promised her, is neither mundane nor masculine, but it is a miracle play with trapdoors and sequins and jokes on the living.

In the sixteenth century, when Indians were demoralized by the routing of their gods, when millions of Indians were dying from the plague of Europe, the Virgin Mary appeared pacing on a hillside to an Indian peasant named Juan Diego—his Christian name, for Juan was a convert. It was December 1531.

On his way to mass, Juan passed the hill called Tepayac . . .

Just as the East was beginning to kindle
To dawn. He heard there a cloud
Of birdsong bursting overhead
Of whistles and flutes and beating wings
—Now here, now there—
A mantle of chuckles and berries and rain
That rocked through the sky like the great Spanish bell
In Mexico City;
At the top of the hill there shone a light
And the light called out a name to him
With a lady's voice.
Juan, Juan,
The Lady-light called.
Juan crossed himself, he fell to his knees,
He covered his eyes and prepared to be blinded.

He could see through his hands that covered his face
As the sun rose up from behind her cape,
That the poor light of day
Was no match for this Lady, but broke upon her
Like a waterfall,
A rain of rings.
She wore a gown the color of dawn.
Her hair was braided with ribbons and flowers
And tiny tinkling silver bells. Her mantle was sheer
And bright as rain and embroidered with thousands of twinkling stars.
A clap before curtains, like waking from sleep;
Then a human face,
A mother's smile;
Her complexion as red as cinnamon bark;
Cheeks as brown as pérsimmon.

Her eyes were her voice,
As modest and shy as a pair of doves
In the eaves of her brow. Her voice was
Like listening. This lady spoke
In soft Nahuatl, the Aztec tongue
(As different from Spanish
As some other season of weather,
As doves in the boughs of a summer tree
Are different from crows in a wheeling wind,
Who scatter destruction and
Caw caw caw caw)—
Nahuatl like rain, like water flowing, like drips in a cavern,
Or glistening thaw,
Like breath through a flute,
With many stops and plops and sighs . . .

Peering through the grille of her cigarette smoke, Lynn heard and she seemed to approve the story.

At the Virgin's behest, this Prufrock Indian must go several times to the bishop of Mexico City. He must ask that a chapel be built on Tepayac where his discovered Lady may share in the sorrows of her people. Juan Diego's visits to the Spanish bishop parody the conversion of the Indians by the Spaniards. The bishop is skeptical.

The bishop wants proof.

The Virgin tells Juan Diego to climb the hill and gather a sheaf of roses as proof for the bishop—Castilian roses—impossible in Mexico in December of 1531. Juan carries the roses in the folds of his cloak, a pregnant messenger. Upon entering the bishop's presence, Juan parts his cloak, the roses tumble; the bishop falls to his knees.

In the end—with crumpled napkins, torn carbons, the bitter dregs of coffee—Lynn gave the story over to the Spaniards.

The legend concludes with a concession to humanity—proof more durable than roses—the imprint of the Virgin's image upon the cloak of Juan Diego . . .

A Spanish trick, Lynn said. A recruitment poster for the new religion, no more, she said (though sadly). An itinerant diva with a costume trunk. Birgit Nilsson as Aïda.

Why do we assume Spain made up the story?

The importance of the story is that Indians believed it. The jokes, the vaudeville, the relegation of the Spanish bishop to the role of comic adversary, the Virgin's chosen cavalier, and especially the brown-faced Mary—all elements spoke directly to Indians.

The result of the apparition and of the miraculous image of the Lady remaining upon the cloak of Juan Diego was a mass conversion of Indians to Catholicism.

The image of Our Lady of Guadalupe (privately, affectionately, Mexicans call her La Morenita—Little Darkling) has become the unofficial, the private flag of Mexicans. Unique possession of her image is a more wonderful election to Mexicans than any political call to nationhood. Perhaps Mexico's tragedy in our century, perhaps Mexico's abiding grace thus far, is that she has no political idea of herself as compelling as her icon.

The Virgin appears everywhere in Mexico. On dashboards and on calendars, on playing cards, on lampshades and cigar boxes; within the loneliness and tattooed upon the very skins of Mexicans.

Nor is the image of Guadalupe a diminishing mirage of the sixteenth century, but she has become more vivid with time, developing in her replication from earthy shades of melon and musk to bubble-gum pink, Windex blue, to achieve the hard, literal focus of holy cards or baseball cards; of Krishna or St. Jude or the Atlanta Braves.

Mexico City stands as the last living medieval capital of the world. Mexico is the creation of a Spanish Catholicism that attempted to draw continents together as one flesh. The success of Spanish Catholicism in Mexico resulted in a kind of proof—a profound concession to humanity: the *mestizaje.*

What joke on the living? Lynn said.

The joke is that Spain arrived with missionary zeal at the shores of contemplation. But Spain had no idea of the absorbent strength of Indian spirituality.

By the waters of baptism, the active European was entirely absorbed within the contemplation of the Indian. The faith that Europe imposed in the sixteenth century was, by virtue of the Guadalupe, embraced by the Indian. Catholicism has become an Indian religion. By the twenty-first century, the locus of the Catholic Church, by virtue of numbers, will be Latin America, by which time Catholicism itself will have assumed the aspect of the Virgin of Guadalupe.

Brown skin.

* * * * *

Time magazine dropped through the chute of my mailbox a few years ago with a cover story on Mexico entitled "The Population Curse." From the vantage point of Sixth Avenue, the editors of Time-Life peer down into the basin of Mexico City—like peering down into the skull of a pumpkin—to contemplate the nightmare of fecundity, the tangled mass of slime and hair and seed.

America sees death in all that life; sees rot. Life—not illness and poverty; not death—life becomes the curse of Mexico City in the opinion of *Time* magazine.

For a long time I had my own fear of Mexico, an American fear. Mexico's history was death. Her stature was tragedy. A race of people that looked like me had disappeared.

I had a dream about Mexico City, a conquistador's dream. I was lost and late and twisted in my sheet. I dreamed streets narrower than they actually are—narrow as old Jerusalem. I dreamed sheets, entanglements, bunting, hanging larvaelike from open windows, distended from balconies and from lines thrown over the streets. These streets were not empty streets. I was among a crowd. The crowd was not a carnival crowd. This crowd was purposeful and ordinary, welling up from subways, ascending from stairwells. And then the dream followed the course of all my dreams. I must find the airport—the American solution—I must somehow escape, fly over.

Each face looked like mine. But no one looked at me.

I have come at last to Mexico, to the place of my parents' birth. I have come under the protection of an American credit-card company. I have canceled this trip three times.

As the plane descends into the basin of Mexico City, I brace myself for some confrontation with death, with India, with confusion of purpose that I do not know how to master.

Do you speak Spanish? the driver asks in English.

Andrés, the driver employed by my hotel, is in his forties. He lives in the Colonia Roma, near the airport. There is nothing about the city he does not know. This is his city and he is its memory.

Andrés's car is a dark-blue Buick—about 1975. Windows slide up and down at the touch of his finger. There is the smell of disinfectant in Andrés's car, as there is in every bus or limousine or taxi I've ridden in Mexico—the smell of the glycerine crystals in urinals. Dangling from Andrés's rearview mirror is the other appliance common to all public conveyance in Mexico—a rosary.

Andrés is a man of the world, a man, like other working-class Mexican men, eager for the world. He speaks two languages. He knows several cities. He has been to the United States. His brother lives there still.

In the annals of the famous European discoverers there is invariably an Indian guide, a translator—willing or not—to facilitate, to preserve Europe's stride. These seem to have become fluent in pallor before Europe learned anything of them. How is that possible?

The most famous guide in Mexican history is also the most reviled by Mexican histories—the villainess Marina—"La Malinche." Marina became the lover of Cortés. So, of course, Mexicans say she betrayed India for Europe. In the end, she was herself betrayed, left behind when Cortés repaired to his Spanish wife.

Nonetheless, Marina's treachery anticipates the epic marriage of Mexico. La Malinche prefigures, as well, the other, the beloved female aspect of Mexico, the Virgin of Guadalupe.

Because Marina was the seducer of Spain, she challenges the boast Europe has always told about India.

I assure you Mexico has an Indian point of view as well, a female point of view:

I opened my little eye and the Spaniard disappeared.

Imagine a dark pool; the Spaniard dissolved; the surface triumphantly smooth.

My eye!

The spectacle of the Spaniard on the horizon, vainglorious—the shiny surfaces, clanks of metal; the horses, the muskets, the jingling bits.

Cannot you imagine me curious? Didn't I draw near?

European vocabularies do not have a silence rich enough to describe the force within Indian contemplation. Only Shakespeare understood that Indians have eyes. Shakespeare saw Caliban eyeing his master's books—well, why not his master as well? The same dumb lust.

WHAT DAT? is a question philosophers ask. And Indians.

Shakespeare's comedy, of course, resolves itself to the European's applause. The play that Shakespeare did not write is Mexico City.

Now the great city swells under the moon; seems, now, to breathe of itself—the largest city in the world—a Globe, kind Will, not of your devising, not under your control.

The superstition persists in European travel literature that Indian Christianity is the thinnest veneer covering an ulterior altar. But there is a possibility still more frightening to the European imagination, so frightening that in five hundred years such a possibility has scarcely found utterance.

What if the Indian were converted?

The Indian eye becomes a portal through which the entire pageant of European civilization has already passed; turned inside out. Then the baroque is an Indian conceit. The colonial arcade is an Indian detail.

Look once more at the city from La Malinche's point of view. Mexico is littered with the shells and skulls of Spain, cathedrals, poems, and the limbs of orange trees. But everywhere you look in this great museum of Spain you see living Indians.

Where are the *conquistadores?*

Postcolonial Europe expresses pity or guilt behind its sleeve, pities the Indian the loss of her gods or her tongue. But let the Indian speak for herself. Spanish is now an Indian language. Mexico City has become the metropolitan see of the Spanish-speaking world. In something like the way New York won English from London after World War I, Mexico City has captured Spanish.

The Indian stands in the same relationship to modernity as she did to Spain—willing to marry, to breed, to disappear in order to ensure her inclusion in time; refusing to absent herself from the future. The Indian has chosen to survive, to consort with the living, to live in the city, to crawl on her hands and knees, if need be, to Mexico City or L.A.

I take it as an Indian achievement that I am alive, that I am Catholic, that I speak English, that I am an American. My life began, it did not end, in the sixteenth century.

The idea occurs to me on a weekday morning, at a crowded intersection in Mexico City: Europe's lie. Here I am in the capital of death. Life surges about me; wells up from subways, wave upon wave; descends from stairwells. Everywhere I look. Babies. Traffic. Food. Beggars. Life. Life coming upon me like sunstroke.

Each face looks like mine. No one looks at me.

Where, then, is the famous conquistador?

We have eaten him, the crowd tells me, *we have eaten him with our eyes.*

I run to the mirror to see if this is true.

It is true.

In the distance, at its depths, Mexico City stands as the prophetic example. Mexico City is modern in ways that "multiracial," ethnically "diverse" New York City is not yet. Mexico City is centuries more modern than racially "pure," provincial Tokyo. Nothing to do with computers or skyscrapers.

Mexico City is the capital of modernity, for in the sixteenth century, under the tutelage of a curious Indian whore, under the patronage of the Queen of Heaven, Mexico initiated the task of the twenty-first century—the renewal of the old, the known world, through miscegenation. Mexico carries the idea of a round world to its biological conclusion.

* * * * *

For a time when he was young, Andrés, my driver, worked in Alpine County in northern California.

And then he worked at a Lake Tahoe resort. He remembers the snow. He remembers the weekends when blond California girls would arrive in their ski suits and sunglasses. Andrés worked at the top of a ski lift. His job was to reach out over a little precipice to help the California girls out of their lift chairs. He would maintain his grasp until they were balanced upon the snow. And then he would release them, watch them descend the winter slope—how they laughed!—oblivious of his admiration, until they disappeared.

9. The Mexican-American and the Church

CÉSAR E. CHAVEZ

The following article was prepared by Mr. Chavez during his 25-day "spiritual fast" and was presented to a meeting on "Mexican-Americans and the Church" at the Second Annual Mexican-American Conference in Sacramento, California, on March 8–10, 1968.

The place to begin is with our own experience with the Church in the strike which has gone on for thirty-one months in Delano. For in Delano the Church has been involved with the poor in a unique way which should stand as a symbol to other communities. Of course, when we refer to the Church we should define the word a little. We mean the whole Church, the Church as an ecumenical body spread around the world, and not just its particular form in a parish in a local community. The Church we are talking about is a tremendously powerful institution in our society, and in the world. That Church is one form of the Presence of God on Earth, and so naturally it is powerful. It is powerful by definition. It is a powerful moral and spiritual force which cannot be ignored by any movement. Furthermore, it is an organization with tremendous wealth. Since the Church is to be servant to the poor, it is *our* fault if that wealth is not channeled to help the poor in our world.

In a small way we have been able, in the Delano strike, to work together with the Church in such a way as to bring some of its moral and economic power to bear on those who want to maintain the status quo, keeping farm workers in virtual enslavement. In brief, here is what happened in Delano.

Some years ago, when some of us were working with the Community Service Organization, we began to realize the powerful effect which the Church can have on the conscience of the opposition. In scattered instances, in San Jose, Sacramento, Oakland, Los Angeles and other places, priests would speak out loudly and clearly against specific instances of oppression, and in some cases, stand with the people who were being hurt. Furthermore, a small group of priests, Frs. McDonald, McCollough, Duggan and others, began to pinpoint attention on the terrible situation of the farm workers in our state.

At about that same time, we began to run into the California Migrant Ministry in the camps and fields. They were about the only ones there, and a lot of us were very suspicious, since we were Catholics and they were Protestants. However, they had developed a very clear conception of the Church. It was called to serve, to be at the mercy of the poor, and not to try to use them. After a while this made a lot of sense to us, and we began to find

---

"The Mexican-American and the Church", by César E. Chávez, presented at the Second Annual Mexican-American Conference in Sacramento, California on March 8–10, 1968.

ourselves working side by side with them. In fact, it forced us to raise the question why OUR Church was not doing the same. We would ask, "Why do the Protestants come out here and help the people, demand nothing, and give all their time to serving farm workers, while our own parish priests stay in their churches, where only a few people come, and usually feel uncomfortable?"

It was not until some of us moved to Delano and began working to build the National Farm Workers Association that we really saw how far removed from the people the parish Church was. In fact, we could not get any help at all from the priests of Delano. When the strike began, they told us we could not even use the Church's auditorium for the meetings. The farm workers' money helped build that auditorium! But the Protestants were there again, in the form of the California Migrant Ministry, and they began to help in little ways, here and there.

When the strike started in 1965, most of our "friends" forsook us for a while. They ran—or were just too busy to help. But the California Migrant Ministry held a meeting with its staff and decided that the strike was a matter of life or death for farm workers everywhere, and that even if it meant the end of the Migrant Ministry they would turn over their resources to the strikers. The political pressure on the Protestant Churches was tremendous and the Migrant Ministry lost a lot of money. But they stuck it out, and they began to point the way to the rest of the Church. In fact, when 30 of the strikers were arrested for shouting Huelga, 11 ministers went to jail with them. They were in Delano that day at the request of Chris Hartmire, director of the California Migrant Ministry.

Then the workers began to raise the question: "Why ministers? Why not priests? What does the Bishop say?" But the Bishop said nothing. But slowly the pressure of the people grew and grew, until finally we have in Delano a priest sent by the new Bishop, Timothy Manning, who is there to help minister to the needs of farm workers. His name is Father Mark Day and he is the Union's chaplain. *Finally,* our own Catholic Church has decided to recognize that we have our own peculiar needs, just as the growers have theirs.

But outside of the local diocese, the pressure built up on growers to negotiate was tremendous. Though we were not allowed to have our own priest, the power of the ecumenical body of the Church was tremendous. The work of the Church, for example, in the Schenley, Di Giorgio, Perelli-Minetti strikes was fantastic. They applied pressure—and they mediated.

When poor people get involved in a long conflict, such as a strike, or a civil rights drive, and the pressure increases each day, there is a deep need for spiritual advice. Without it we see families crumble, leadership weaken, and hard workers grow tired. And in such a situation the spiritual advice must be given by a *friend,* not by the opposition. What sense does it make to go to Mass on Sunday and reach out for spiritual help, and instead get sermons about the wickedness of your cause? That only drives one to question and to despair. The growers in Delano have their spiritual problems . . . we do not deny that. They have every right to have priests and ministers who serve their needs. BUT WE HAVE DIFFERENT NEEDS, AND SO WE NEEDED A FRIENDLY SPIRITUAL GUIDE. And this is true in every community in this state where the poor face tremendous problems.

But the opposition raises a tremendous howl about this. They don't want us to have our spiritual advisors, friendly to our needs. Why is this? Why indeed except that THERE IS TREMENDOUS SPIRITUAL AND ECONOMIC POWER IN THE CHURCH. The rich know it, and for that reason they choose to keep it from the people.

The leadership of the Mexican-American Community must admit that we have fallen far short in our task of helping provide spiritual guidance for our people. We may say, "I don't feel any such need. I can get along." But that is a poor excuse for not helping provide such help for others. For we can also say, "I don't need any welfare help. I can take care of my own problems." But we are all willing to fight like hell for welfare aid for those who truly need it, who would starve without it. Likewise we may have gotten an education and not care about scholarship money for ourselves, or our children. But we would, we should, fight like hell to see to it that our state provides aid for any child needing it so that he can get the education he desires. LIKEWISE WE CAN SAY WE DON'T NEED THE CHURCH. THAT IS OUR BUSINESS. BUT THERE ARE HUNDREDS OF THOUSANDS OF OUR PEOPLE WHO DESPERATELY NEED SOME HELP FROM THAT POWERFUL INSTITUTION, THE CHURCH, AND WE ARE FOOLISH NOT TO HELP THEM GET IT.

For example, the Catholic Charities agencies of the Catholic Church has millions of dollars earmarked for the poor. But often the money is spent for food baskets for the needy instead of for effective action to eradicate the causes of poverty. The men and women who administer this money sincerely want to help their brothers. It should be our duty to help direct the attention to the basic needs of the Mexican-Americans in our society . . . needs which cannot be satisfied with baskets of food, but rather with effective organizing at the grass roots level.

Therefore, I am calling for Mexican-American groups to stop ignoring this source of power. It is not just our right to appeal to the Church to use its power effectively for the poor, it is our duty to do so. It should be as natural as appealing to government . . . and we do that often enough.

Furthermore, we should be prepared to come to the defense of that priest, rabbi, minister, or layman of the Church, who out of commitment to truth and justice gets into a tight place with his pastor or bishop. It behooves us to stand with that man and help him see his trial through. It is our duty to see to it that his rights of conscience are respected and that no bishop, pastor or other higher body takes that God-given, human right away.

Finally, in a nutshell, what do we want the Church to do? We don't ask for more cathedrals. We don't ask for bigger churches or fine gifts. We ask for its presence with us, beside us, as Christ among us. We ask the Church to *sacrifice with the people* for social change, for justice, and for love of brother. We don't ask for words. We ask for deeds. We don't ask for paternalism. We ask for servanthood.

10. In Search of Aztlán

Luis Leal

One of the functions of the critic is to discover and analyze literary symbols with the object of broadening the perception that one has of a certain social or national group, or of humanity in general. In the case of Chicano literature, a literature that has emerged as a consequence of the fight for social and human rights, most of the symbols have been taken from the surrounding social environment.

For that reason, Chicano literary symbolism cannot be separated from Chicano cultural background. In order to study this symbolism, it is necessary to see it in context with the social ideas that predominate in Chicano contemporary thought. Therefore, we must consult the large bibliography that already exists and pertains to the social, racial, linguistic, and educational problems that the Chicano has confronted since 1848. The social and literary symbols, as we shall see, are the same. Their origin is found in the sociopolitical struggle, from where they have passed on to literature.

The symbols that have served to give unity to the Chicano movement and that appear in literature are many: Aztlán, the black eagle of the farmworkers; the Virgin of Guadalupe; *la huelga* (the strike); the expression *¡Viva la raza!;* and the characteristic handshake, the latter, of course, being outside of the literary field. The greatest part of these symbols, which give form to the concept of Chicanismo, are of recent origin; they were born with the political and social movement that was initiated with the strike in Delano, California, in 1965. But they have their roots in Mexico's historic past. The Virgin of Guadalupe was one of the symbols that helped to create Mexican nationality and political independence, her image having been hoisted by Father Miguel Hidalgo in 1810. The eagle the farmworkers used has an older origin, dating back to the foundation of Tenochtitlán by the Aztecs in 1325, where the people from Aztlán found on an island an eagle sitting on a nopal devouring a serpent. César Chávez, the creator of this Chicano symbol, said to *Ramparts* magazine:

> *I wanted desperately to get some color into the movement, to give people something they could identify with, like a flag. I was reading some books about how various leaders discovered what colors contrasted and stood out the best. The Egyptians had found that a red field with a white circle and a black emblem in the center crashed into your eyes like nothing else. I wanted to use the Aztec eagle in the center, as on the Mexican flag. So I told my cousin Manuel, "Draw an Aztec Eagle." Manuel had a little trouble with it, so we modified the eagle to make it easier for people to draw.*

According to accepted definitions, the symbol is a sensory image, which represents a concept or an emotion that cannot be expressed in its totality by any other method. The symbol expresses, with that sensory image, the significance of the spiritual. The image that we see reveals to us or makes us aware of the existence of something beyond the material. In other words, the sensory image, or symbol, is associated with a concept or an emotion (the symbolized thing). Therefore, it is necessary to interpret the symbol (the thing expressed) in terms of what is not expressed. Since the symbol can be social and not necessarily archetypal or mythical, it often has significance only for the group that has produced it and, frequently, only for the artist who has created it.

As a visual symbol, and not a literary one, the black eagle in the white circle over a red background symbolized for the Chicano the triumph over economic injustice by means of the farmworkers' union, whose aim is to obtain a better standard of living and also cultural identity. For those who are not Chicanos, the symbol loses its significance. Nevertheless, since the colors red, black, and white have a universal symbolic meaning, the image has a broad emotional significance, although not necessarily the same for all as the one that the Chicano understands. At the same time, the use of the eagle from the Mexican flag and of the colors red and white has a symbolic meaning for the *mexicano,* since it reminds him or her of the national flag. The eagle, Aztlán, the Quinto Sol, and other Chicano symbols of Mexican origin form a part of a mythic system, a characteristic often attributed to the symbol. An excellent example of the symbolic use of colors is the creation of Haiti's flag by the former slave Jean-Jacques Dessalines, who ripped the white color out of the French flag and sewed together the red and blue, symbolizing the expulsion of the white people from the country.

Aztlán, which we propose to examine in this study, is as much symbol as it is myth. As a symbol, it conveys the image of the cave (or sometimes a hill) representative of the origin of man; and as a myth, it symbolizes the existence of a paradisiacal region where injustice, evil, sickness, old age, poverty, and misery do not exist. As a Chicano symbol, Aztlán has two meanings: first, it represents the geographic region known as the Southwest of the United States, composed of the territory that Mexico ceded in 1848 with the Treaty of Guadalupe Hidalgo; second, and more important, Aztlán symbolizes the spiritual union of the Chicanos, something that is carried within the heart, no matter where they may live or where they may find themselves.

As a region in mythical geography, Aztlán has a long history. According to the Nahuatlan myth, the Aztecs were the last remaining tribe of seven, and they were advised by their god Huitzilopochtli to leave Aztlán in search of the Promised Land, which they would know by an eagle sitting on a nopal devouring a serpent. Later, the Aztecs, whose name is derived from Aztlán, remembered the region of their origin as an earthly paradise. During the fifteenth century, Moctezuma Ilhuicamina (1440–49) sent his priests in search of Aztlán. The historian Fray Diego Durán, in his *Historia de las Indias de Nueva España e Islas de Tierra Firme*, a work finished in 1581, says that Moctezuma I, desiring to know where the Aztecs' ancestors had lived, what form those seven caves had, and the relation between the people's history and their memory of it, sent for Cuauhcóatl, the royal historian, who told him:

> *O mighty lord, I, your unworthy servant, can answer you. . . . Our forebears dwelt in that blissful, happy place called Aztlán, which means "Whiteness." In that place*

> *there is a great hill in the midst of the waters, and it is called Culhuacan because its summit is twisted; this is the Twisted Hill. On its slopes were caves or grottos where our fathers and grandfathers lived for many years. There they lived in leisure, when they were called Mexitin and Azteca. There they had at their disposal great flocks of ducks of different kinds, herons, waterfowl, and cranes. Our ancestors loved the song and melody of the little birds with red and yellow heads. They also possessed many kinds of large beautiful fish.*
>
> *They had the freshness of groves of trees along the edge of the waters. They had springs surrounded by willows, evergreens, and alders, all of them tall and comely. Our ancestors went about in canoes and made floating gardens upon which they sowed maize, chili, tomatoes, amaranth, beans, and all kinds of seeds which we now eat and which were brought here from there.*
>
> *However, after they came to the mainland and abandoned that delightful place, everything turned against them. The weeds began to bite, the stones became sharp, the fields were filled with thistles and spines. They encountered brambles and thorns that were difficult to pass through. There was no place to sit, there was no place to rest; everything became filled with vipers, snakes, poisonous little animals, jaguars, and wildcats and other ferocious beasts. And this is what our ancestors forsook. I have found it painted in our ancient books. And this, O powerful king, is the answer I can give you to what you ask of me.*

Moctezuma I called for all of his sorcerers and magicians and sent them in search of Aztlán and of Coatlicue, the mother of Huitzilopochtli. The sorcerers in Coatepec, a province of Tula, transformed themselves through the art of magic into birds, tigers, lions, jackals, and wildcats, and in this way arrived at that lagoon in the middle of which is the hill of Culhuacan. They again took the form of humans and asked for Coatlicue "and the place which their ancestors left, which was called Chicomostoc [seven caves]."

The emissaries were taken in canoes to the island of Aztlán, where the hill is. "They say," relates Durán, "that the top half of the hill is made up of a very fine sand." There they found Coatlicue, who demonstrated to them that in Aztlán men never become old. She tells them:

> *"Stop so that you can see how men never become old in this country! Do you see my old servant? Watch him climb down the hill! By the time he reaches you he will be a young man."*
>
> *The old man descended and as he ran he became younger and younger. When he reached the Aztec wizards, he appeared to be about twenty years old. Said he, "Behold, my sons, the virtue of this hill; the old man who seeks youth can climb to the point on the hill that he wishes and there he will acquire the age that he seeks."*

The emissaries again transformed themselves into animals in order to make the return trip, which many of them did not succeed in completing because of having been eaten by wild beasts on the way. That is the Aztlán of the Aztec myth, the Aztlán that, like the mythical Atlantis, has never been pinpointed in geography. The search for it, like that for the fountain of youth, has never ceased. Cecilio Robelo, the Mexican historian of Nahuatlan mythology, tells us, "It's generally believed that Aztlán was located to the north of the Gulf of California." But not even that conjecture is accepted, since later he adds, "The inexorable question, then, of the place where the Mexica came from, still remains." And the inexorable question still stands, in spite of the efforts of erudite historians, whether they be Mexican, European, or American, such as Clavijero, Humboldt, Prescott, Orozco y Berra, Eustaquio Buelna, Chavero, Fernando Ramírez, Lapham, Wickersham, or Seler. There was even a book published in 1933 by S. A. Barrett titled *Ancient Aztalan,* which tried to prove that Aztlán can be found in the lakes of Wisconsin. Others have said that it was in Florida; others believe that it was in New Mexico; and still others in California. It was even said that Aztlán was to be found in China. The historian of Santa Barbara, California, Russell A. Ruíz, in a pamphlet published during the summer of 1969 that treats of the passing of the expedition of Portolá through the region, tells us that when the governor arrived on August 20, 1769, at what is today Goleta, California, he baptized the land with the name Pueblos de la Isla, which Father Crespí, who accompanied him, called Santa Margarita de Cortona, and to which the soldiers gave the name Mescaltitlán, believing that they had found themselves in the legendary place of origin of the Aztecs. In a few words, Ruiz says, "Mescaltitlán was another name for Aztlán, the legendary place of origin of the Aztecs or Mexican people. The Aztecs described it as a terrestrial paradise."

What interests us is not determining where Aztlán is found, but documenting the rebirth of the myth in Chicano thought. It is necessary to point out the fact that before March 1969, the date of the First National Chicano Liberation Youth Conference in Denver, no one mentioned Aztlán in writing. In fact, the first time that it was mentioned in a Chicano document was in "El plan espiritual de Aztlán" ("The Spiritual Plan of Aztlán"), which was presented in Denver at that time. Apparently, the rebirth of Aztlán owes its creation to the poet Alurista who already, in autumn 1968, had spoken about Aztlán in a class about Chicano culture held at San Diego State University.

"El plan espiritual de Aztlán" is important because in it the Chicano recognizes his Aztec origins ("We, the Chicano inhabitants and civilizers of the northern land of Aztlán, from whence came our forefathers"); because it established that Aztlán is the Mexican territory ceded to the United States in 1848; and because, following one of the basic ideas of the Mexican Revolution, it recognizes that the land belongs to those who work it ("Aztlán belongs to those that plant the seeds, water the fields, and gather the crops"); and finally, it identifies the Chicano with Aztlán ("We are a nation, we are a union of free pueblos, we are *Aztlán*").

Those words were published in March 1969. Beginning with that date, Aztlán has become the symbol most used by Chicano authors who write about the history, the culture, or the destiny of their people; and the same thing occurs among those who write poetic novels or short stories. During the spring of the following year, 1970, the first number of the journal *Aztlán* was published, and in it the plan was reproduced in both English and Spanish.

The prologue consists of a poem by Alurista called "Poem in Lieu of Preface," which united the mythical Aztec past with the present:

it is said
    that MOTECUHZOMA ILHUICAMINA
  SENT
    AN expedition
    looking for the NortherN
  mYthical land
  wherefrom the AZTECS CAME
    la TIERRA
  dE
  AztlÁN
  mYthical land for those
    who dream of roses and
    swallow thorns
    or for those who swallow thorns
  in powdered milk
  feeling guilty about smelling flowers
about looking for AztlÁN

In the following year, Alurista published the anthology *El ombligo de Aztlán* (*Aztlán's Navel*), and a year later his *Nationchild Plumaroja* appeared, published in San Diego by Toltecas de Aztlán. The title *Nationchild* refers, of course, to the Chicanos of Aztlán. From here on, books in whose title the word *Aztlán* appears would multiply.

In fiction also, especially in the novel, the symbol has been utilized with advantage for artistic creation. The novels of Méndez, *Peregrinos de Aztlán* (*Pilgrims of Aztlán,* 1974), and of Anaya, *Heart of Aztlán* (1976), are works representative of that tendency. It is fitting to point out that both works have antecedents in Mexican narrative. Gregorio López y Fuentes published in 1944 his novel *Los peregrinos inmóviles* (*Motherless Pilgrims*), and in 1949 María de Lourdes Hernández printed hers, *En el nuevo Aztlán* (*In the New Aztlán*). There is no direct influence between these Mexican and Chicano novels. Nevertheless, the elements that they have in common are significant and permit us to make a comparison. The theme of *Los peregrinos inmóviles* is the search for the Promised Land; in that novel, López y Fuentes re-creates the mythical pilgrimage of the Aztecs. In *Peregrinos de Aztlán* the theme is identical, only that the pilgrimage is in reverse. We read in Méndez's novel: "My imagination got the best of me and I saw a pilgrimage of many Indian people who were being trod upon by the torture of hunger and the humiliation of despoilment, running back through ancient roads in search of their remote origin." López y Fuentes had already written: "We walked all afternoon and part of the night. . . . We were going to the land of abundance: that was the message of the eagle, and we were on the right track."

Another important incidence is that in both works the narrator is an old Indian who remembers the history of his village. For the old Yaqui Loreto Maldonado, in Tijuana, the memories of his fallen and abused people torment him; and for the old Marcos, the memory of the original pilgrimage gives him courage to guide his own people. The first part of *Los peregrinos inmóviles* is titled "Heart of the World." And years later, Rudolfo Anaya would publish his novel with the title *Heart of Aztlán,* in which there is also a pilgrimage that the protagonist makes in search of Aztlán in a vision. Here he has the help of a magic stone instead of the eagle.

A greater similarity exists between *Heart of Aztlán* and *En el nuevo Aztlán.* In both novels the theme is the search for Aztlán, the lost paradise. In the work of Hernández, a group of Aztecs, immediately after the fall of Cuauhtémoc, takes refuge in a secret valley to which they can travel only by means of a mysterious river, which runs inside the grottos of Cacahuamilpa. In that valley, they founded a kind of Shangri-la, a perfect society. In the novel of Anaya, which develops in Barelas, a barrio in Albuquerque, the protagonist Clemente Chávez, not an old man but a man of some years, goes to the mountains, guided by the blind minstrel Crispín, in search of Aztlán on a truly imaginary pilgrimage: "They moved north, and there Aztlán was a woman fringed with snow and ice; they moved west, and there she was a mermaid singing by the sea. . . . They walked to the land where the sun rises, and . . . they found new signs, and the signs pointed them back to the center, back to Aztlán."

It is here where they find out that Aztlán symbolizes the center: "Time stood still, and in that enduring moment he felt the rhythm of the heart of Aztlán beat to the measure of his own heart. Dreams and visions became reality, and reality was but the thin substance of myth and legends. A joyful power coursed from the dark womb-heart of the earth into his soul and he cried out *I am Aztlán!*"

The search, for Clemente, has ended. And that is the way it must be for all Chicanos: whosoever wants to find Aztlán, let him or her look for it, not on the maps, but in the most intimate part of his being.

11. El Aposento Alto

ARLENE M. SANCHEZ WALSH

Among Protestant groups, what made Pentecostals stand out was their reliance on the Holy Spirit as the central experience from which one could partake to equip oneself to lead the sanctified life Methodists talked about, and to modify one's behavior as other conservative Protestants stressed. When faced with the choice of Unitarian-Trinitarian Pentecostalism, the marketplace became more competitive. In this case, Pentecostals were pitted against Pentecostals, including the Oneness groups willing to compete fiercely for congregants. Oneness Pentecostals offered similar spiritual experiences but stressed that their baptism in the Holy Spirit was just as efficacious as Trinitarians—meaning that believers spoke in tongues as evidence of the Spirit's indwelling. Oneness Pentecostals stressed that their baptismal formula of baptizing in the name of Jesus was correct, because there was a biblical verse and an Apostle who appeared to have baptized in that way (Acts 10:48). Oneness Pentecostals competed successfully for Latino congregants because they ministered to them where they were, as will be seen later; on a theological level, they convinced a sufficient number of people that their view of the Pentecostal outpouring and view of God was as biblically orthodox, if not more so, than their Trinitarian brethren. The significance of these parallels are that religious choice existed, and was partaken of, on a regular basis; the Pentecostal faith continued a long line of Protestant faiths that Mexicanos adhered to and promoted. Within the larger framework of Pentecostalism, the choices included the Unitarian-Trinitarian bodies, and later the movement led by famed evangelist Francisco Olazábal.

Here I shall turn our focus to the early years of the movement at the Azusa Street mission, to the breaking away of Oneness Pentecostals, and, finally, to the institutionalizing processes of the Assemblies of God.

Azusa Street's worshippers were a diverse population, some of whom spoke no English, but, as William Seymour expressed in his *Apostolic Faith* (hereafter, AF), that did not matter: "It is noticeable how free all nationalities feel. If a Mexican or German cannot speak English, he gets up and speaks in his own tongue and feels quite at home for the spirit interprets through the face and people say amen." Pentecost broke down linguistic barriers. For Pentecostals, Azusa Street was part of a continuum, since the day of Pentecost marked the beginning of the Christian Church. From its inception, this revival became a worldwide phenomenon. Frank Bartleman, a Pentecostal missionary, wrote: "Pentecost has come to Los Angeles, the American Jerusalem. Every sect, creed, and doctrine under heaven . . . as well as every nation is represented." Both Seymour and Bartleman noted the diversity among people at the

"El Aposento Alto", *Latino Pentecostal Indentity: Evangelical Faith, Self, and Society,* by Arlene M. Sanchez Walsh.

mission. This diversity worked in favor of the evangelist Seymour who received instruction from Charles Parham on the importance of speaking in tongues; language was now a gift from God, regardless of one's original language. This experience allowed the Spanish speaker to communicate with the German speaker, with the English speaker, and so on.

The revival began in house church gatherings held by Seymour. Eventually, their tarrying for an outpouring of the Holy Spirit was answered when, on 6 April 1906, Pentecost descended on Seymour and his followers, in keeping with the biblical pronouncement of spiritual outpouring. Speaking in tongues, healing, prophecy, and other signs brought in crowds so large that Seymour rented a larger church on nearby Azusa Street. The revival continued for three years, and converts at the mission exported the revival to the Midwest and southern United States.

One of the few accounts of conversion among Mexicans came from A. C. Valdez, who was ten years old when his mother brought him to Azusa Street. Valdez's mother, Susie, converted from Catholicism and became Yoakum's helper at his Pisgah House mission for prostitutes and alcoholics. Valdez writes of his family's early years of evangelism from 1906 to 1916, a time he describes as the worst years of persecution. He tells of being thrown in jail while others were horsewhipped, clubbed, or stoned. He claims that some Pentecostals were martyred. Other sources corroborated Valdez's accounts of harassment and violence, but I have found no evidence of martyrdom. Aside from Susie Valdez's work with Yoakum, A.C. did not record another time when he or his family ministered to Spanish speakers. This was not the case with other Azusa Street converts.

Historian Mel Robeck's important work on Latinos at Azusa Street places their roles in the context of Pentecostal history of the early twentieth century. Abundio López and his wife, Rosa, converted to Pentecostalism at Azusa Street and became emissaries of the Pentecostal faith to other Mexicans. It seems that the Lópezes had embraced the Protestant faith before Azusa Street as the Reverend Alexander Moss Merwin, pastor of the Spanish Presbyterian Church, officiated at their wedding in 1902. They attended the revival on 29 May 1906, and converted the following month. Rosa was not mentioned in the Los Angeles City Directory, but Abundio was listed in the 1920 edition. He is listed as the pastor of the Apostolic Faith Church, a Spanish-speaking congregation that doubled as a Euro American church named Victoria Hall on Spring Street. The "Apostolic Faith" was the first name given to the nascent Pentecostal movement at Azusa Street. The couple's ministry caught the attention of Seymour, who wrote about their work at the mission: "There are a good many Spanish-speaking people in Los Angeles. The Lord has given them language, and now a Spanish preacher, who, with his wife, are preaching the gospel in open air meetings on the Plaza, having received their Pentecost." One month later the Lópezes became Seymour's helpers. "Brother and Sister López, Spanish people who are filled with the Holy Ghost, are being used of God in street meetings and helping Mexicans at the altar at Azusa Street." The Lópezes eventually left Los Angeles to minister to Mexicans in the borderlands. The specter of a Mexican preaching in the open-air plaza of Los Angeles, which, at the time of Azusa Street, contained within the plaza eleven Catholic churches, adds another important dimension to the creation of a Pentecostal identity. Pentecostalism liberated immigrants from language, and also from the enclosed sacred spaces of the plaza that, for decades, symbolized the Catholic Church's strength within the Mexican community. Protestants contested that space by building churches and training their Spanish-speaking ministers in the plaza as early as the 1880s. Pentecostals like the Lópezes zealously sought converts and did so in the heart of Catholic Los Angeles. To the eventual (and continuing) dismay of the Church, they succeeded.

Language for the Pentecostal took on a sacred meaning that other Protestant denominations working in Mexican communities did not have. The following report from Seymour demonstrates what spiritual language did for the convert. On 11 August 1906, a native Mexican from Central Mexico interpreted the language of a German woman to be his own. "He understood, and through the message that God gave him through her, he was most happily converted. . . . All the English he knew was Jesus Christ and Hallellujah." The Pentecostal baptism, according to converts, gave them the ability to transcend language barriers and proved key to gaining converts who did not speak English. Speaking in tongues transcended the temporal boundaries of human language and introduced the mostly working-class Mexican immigrant population to the ethereal world of the Spirit. Many reports describe what Wacker termed *missionary tongues* during the early years of the Pentecostal movement. This gift centered on the ability to speak in the language of the mission field so that the gospel could be preached all over the world in native languages. Wacker notes that no evidence of such a gift existed, aside from personal testimonials filling the pages of Pentecostal magazines and pulpits. He views missionary tongues as a pragmatic strategy employed by Pentecostals to continue their worldwide missionary efforts. Missionary tongues were needed, Pentecostals reasoned, because Jesus was coming soon, the "heathen" was perishing without the gospel, and it was not too far-fetched to assume that the Holy Spirit would give Pentecostals this gift to meet a practical need, another example of the pragmatic approach to seeking converts.

Another key to conversion efforts lay in the places where Euro American evangelists sought converts—homes, social missions, plazas, and jails—sites where a marginal population might find themselves in early twentieth-century Los Angeles. A lay missionary in jail in Whittier began ministering to the Mexican population, and, as he described it: "The Lord gave me their tongue, the Mexican language. . . . I did not have that tongue, until I went into jail . . . most of the men are Mexicans, the men in jail asked me where the mission was, and they were going to come down as soon as they get out." Pentecostals, then as now, have never been intimidated by the often dour and dark surroundings of prisons, migrant field houses, and the modest homes of working-class Mexicanos. In the same issue of *AF*, another unnamed missionary offered insight into the motivations behind this conversion strategy after the initial Azusa Street revival in April 1906: "I bless God that it did not start in any church in this city, but in a barn, so that we might all come and take part in it. If it had started in a fine church, poor, colored people, and Spanish people would not have got it." Pentecostals recognized the segregation that comprised much of churchgoing in Los Angeles, cognizant that had the revival occurred anywhere else, people of color would have been excluded.

Azusa Street initiated the Mexican population into the evangelical world of Pentecostals. This revival and the ensuing push to convert others signified something more than the beginning of a new religious movement. The Protestant Los Angeles Singleton, found in

1907, now included a zealous and growing movement whose characteristics included more than a voluntaristic impulse. Pentecostalism delivered a message to the burgeoning immigrant population that extolled the virtues of a spiritual experience offering certain salvation. But almost as soon as Azusa Street waned, around 1909, Pentecostalism's discordant voices began to give way to schism.

A new theological issue casting doubt on the Trinitarian nature of God split the small but growing Mexican convert population. The nascent Mexican Pentecostal movement experienced its first theological division, and, with that, Oneness Pentecostals felt the urge to spread their new message to their own. The significance of this break lies in the fact that the Mexican converts established churches and spread the Oneness message independently of the larger, Euro American Oneness group that separated from the Assemblies of God in 1914. Even more significant, for the purposes of unfurling the layers of a Pentecostal identity, is the establishment of a Mexican Oneness Pentecostal movement in Los Angeles by 1909 and its growth to the borderlands and Mexico by 1912. The first known Apostolic church (Oneness churches are still commonly referred to as Apostolic), the "Spanish Apostolic Faith Mission," opened on Alpine Street in 1912, pastored by Genaro Valenzuela Mexican converts began to challenge the established norms of Trinitarian Pentecostalism, and, within three years of their initiation, a separate Pentecostal identity began to take shape. The origins of the Oneness movement are not entirely clear. The movement began in house churches in and around Los Angeles, ministered by Mexicanos, who converted Azusa Street converts like Luis López and Romanita Valenzuela.

Romanita Carbajal de Valenzuela gathered followers in Los Angeles and rebaptized them in the name of Jesus. She returned to Chihuahua and converted her family. The church she established, La Iglesia Cristiana Espiritual (the Christian Spiritual Church), became one of the largest Protestant bodies in Mexico. The U.S. counterpart, La Asamblea Apostólica (Apostolic Assembly), spread quickly throughout southern California and the Southwest. Valenzuela also did work along the border of California, Texas, and Arizona. Though there is little biographical information on him, Luis López was baptized at Azusa Street in 1909. The revival also produced evangelist Juan Navarro. López and Navarro were rebaptized in the name of Jesus later that year. They established a mission and converted many of the future leaders of the Asambleas Apostólicas. One convert, Antonio C. Nava, copastored a small Apostolic church in Los Angeles, on Angeles and Aliso Streets, one of the denomination's first churches in Los Angeles. By 1919 Apostolics had established churches in Watts, Oxnard, Los Angeles, San Fernando, San Diego, San Bernardino, and Riverside, usually establishing missions among migrant farm workers. By 1925 there were at least twenty-three churches and twenty-five pastors scattered from Baja, California, to New Mexico.

As Daniel Ramírez notes, the preponderance of the Apostolic Assemblies churches were planted among migrant labor camps of southern California. Ramírez contends that the movement which began in the plaza area of Los Angeles became increasingly rural and focused its attention on farm workers: "A nucleus of farm worker converts in the Coachella Valley proved key in subsequent evangelization work in Mexico." The dire surroundings facing Apostolic Assembly members, and indeed most laborers in the fields, caught the attention of a rival missionary, Assemblies of God minister John Preston, who wrote of conditions in the Imperial Valley in 1918. "This is a very needy place. . . . There is absolutely nothing being done for the Mexicans on either side of the line by any of the Protestant churches, and so it is all over the Imperial Valley, the Mexicans are neglected." Judging by the requests missionaries made for donations, the remedy for this neglect focused not so much on a social mission but on a spiritual mission offering laborers a better life through Pentecostalism with fellow laborers leading the way, establishing churches and bringing laborers out of the fields they plowed together. The ease with which church members crossed the border to evangelize and create churches ceased with the deportation of many Apostolic members during the 1930s. During their stay in Mexico, Apostolic members spent their time evangelizing and building churches. Oneness Pentecostals established a separate identity from their Trinitarian brethren as early as 1912. Their desire to build on that difference is demonstrated by their commitment to evangelize their fellow immigrants and their former homeland. What attracted them to Oneness? To Pentecostalism? The spiritual gifts of tongues and healing were and remain two of the most important phenomena feeding the desire to become Pentecostal. In the pages of *AF* and in the experiences converts describe, several clues are provided.

What did Azusa Street represent to those who visited the mission? What did the emerging Oneness movement represent to the convert? What happened at the mission that so impressed people that they chose to adopt Pentecostalism, even for only a moment but often a lifetime? Two feats, in particular, appealed to visitors of Azusa Street: speaking in tongues and healing. Abundio López, Rosa López, Brigido Pérez, Luis López, Juan Navarro, and the unidentified native Mexican all experienced the baptism of the Holy Spirit. Both the native Mexican and Abundio López reported that they had been given the gift of healing or were healed themselves. The native Mexican laid hands on a woman at the mission, and she reported being healed of tuberculosis, "de almas y de cuerpos" (of soul and body). Information on early Oneness converts is scanty, revealing only that they claimed to experience Spirit baptism. Antonio C. Nava, on an evangelism tour of Yuma, Arizona, prayed for his sister, and she was reportedly healed of cancer. This resulted in the entire family converting to Oneness Pentecostalism. Like the native Mexican, healing facilitated the opening of Pentecostalism to others who sought the same experience. This is not to suggest, however, that Pentecostalism introduced religious healing to the Mexican community. The desire to alleviate physical suffering by means of divine intervention has a long tradition among Mexican immigrants, who, years before they entered the Azusa Street mission, visited the homes of curanderas like Teresa Urrea and took the prescriptions of curanderos like: Don Pedrito Jaramillo.

Urrea brought her healing powers to the Mexican population of Los Angeles in 1902 in exile. "The halt, the blind, the inwardly distressed, paralytics almost helpless, and others ravaged by consumption, are helped to her doors each day by friends, and relatives and none go there without the belief that by the laying on of her magic hands, they will be cured." Urrea purchased a home in Boyle Heights on Brooklyn Avenue and State Street, and, according to the *Los Angeles Times,* a continual stream of "invalids" visited her. Urrea's exile began when she became a larger threat to the Mexican government, who did not appreciate the moral support she gave to native Mexican uprisings. Faith healer Don Pedrito Jaramillo, the healer of Los Olmos, ministered to the Mexican population of southern Texas and northern Mexico from 1881 until his death in 1907. Jaramillo wrote unusual prescriptions for his followers, as the patients informed his assistant of their symptoms. During one engagement in San Antonio in 1897 between March 24 and April 11, Jaramillo received and prescribed cures for 11,583 people, sometimes sending telegrams as far away as New Orleans.

There are significant differences and a few similarities between the healing arts legacy within the Mexican community of Urrea and Jaramillo and the Pentecostal healing converts at Azusa Street experienced. Both the Pentecostals and Urrea used the laying on of hands to transmit healing. Both Urrea and Jaramillo became associated with the Latino Catholic lexicon of folk saints, a lexicon Pentecostals reject as having any part in their healing. For example, Tomochic rebels attempting to invade Mexico on behalf of Santa Teresa wore her picture on their person to help ward off bullets from Mexican government soldiers. Don Jaramillo's grave became a pilgrimage site. Pentecostals, implicitly if not explicitly, tried to remove any hint of popular Catholicism from the healing experience. Although similarities exist between the trance possession curanderos report when channeling spirits and the Pentecostal act of being "slain in the Spirit," Pentecostals diligently discourage any theological link to practices of folk religion in an attempt to create boundaries of orthodox/heterodox religion. Another experiential similarity exists between the healing tradition of Spiritualists and Pentecostals—both claim the supernatural ability to speak in tongues. Though this phenomenon has been recorded by both curanderos who are *espritualistas* and U.S. Spiritualists, it is again relegated outside the boundaries of orthodox religious practice.

While the healing traditions of the curanderos and santos have ancient roots among Mexicanos, the healing tradition brought to them through Pentecostalism bears little resemblance to the healing traditions of the past. The chief and, for Pentecostals, most important difference is their claim that their tradition receives its supernatural commandments from the New Testament's injunctions to use the power Jesus gave to heal to the Apostles as part of their reclaiming of the Apostolic tradition. Pentecostals would disavow any linkages—cultural, spiritual, or otherwise—to any healing traditions outside Christianity.

The power of Pentecostalism is in its immediacy and the implicit acceptance of the miraculous. God mandated the end of the exclusiveness of language by making spiritual language available to all who asked for the Spirit baptism. Among those who accepted the baptism, a handful of Mexicanos became evangelists for a new faith. Problems for these evangelists and for their new faith were not far behind. One of the problems, according to Robeck, was culture: "When Hispanic Pentecostals such as Lopez, Pérez, or the Valdez families did choose to share their personal testimony with other Hispanics and encourage them to seek the same thing thereby evangelizing them, have they actually violated their own culture?" Does preaching for Pentecostalism mean preaching against Catholicism? Did that, in turn, mean a betrayal of the cultural marker of Catholicism imbued so deeply that its loss signified a cultural death? Some of the more introspective analysis on Latino Pentecostals and the question of ethnicity and culture have come from Catholic priest/scholar Allen Figueroa Deck.

> *The thoughtful Hispanic will view evangelical efforts to convert Hispanics as a particularly vicious attack on his or her cultural identity. Even though the Hispanic*

> *American may not be active in practicing the Catholic faith, he or she perceives that the culture is permeated by a kind of Catholic ethos and symbols that revolves around a rich collection of rites and symbols. Many of these rites and symbols are imbued with a certain Catholic spirit. The evangelical penchant for reducing the mediation between God and humanity to the Scriptures is antithetical to the Hispanic Catholic tendency to multiple mediations. . . . Hispanics have often experienced serious family divisions when a member becomes Protestant. In Hispanic culture, this is not just a religious matter. It is a profound cultural, social, and familial rupture.*

Examining Figueroa Deck's words explicates the dilemma that early Pentecostal converts experienced and, to some extent, still do. As Figueroa Deck described in another work, it is the reactionary impulse of the Catholic Church and the indifference of mainline Protestantism to the "Hispanic shift" toward Pentecostalism that has given rise to a culture of suspicion and animosity. All sides that have failed to understand the shift toward Pentecostalism feed this culture, ascribing to a premise based more on the proprietary concern of the Catholic Church and its desire to be seen as the Mother Church. Add to this the lack of attention Latino Protestants received in mainline Protestant churches, where, for nearly two centuries, becoming a Christian has been equated with becoming Euro American.

Although Figueroa Deck writes more about contemporary conversions than does Robeck in his historical analysis, the former recognizes the profound tensions created around conversion, but his insistence on placing it in a Catholic context does not help us ascertain how a Pentecostal identity is created among mainline Protestant or agnostic converts who have never been Catholic. In my research for the succeeding chapters, I interviewed many converts who did not have ties to Catholicism before conversion, and to suggest, as Figueroa Deck does, that Latinos have an innate Catholic ethos requires rigorous examination. If Figueroa Deck limits his scope to Catholic converts, then the problem becomes, of course, how these converts work out their faith life as an ex-Catholics, who may or may not still be involved in popular Catholic practices, and how they deal with familial tensions. But if we want to examine the larger picture of Latino converts, we cannot assume a Catholic ethos for non-Catholics nor even for nominal Catholics. However, we may be able to assert a symbolic religious identity for Latino Catholics, who are nonpracticing and are quite ambivalent about the Church but would never think of leaving. By this I wish to suggest that Latino Pentecostals developed a historical memory and religious identity separate from Catholicism and that, by maintaining certain faith traditions, these Pentecostal identities continue to this day, operating separately from Catholicism's historical memory and religious identity. Ruiz posits another perspective on ethnicity and religious identity called "cultural coalescence." "Immigrants and their children pick, borrow, retain, and create distinctive cultural forms. There is not a single hermetic Mexican or Mexican American culture but rather permeable cultures rooted in generation, region, class, and personal experience." If there is no single culture, then presumably there is no single religious heritage informing the faith lives of Latinos. Assumptions anchoring scholarship about Latinos and religion need reconceptualization. The permeability of cultures certainly finds support in the Pentecostal experience of Latinos, who not only chose their religious identity but also began forming it early on as they sifted through varieties of Pentecostalism. Sociologists Rubén Rumbaut and Alejandro Portes offer another theory that does not deal explicitly with religious identity but may help to explain why Latino immigrants, especially Mexican immigrants, enter into the acculturation process and form identities at different rates than other immigrant groups.

Portes's and Rumbaut's segmented assimilation idea suggests that a host of factors determines how second-generation immigrants, in particular, acculturate effectively into American society. The two describe three levels of acculturation based on their findings. Unfortunately, like most sociologists who do not deal with religion, there is no factor attached to this topic. In fact, in their entire book on second-generation immigrants, Portes and Rumbaut make only one reference to religion, and it focuses narrowly on Chinese immigrants and Buddhism. Nevertheless, this and other theoretical models are helpful in contributing to an understanding of the larger picture of Mexican immigration and how Pentecostalism figures into the acculturation process. Certain questions should be kept in mind as the story continues: Does Pentecostalism offer anything with regard to human capital? Does it ease modes of incorporation? Does it buffer family structures? How does Pentecostalism help successive generations of Latinos acculturate, and what does that do to their identity as Latinos? To answer these questions, we continue.

The very nature of Pentecostalism as an independent faith would be the cause of its unraveling within a few years of its inception. The evangelists would then have to organize churches, build Bible schools, and solidify a Pentecostal identity among the Mexican communities from California to Texas. In order to maintain our focus on the institutionalization of Pentecostalism within Mexican communities, attention here shifts to the Assemblies of God, one of the most productive of Pentecostal groups, who, by 1918, had missionaries committed to Latinos in the United States despite the breakaway movement of the Mexican healing evangelist, Francisco Olazábal.

Olazábal, born in El Verano, Sinaloa, Mexico, on October 12, 1886, was the mayor's son. After his mother converted to Methodism, he was sent to the United States to study for the ministry. After a stint at the Moody Bible Institute in Chicago, Olazábal worked at the Glad Tidings Tabernacle in San Francisco and then pastored at Misión Mexicana de Pasadena, founded in 1907. During that time he founded a cooperative laundry for Mexican immigrant women in Pasadena. Olazábal's Pentecostal conversion occurred under the ministry of Carrie and George Montgomery.

The Montgomerys worked in Arizona and California. Their Pentecostal lineage is not traced to Azusa Street but to the "come-out" movement within the Holiness denominations at the turn of the century. The Montgomerys "came out" of the Christian Missionary Alliance, a denomination particularly rife with contention over the alleged unsavory character of Pentecostalism. For years, Holiness converts to Pentecostalism tried unsuccessfully to win approval from the Alliance founder A. B. Simpson, who never accepted the more elaborate doctrines of Pentecostalism, especially speaking in tongues. Carrie's fame as a healer-evangelist grew within the Holiness community as her husband, George, funded her nationwide revivals with the profits of his northern Mexico mining business. On a trip to Los Angeles, they visited Misión Mexicana in Pasadena and met Olazábal, who told George that his own conversion to Pentecostalism came through George's healing experience which he had read about in a Spanish Bible tract.

Olazábal was one of the first Mexican Pentecostal leaders to leave any written record of his ministry. Not only do his writings piece together the early history of the movement but they also provide clues to the creation of a Latino Pentecostal identity. Olazábal demonstrated a typical nineteenth-century Protestant education in a speech before the Methodist Epworth League in Gardena, California, in May 1913, his predisposition to anti-Catholic sentiment having been set years before he became Pentecostal.

> *In the critical moments through which my country is passing, when nearly the entire world considers my people to be barbarous and uncivilized because of the fratricidal war that is desolating the fields and cities of Mexico . . . I do not believe in the armed intervention of your country because it is not what we need and you can bear it to us: the intervention of the Gospel and of Christian love.*

The Mexican, according to Olazábal, would prefer death rather than be subject to armed intervention. In an ironic twist, Olazábal's nationalism echoed what conservative Mexican Catholics said at the time on the need to respect the sovereignty of the Mexican nation. The obvious difference was that nationalist Catholics viewed Protestant missionaries in Mexico as part of the U.S. invasion, not as part of the solution to the nation's problems. Catholic detractors accused triumphant revolutionaries of Protestantism. Historian Deborah Baldwin believes that conservative Catholics saw the revolution as "culturally incongruous," since being both Protestant and Mexican was unacceptable. Not only did Olazábal see no incongruity in conversion, he encouraged the continued conversion of Mexican and Mexican Americans.

Olazábal, the Methodist, blamed the Catholic Church for Mexico's misfortunes. He explained: "I was born in that faith, and the first instruction which I received was Roman Catholic." Olazábal echoed a familiar refrain at the end of his speech, the idea that Catholicism was not Christian. "When Mexico shall come to be a Christian country, which it surely will be if we do our part, let its best friend be the U.S." Ruiz's contention that cultures permeate and create identities from various sources finds strength in Olazábal life. Olazábal, the Mexican nationalist Protestant with strong ties to the American Protestant community, pleads for the United States not to invade Mexico militarily but, instead, to invade Mexico with more American missionaries. Another ironic twist to this story is that the Americans who heeded similar calls from Olazábal and others to "save" Mexico turned out to be missionaries like Henry Ball—an Assemblies of God pastor whom Olazábal would break away from over allegations of racism.

Olazábal continued working for the Misión Mexicana Church in Pasadena until 1916 when he moved to Texas and began to work with the Assemblies of God mission to Mexicans. Olazábal was ordained into the Assemblies of God on 24 September 1916, and soon afterward moved to El Paso to pastor. Within three years the mission was in financial trouble, and Olazábal wrote to Montgomery for support. In response, Montgomery sent him forty-five dollars toward a new church building. In thanking him, Olazábal asked for prayer and more workers for his growing mission. The El Paso mission flourished in the midst of revival but not without repercussions. Olazábal described the difficulty of operating in a Catholic stronghold: "We had to fight against the powers of the Catholic Church. The tent was stoned, threatened to be set on fire, etc." Along with Spirit baptisms, the members reported healings, visions of Jesus and the Second Coming, and prophetic utterances regarding the future of the church. Olazábal concluded his column by asking for support for his ministry and hinting about a Bible school for Mexican men and women preparing for the ministry. In 1921 an unknown writer pleaded Olazábal's case to the readers of *Pentecostal Evangel* (hereafter, *PE*), the weekly magazine of the Assemblies of God. The writer notes the lack of workers for the masses of Mexicans who attend services in El Paso in a church that needs expansion to accommodate the crowds. During the first three years of his ministry with the Assemblies of God, Olazábal appeared to receive support and encouragement for his work. Apparently, however, as his ministry continued to grow and require more donations, his fund-raising activities on behalf of the church made the Assemblies of God uncomfortable. Depending on which version of the story one chooses to accept, Olazábal was either asked to leave or he resigned.

In January 1923 J. R. Flower, the Assemblies superintendent, wrote a column in *PE* describing Olazábal's situation. According to Flower, Olazábal's attempts to begin a school in El Paso failed so badly that Flower, Ball, Olazábal, Luce, and the missionary to Mexico George Blaisdell attended an emergency meeting in December 1922. According to Flower, the El Paso school was too far away from Mexicans to be effective. He also cited the poverty of the Mexicans of El Paso as a reason why the school failed. Flower said, quoting Olazábal: "He agreed that he would devote his time and energies to the ministry rather than to attempt to build up a school or other institution which would take him from the field." Flower moved the efforts to build a school to San Antonio and placed it under the supervision of the Missionary Commission of the General Council of the Assemblies of God. Ball took charge of the administration of the school, and Luce took charge of the faculty.

According to Miguel Guillen, the official chronicler of Olazábal's story and former minister with the Texas mission of the Assemblies of God, Olazábal did not leave the denomination voluntarily but was asked to leave because of problems related to his fund-raising for the school, which caused the leadership concern. According to Guillen, the Assemblies of God was intent on not allowing Olazábal any position of leadership and terminated his ministry in an effort to silence his powerful presence amid the growing Mexican Pentecostal community. In 1922 the Mexican members of the Texas Assemblies of God voted to start their own district council, which Olazábal would head. According to Isabel Flores (another former member of the Assemblies of God), the plan required Olazábal to run the council from his El Paso church while starting a Bible institute and a printing press. Opposition to Olazábal's promotion came from the Euro American members of the Assemblies of God, who, according to Flores, believed that "el pueblo Mexicano no estaba capacitado para dirigir el trabajo" (the Mexican people were not qualified to direct the work).

In December 1923 Guillen interviewed Olazábal at his home in Port Arthur, Texas, and the interview supported Flores's account. Olazábal recalls meeting with Assemblies of God leaders to explain why he raised money for his church. He mentioned Alice Luce's philosophy of autonomous Mexican leadership. The leadership was offended at his reference to Luce and suggested he showed disrespect. When Flower, the Assemblies of God leader, asked who had authorized his fund-raising, Olazábal answered that he had received authority to raise funds at the last Texas Assemblies of God convention (1918) from Flower himself. Olazábal's response to his dismissal was this: "Yo salí de entre los Metodistas y creí que había entrado entre mas cristianos, pero ahora veo que un Ruso, un Griego, puede ser misionero, menos un Mexicano." (I left the Methodists and I thought I had been among Christians, but now I see that a Russian, a Greek, can be a missionary, but not a Mexican). With that, Olazábal set off to found his own church. In 1923 El Concilio Latino Americano de lglesias Cristianas began.

The Assemblies of God recollection of events differs significantly from Olazábal's. Glenn Gohr, an Assemblies of God historian, believes that Olazábal became "disconcerted" with the predominantly Euro American denomination. Other Assemblies of God recollections of the Olazábal controversy are sparse. Henry Ball commented on the controversy in a 1940 retrospective on his career:

> *El hermano Francisco Olazábal se retiró de las Asambleas de Dios el dia de 13 de Enero de 1923. Era un gran evangelista y se retiró de nuestro movimiento que causó disturbios de caracter serio; indudablemente estariamos mas avanzados.*
>
> *[Brother Francisco Olazábal withdrew from the Assemblies of God in January 1923. He was a grand evangelist. His retirement from the movement caused a great disturbance in the character (of the movement). Unquestionably, we would have been much more advanced].*

Ball concluded that the Assemblies of God mission would have been much stronger had Olazábal stayed with the church. Despite his popularity in the Assemblies, Olazábal left and convinced a core group of Assemblies of God ministers, including the future church superintendent Demetrio Bazán, to leave the church to join Olazábal in establishing churches in Texas and California. This episode between Olazábal and another Pentecostal denomination clearly speaks to the tenor of the times in which Olazábal preached and reflects how Euro American leadership viewed him.

After Olazábal left the Assemblies, he continued his healing campaigns. One campaign in East Los Angeles in 1927 attracted the attention of Foursquare founder Aimee Semple McPherson. McPherson and Olazábal were invited to preach in each other's churches, but this cozy relationship did not last long. When McPherson asked Olazábal to merge his new denomination with her's, the Concilio membership defeated the proposal. Undoubtedly, in the aftermath of the Assemblies of God split, Mexican members had had enough of Euro American leadership. McPherson did not take the rejection well and requested the return of her $100 "love offering." When Olazábal refused, McPherson set out to counter Olazábal's work in Los Angeles by starting Foursquare's own Spanish-speaking churches. From its inception, Olazábal's vision of Pentecostal revival and salvation for Mexico in the "last days" powered the Concilio.

In 1923 Olazábal wrote to the Pentecostal minister Richey and asked for support to fund a campaign Olazábal planned for Mexico. He offered two reasons for the campaign: (1) the millennial inspiration of the Second Coming; and (2) the need to "save" Mexico from "'a avaricia y absolutismo del clero romano, que por cuatro centurias ha esclavizado la consciencia de ese pueblo en el 99 por cento de su población" (the avarice and absolutism of the Roman clergy, who, for four centuries, has enslaved the conscience of 99 percent of the population). Although Richey did not respond to this request, Olazábal's frequent campaigns across the United States seem to indicate that he soon became a very popular healing evangelist.

Olazábal's campaigns focused on healing and educating converts on the theological nuances of what Pentecostals believed. He writes of a campaign in Texas:

> *Muy pocos de los que han sido sanados en mis servicios de sanidad han vuelto la cara atras y casi todos los que han sido salvados por la operación de los milagros y la sanidades han sido completamente regenerados y llevan hoy una vida ejemplar.*
>
> *[Very few of those who have been healed in my healing services have turned back, and almost all those that have been saved through the working of miracles and healings have been completely renewed and today lead exemplary lives.]*

Healing changes lives and, in so doing, gives converts the opportunity to lead exemplary lives. Olazábal brought his campaigns to San Fernando, California, El Paso, Cleveland, Tennessee, New York, and Puerto Rico.

Reporting on his crusades, the media noted the great crowds and miraculous healings. The *Cleveland Daily* Banner pointed out the unusual nature of an all-night service, where the "Aztec missionary" Olazábal led the crowd in an all-night prayer meeting. The paper also notes the merger of his church with the Church of God, claiming Olazábal could deliver fifty thousand Mexicans to the denomination. Why Olazábal would leave the predominantely Euro American Assemblies of God for the predominantly Euro American Church of God is unclear. When Olazábal died in a car accident in 1937, the merger had not been completed. Another publication, the *Christian Herald,* wrote of Olazábal's growing ministry and the success the "great Aztec" had in ministering to Mexicans. The Aztec imagery reflects the racial component intoned by many Euro American observers and missionaries when writing about Mexican ministers and converts. The author of an article about Olazábal's New York ministry prefaced the piece by suggesting that the "barbaric" nature of Aztec priests and the "jungle dances" of Harlem bespeak an impossible situation for anything positive to come out of Harlem, where Olazábal's outreach reportedly converted and healed hundreds. What makes Olazábal acceptable? Despite his Aztec ancestry, his Protestantism legitimizes him as civilized and godly—unlike his ancestors. Commenting on contemporary racial attitudes, Roberto Almaraz, an Assemblies of God minister, says that this patronizing attitude plagues Latino/Euro American Pentecostal relations to this day. Says Almaraz: "The problem is that they [Assemblies of God continue to view us as a mission field, as converts . . . not as equals. The stereotypical language, using Aztec iconography, employed by the writer in the *Christian Herald* continues to this day by Olazábal's admirers themselves, who call him "el Azteca" as a term of affection.

As part of his two-tiered ministry, Olazábal took time out of his healing services and campaigns to answer questions about Pentecostalism and wrote responses in the church's magazine. During the 1930s the Pentecostal movement was considered "bizarre," and the misinformation about their spiritual practices was widespread. On several occasions the prejudice descended into verbal and physical violence. Detractors accused Pentecostals of practicing witchcraft, devil worship, and sexual promiscuity. They threw rocks and garbage, mobbed Pentecostal meetings, slashed meeting tent ropes, and set churches afire. With this history of contention, Olazábal's role as a promoter of Pentecostalism meant that he had to promote its acceptance as a part of orthodox Christianity. A question came from an unnamed person who wanted to know if Pentecostalism was equivalent to Spiritualism. Olazábal responded:

> *No, en ninguna manera si el pueblo conciente que pertenece al dicho movimiento Pentecostal es responsable de lo malo que encontrate en este o en aquel individuo por el hecho de que el dicho individuo asegura pertenecer al dicho movimiento . . . el movimiento Pentecostal enseña que es error todo lo que contradice, el material de doctrina, lo que está escrito en la Biblia; considera como pecado toda rebeldia contra la voluntad de Dios y toda desobediencia de su santa ley.*
>
> *[No, in no manner is the Pentecostal movement responsible for such bad things. The Pentecostal movement teaches that [Spiritualism] is in error in doctrinal matters, in what is written in the Bible; it is considered a sin and rebellion for such bad things. The Pentecostal movement teaches [that Spiritualism] is in error in doctrinal manners, in what is written in the Bible; it is considered a sin and rebellion against God and totally disobedient of His Holy law].*

Olazábal had two concerns: (1) to educate his growing congregation, and (2) to convince his flock of the uncomplimentary practices of Spiritualism. Spiritualists, along with using intermediaries to attempt contact with the deceased, practiced speaking in tongues. This practice for a time made Spiritualism an attractive option for Pentecostals who where "deceived" into attending Spiritualist churches.

Olazábal's crusades and teaching came to an end in 1937, when he died in a car accident on his way back from a campaign in Texas. The denomination he started did not merge with any other Pentecostal denomination and, for the most part, had relied on generational growth to continue to fill its churches. Holland calls the Concilio "the most conservative and introverted of the Pentecostal denominations." This observation is supported by a personal conversation with Latino Pentecostal ministers who have close ties to the Concilio, one of whom, a family friend of the Olazábal family, told me that the church has little interest in working with others, rarely grants interview requests, and, in his estimation, is still suffering the effects of the Olazábal split with the Assemblies of God more than seventy years ago. Despite the church's reluctance to discuss its history or current work, what should be kept in mind is Olazábal's work in the early years of Latino Pentecostalism, and his insistence on autonomy—an insistence that would be bolstered by the writing and work of Alice Luce.

Alice Luce began her "Mexican work" as a missionary to Mexico. Forced to leave on the eve of the Revolution, she became a missionary to Mexicans in California. She wrote an open letter to the Assemblies of God warning them of lost opportunities if they did not support the Mexican work. In order for this mission to work, the Assemblies of God would have to send many more workers to the border. Luce's missionary impulse concentrated on two points: (1) to spread the word about the Pentecostal cause among. Mexicans, and (2) to "save" Mexicans from the continuing influence of the Catholic Church. She writes: "We are proving the good old gospel to be the power of God unto salvation for these poor, dark, Mexicans, just as for the white people. The opposition of the priests has been terrible." Luce's sentiments demonstrate some ideas commonly held by Protestants raised in the nineteenth century, (Luce was the daughter of an Anglican bishop) that Catholicism kept people in darkness. But her idea that evangelization efforts succeeded in converting "white" people as well as "poor, dark" Mexicans displays a crucial element she had for her missions: that they be turned over to Mexican control as soon as possible. It should be noted, however, that Luce's partner, Henry Ball, did not have the same idea regarding Mexican control. Ball writes: "We need more American missionaries. I have in the past two years, trained several Mexican workers, but while they are excellent workers, they need American oversight." Creeping paternalism as it worked its way into Protestant missions to Mexicans before Pentecostalism continued despite the gains made by Mexican pastors and Luce's work.

Luce founded a Pentecostal mission in the Placita in 1917. El Aposento Alto was located on Los Angeles Street. Like other Protestant missions who set up in the plaza decades earlier, a distinct Pentecostal presence that had begun at the Azusa Street mission continued with Luce's mission and continued to reap the benefits of a large Mexican population of religious seekers. In 1922 Luce took a failed Pentecostal mission in the Belvedere section of Los Angeles and moved her fledgling mission to what the Reverend Samuel Ortegón in 1932 described as the largest, most progressive settlement of Mexicans in East Los Angeles.

A large percentage of the 20,125 East Los Angeles residents were Mexican and Mexican Americans. Ortegón counted eight churches in the area. A Presbyterian church and settlement house, two Pentecostal churches, a Spiritualist church, a Baptist church, and two Catholic churches. Belvedere's progressive status did not mean that other areas of East Los Angeles fared as well. Ortegón noted that Maravilla Park, just east of Belvedere, was the poorest section, with people "living in shacks, and eating practically nothing." He mentioned that the two Pentecostal churches, Misión Mexicana McPherson and the Iglesia Pentecostal Bethel, Olazábal's church, had fifty members: The McPherson church was a part of the International Church of the Foursquare Gospel Church in Boyle Heights. Ortegón reports that most of the members came from other Pentecostal churches. The church sat eight hundred and had five hundred members. Ortegón, a Baptist minister, comments on the appeal of Pentecostalism: "The healing services . . . appeal strongly to the Mexican mind." The mission's other appealing features were its women's society, the clothes sale, and the food giveaways, which, during the Depression, fed four hundred every week. In addition to these churches, the Latter-Day Saints rented a hall for services, and the Catholic Church, in addition to its churches, had three settlement houses in Boyle Heights, Los Angeles, and Maravilla Park. The religious choices facing the burgeoning population in East Los Angeles must have made for a competitive and lively contest for the allegiance of the recent immigrant and long-time resident alike. Pentecostals proved to be well equipped for the fight.

Luce relied heavily on Mexican workers to help run El Aposento Alto, placing Francisco and Natividad Nevarez in charge soon after its move. The Nevarezes received the Pentecostal baptism in 1916 at Luce's tent revival in Los Angeles; they had converted from Presbyterianism. They ran the church until the 1950s, when they left to develop other Pentecostal missions to Mexicans in Mexico and Mexicans in East Los Angeles and Watts. According to Victor De Leon (an Assemblies of God minister who wrote the first and one of the only histories of Latino Pentecostals), many Mexicans who received Spirit baptism in these early years came from the Presbyterian, Baptist, and Methodist churches in East Los Angeles. Though he offers little evidence for his assertion, his description matches that of the Nevarezes. Mainline denominations offered a gateway to Pentecostalism for a variety of reasons. For one, Holiness denominations like the Methodists experienced the "come-out" movement and lost many members to Pentecostal groups. For another, Protestants, such as the former Baptist Arnulfo López, had nowhere else to go once they experienced Spirit baptism. For them, the Assemblies of God served as a new home and refuge: "Bro. A.M. Lopez . . . a young Spanish brother of considerable ability . . . received the baptism of the Holy Ghost . . . here in Austin last winter, on account of which church officials rejected him." López went to work for Ball's church in Texas and was instrumental in introducing the future Latino leader Demetrio Bazán to Pentecostalism by praying for him to receive Spirit baptism. Natividad Nevarez also recalls that from 1916 to the 1930s she encountered many Latinos open to proselytism by Pentecostals. This view may be supported by the thirty-four Pentecostal missions, of various denominational persuasions, throughout southern California.

Despite the presence of other Pentecostal groups, the Assemblies of God was still the most predominant. Why? Because it had the most extensive foreign-language ministry among Latinos. Healing and spiritual gifts certainly account for some of the popularity of Pentecostalism among a people not estranged from supernatural religious expression. Pentecostalism became a faith easily communicated through a common language of salvation, often spoken in Spanish. The acceptance of an active supernatural life made the acceptance of Pentecostal spirituality all the more enticing. Simply put, Pentecostalism nullifies the doubt one might have about the existence and efficacy of God through direct personal experience. Olazábal's healing ministry, the mission to Mexicans in their own language and within their own communities, and the Pentecostal baptism offered by all missionaries meant that this faith, far from being "bizarre" to Latinos, became quite natural. No church organized, institutionalized, or laid a better foundation for posterity than the Assemblies of God and the work of Henry Ball and Alice Luce.

12. The Fire between Them

Cristina García

Felicia del Pino doesn't know what brings on her delusions. She knows only that suddenly she can hear things very vividly. The scratching of a beetle on the porch. The shifting of the floorboards in the night. She can hear everything in this world and others, every sneeze and creak and breath in the heavens or the harbor or the gardenia tree down the block. They call to her all at once, grasping here and there for parts of her, hatching blue flames in her brain. Only the Beny Moré records, played loud and warped as they are, lessen the din.

The colors, too, escape their objects. The red floats above the carnations on her windowsill. The blues rise from the chipped tiles in the kitchen. Even the greens, her favorite shades of greens, flee the trees and assault her with luminosity. Nothing is solid until she touches it. She blames the sun for this, for the false shadows it casts in her house, and she tightens the shutters against enemy rays. When she dares look outside, the people are paintings, outlined in black, their faces crushed and squarish. They threaten her with their white shining eyes. She hears them talking but cannot understand what they say. She never knows the time.

Felicia's mind floods with thoughts, thoughts from the past, from the future, other people's thoughts. Things come back as symbols, bits of conversation, a snatch of an old church hymn. Every idea seems to her connected to thousands of others by a tangle of pulsing nerves. She jumps from one to another like a nervous circus horse. It is worse when she closes her eyes.

Felicia remembers how when she was in grammar school the paraphernalia of faith had proved more intriguing than its overwrought lessons. After mass, long after the priest's words stopped echoing against the cement walls, she remained in church, inspecting the pews for forgotten veils or rosary beads. She collected prayer cards and missals engraved with gold initials and filled glass jars with holy water, which she later used to baptize Ilda Limón's chickens. Once she pried loose a crucifix with an ivory Jesus from a Station of the Cross and blessed her baby brother, Javier, with three mild raps to his forehead.

During high mass, her sister and father recited the Lord's Prayer with loud precision and clung forever to the last syllables of the hymns.

"Alleluiaaaaaaaaaaaaaaaaaaaaa!" they sang, releasing the "a" only when those around them began to stare.

Felicia knew that her mother, who stayed at home reading her books and rocking on the porch swing, had an instinctive distrust of the ecclesiastical. She suspected her mother of being an atheist and only hoped she wouldn't burn in hell for eternity as Lourdes and the nuns said.

Although Celia was not a believer, she was wary of powers she didn't understand. She locked her children in the house on December 4, the feast day of Changó, god of fire and lightning, and warned them that they'd be kidnapped and sacrificed to the black people's god if they wandered the streets alone. For good measure, she forbade Felicia to visit her best friend, Herminia, whose father everyone denounced as a witch doctor.

Lourdes took advantage of their confinement to tell Felicia how the shriveled tin peddler, who rattled by with his trolley at noon, abducted children to caves with flapping bats that nested in human hair. At night, he'd scoop out their eyes with a wooden spoon and drink their blood like milk. Lourdes insisted that the tin man had left the eyes of a dozen sacrificed children under Felicia's bed as an omen. Felicia, her eyes closed tight, cautiously patted the floor until she touched the peeled grapes her sister had left for her there, and screamed to holy hell.

As the summer of coconuts wears on, Felicia hears Saint Sebastian speaking to her inside her head. She can't stop his words, which come in rhymes sometimes or jumbled together like twisted yarn. He doesn't let her think. He reminds her how much she used to love him, how much she has disappointed him over the years.

Felicia first became fascinated with Saint Sebastian before her confirmation. She marveled over how he'd been shot through with arrows and left for dead, how he'd survived his murder only to be beaten to death by the Roman Emperor's soldiers and buried in the catacombs. Sebastian's double death appealed to Felicia. She studied his image, his hands tied above his head, his eyes rolled heavenward, arrows protruding from his chest and sides, and felt a great sympathy for him. But the nuns refused to let Felicia choose Sebastian as her confirmation name.

"Why don't you pick María like your sister?" the nuns had suggested. Their faces were pink, puffy squares cut off at the brows, their pores enlarged from the pressure of their tightly bound habits. "That way Our Blessed Virgin Mother will always look after you."

In the end, Felicia refused to be confirmed at all and Jorge del Pino blamed his daughter's later troubles on that fact.

13. God's Will: Herminia Delgado (1980)

Cristina García

I met Felicia on the beach when we were both six years old. She was filling a pail with cowries and bleeding tooth. Felicia used to collect seashells, then rearrange them on the beach before going home because her mother wouldn't allow them in their house. Felicia designed great circles of overlapping shells on the sand, as if someone on the moon, or farther still, might read their significance. I told her that at my house we had many shells, that they told the future and were the special favorites of Yemayá, goddess of the seas. Felicia listened closely, then handed me her pail.

"Will you save me?" she asked me. Her eyes were wide and curious.

"Sure," I answered. How could I realize then what my promise would entail?

Felicia's parents were afraid of my father. He was a *babalawo,* a high priest of *santería,* and greeted the sun each morning with outstretched arms. His godchildren came from many miles on his saint's day, and brought him kola nuts and black hens.

The people in Santa Teresa del Mar told evil lies about my father. They said he used to rip the heads off goats with his teeth and fillet blue-eyed babies before dawn. I got into fights at school. The other children shunned me and called me *bruja.* They made fun of my hair, oiled and plaited in neat rows, and of my skin, black as my father's. But Felicia defended me. I'll always be grateful to her for that.

Felicia was forbidden to visit my house but she did anyway. Once she saw my father use the *obi,* the divining coconut, to answer the questions of a godchild who had come to consult him. I remember the pattern of rinds fell in *ellife,* two white sides and two brown, a definite yes. The godchild left very pleased, and Felicia's fascination with coconuts began that day.

I never doubted Felicia's love. Or her loyalty. When my oldest son died in Angola, Felicia didn't leave my side for a month. She cooked me *carne asada* and read me the collected plays of Molière, which she borrowed from her mother. Felicia arranged for Joaquín's remains to be brought home for a decent burial, and then she stayed with me until I could laugh again at silly things.

Felicia could be very stubborn, too, but she had a gift that offset her stubbornness, a gift I admired very much. I guess you could say she adapted to her grief with imagination.

Felicia stayed on the fringe of life because it was free of everyday malice. It was more dignified there.

There is something else, something very important. Felicia is the only person I've known who didn't see color. There are white people who know how to act politely to blacks, but deep down you know they're uncomfortable. They're worse, more dangerous than those who speak their minds, because they don't know what they're capable of.

For many years in Cuba, nobody spoke of the problem between blacks and whites. It was considered too disagreeable to discuss. But my father spoke to me clearly so that I would understand what happened to his father and his uncles during the Little War of 1912, so that I would know how our men were hunted down day and night like animals, and finally hung by their genitals from the lampposts in Guáimaro. The war that killed my grandfather and great-uncles and thousands of other blacks is only a footnote in our history books. Why, then, should I trust anything I read? I trust only what I see, what I know with my heart, nothing more.

Things have gotten better under the revolution, that much I can say. In the old days, when voting time came, the politicians would tell us we were all the same, one happy family. Every day, though, it was another story. The whiter you were, the better off you were. Anybody could see that. There's more respect these days. I've been at the battery factory almost twenty years now, since right after the revolution, and I supervise forty-two women. It's not much, maybe, but it's better than mopping floors or taking care of another woman's children instead of my own.

One thing hasn't changed: the men are still in charge. Fixing that is going to take a lot longer than twenty years.

But let me begin again. After all, this story is about Felicia, not me.

Felicia returned to our religion with great eagerness after her disappearance in 1978. She showed up at my house one day, slim and tanned, as if she'd just returned from a vacation at a fancy foreign spa. "Take me to La Madrina," she told me, and I did. Then, during a holy trance, Felicia spoke of her days in a far-off town. She said she'd married a bearish man in an amusement park and that he'd planned to escape Cuba, to take a fishing boat north and go ice skating. I don't know if this part is true, but Felicia said that she'd pushed this man, her third husband, from the top of a roller coaster and watched him die on a bed of high-voltage wires. Felicia said his body turned to gray ash, and then the wind blew him north, just as he'd wished.

She never spoke of this again.

Within a week, Felicia had her old job back at the beauty shop. She worked hard to regain the confidence of her former customers, except, of course, for Graciela Moreira, who'd taken to wearing synthetic wigs imported from Hungary. I sent Felicia a few customers myself from the factory. Those girls *needed* manicures after assembling batteries all day long.

At night, Felicia attended our ceremonies. She didn't miss a single one. For her, they were a kind of poetry that connected her to larger worlds, worlds alive and infinite. Our rituals healed her, made her believe again. My father used to say that there are forces in the universe that can transform our lives if only we'd surrender ourselves. Felicia surrendered, and found her fulfillment.

Felicia's mother discouraged her devotion to the gods. Celia had only vague notions about spiritual possession and animal sacrifice, and suspected that our rites had caused her daughter's mysterious disappearance. Celia revered El Líder and wanted Felicia to give herself entirely to the revolution, believing that this alone would save her daughter. But Felicia would not be dissuaded from the *orishas*. She had a true vocation to the supernatural.

Before long, La Madrina initiated Felicia into the *elekes* and gave her the necklaces of the saints that would protect her from evil. They weren't easy to make. Since the revolution, it's been difficult to obtain the right beads. La Madrina told me she had to fashion Felicia's necklaces from the beaded curtains of a restaurant in Old Havana.

Many initiations followed, but I was not allowed to Felicia's last one, her *asiento*. This ritual has been done in secret since the first slaves worked the sugarcane fields on this island. But Felicia told me what she could.

Sixteen days before the *asiento*, Felicia went to live with La Madrina, who had procured seven white dresses for her, seven sets of underwear and nightclothes, seven sets of bedding, seven towels, large and small, and other special items, all white.

Felicia changed every day to stay pure.

On the morning of her initiation, sixteen *santeras* tore Felicia's clothes to shreds until she stood naked, then they bathed her in river water, rubbing her with soap wrapped in vegetable fibers until her skin glowed. The women dressed Felicia in a fresh white gown and combed and braided her hair, treating her like a newborn child.

That night, after a purifying coconut shampoo, Felicia was guided to a windowless room, where she sat for many hours, alone on a stool. La Madrina slipped the sacred necklace of Obatalá around Felicia's neck. Felicia told me she grew sleepy, and felt as though she were drifting through the heavens, that she was a planet looking at herself from one of her moons.

After many more rituals and a final bath in the *omiero*, the *santeras* led Felicia to Obatalá's throne. The diviner of shells shaved her head as everyone chanted in the language of the Yoruba. They painted circles and dots on her head and cheeks—white for Obatalá, reds and yellows and blues for the other gods—and crowned her with the sacred stones. It was then Felicia lost consciousness, falling into an emptiness without history or future.

She learned later that she'd walked purposefully around the room, possessed by Obatalá. The *santeras* had made eight cuts on her tongue with a razor blade so that the god could speak, but Felicia could not divulge his words. When Obatalá finally left her body, she opened her eyes and emerged from the void.

Once more Felicia was led to the throne. The goats to be sacrificed were marched in one by one, arrayed in silks and gold braids. Felicia smeared their eyes, ears, and foreheads with the coconut and pepper she chewed before the *babalawo* slit their throats. She tasted the goats' blood and spit it toward the ceiling, then she sampled the blood of many more creatures.

Four hours later, the *babalawo,* drenched in sweat and countless immolations, lowered his head near hers.

"*Eroko ashé,*" he whispered. It is done, with the blessings of the gods.

When I visited Felicia the following day, she was dressed in her coronation gown, her crown, and all her necklaces. She sat on a throne surrounded by gardenias, her face serene as a goddess's. I believe to this day she'd finally found her peace.

But when Felicia returned to Palmas Street with her sacred stones and her tureen, her seashells and the implements of her saint, neither her mother nor her children were there to greet her. Felicia was crestfallen, but she was certain that the gods were testing her. She wanted to prove to the *orishas* that she was a true believer, serious and worthy of serving them, so she continued her rituals.

Felicia did everything she was supposed to as a novice *santera*. She dressed only in white, and didn't wear makeup or cut her hair. She never touched the forbidden foods—coconuts, corn, or anything red—and covered the one mirror in her house with a sheet, as she was prohibited from seeing her own image.

When I came to visit her, we settled on the warping floorboards, where Felicia ate her meals with a serving spoon. As she spoke, Felicia rolled the spoon between her palms and watched its clumsy, twirling shadow on the wall.

"Have you spoken with them?" she asked me, referring to her mother, her daughters, her son.

"Your mother says they're frightened, like the summer of coconuts."

"But this is completely different. I have a clarity now. You can see the sun enters here." Felicia indicated the dusty shafts of light. "Did you tell her that even El Líder is initiated? That he's the son of Elleguá?"

I shook my head, saying nothing. Felicia covered her face with her hands. A rash erupted on her neck and cheeks. I noticed the imprint her fingers made on her forehead, the delicate chain of bloodless flesh.

Then Felicia spoke of our faith, of her final healing, and held my hands in hers.

"You've been more than a sister to me, Herminia. You saved me, like you promised on the beach."

That night, I dreamt of Felicia in her bathing suit with her pail of cowries and bleeding tooth.

"Will you save me?" she asked me.

"Sure," I answered, again and again.

I've seen other *santeras* during their first year. They are radiant. Their eyes are moist and clear, their skin is smoothed of wrinkles, and their nails grow strong. When you make a saint, the saint takes good care of you. But Felicia showed none of these blessings. Her eyes dried out like an old woman's and her fingers curled like claws until she could hardly pick up her spoon. Even her hair, which had been as black as a crow's, grew colorless in scruffy patches on her skull. Whenever she spoke, her lips blurred to a dull line in her face.

Over the next weeks, all of us from the *casa de santo* took turns visiting Felicia. We wrapped her wrists with beaded bracelets, gave her castor-oil enemas, packed hot cactus compresses on her brow. We boiled *yerba buena* teas and left yams and swatches of cotton on Obatalá's altar. But nothing seemed to help. Felicia's eyesight dimmed until she could perceive only shadows, and the right side of her head swelled with mushroomy lumps.

La Madrina was beside herself with worry. She performed sacrifices every day in Felicia's behalf. Some of us traveled with our offerings to the mountains, where Obatalá is said to live, and placed white flags around the house on Palmas Street to attract peace.

But each time La Madrina threw the shells, the omen was the same. *Ikú*. Death.

A group of *babalawos* tried a *panaldo,* an exorcism, and thought they had trapped an evil spirit in the rooster they buried in a knotted cloth. But Felicia continued to grow worse. The *babalawos* consulted the oracles with all their powers of divination. The *opelé.* The table of Ifá. Even the *ikin,* the sacred palm nuts. Still, the omen did not change.

"It is the will of the gods," they concluded. "It will be resolved by the spirits of the dead."

Just as the *babalawos* were about to leave, Felicia's mother entered the house on Palmas Street. She was wild-eyed, like a woman who gives birth to an unwanted child.

"Witch doctors! Murderers! Get out, all of you!" she cried, and swept the image of Obatalá off its altar.

We pulled back, afraid of the god's response.

Celia overturned the tureen with the sacred stones and crushed Felicia's seashells under the heels of her leather pumps. Suddenly, she removed her shoes and began stamping on the shells in her bare feet, slowly at first, then faster and faster in a mad flamenco, her arms thrown up in the air.

Then just as suddenly she stopped. She made no sound as she wept, as she bent to kiss Felicia's eyes, her forehead, her swollen, hairless skull. Celia lay with her torn, bleeding feet beside her daughter and held her, rocking and rocking her in the blue gypsy dusk until she died.

14. Pilar (1980)

CRISTINA GARCÍA

I'm browsing in the remainders bins outside a record shop on Amsterdam Avenue when two men call to me halfheartedly from across the street, more out of habit than desire. I sift through old 78 polkas with beribboned women smiling at me from the album covers. There's something grotesque about their grins, fixed for thirty years. Maybe I'd do them a favor by buying their records and breaking them in two. Maybe it'd release them from some terrible Romanian spell.

I find a Herb Alpert record, the one with the woman in whipped cream on the cover. It looks so tame to me now. I read somewhere that the woman who posed for it was three months pregnant at the time and that it was shaving cream, not whipped cream, she was suggestively dipping into her mouth.

In the last bin, I find an old Beny Moré album. Two of the cuts are scratched but I buy it anyway for fifty cents. The cashier's features are compressed beneath a bulbous forehead. When I thank him in Spanish, he's surprised and wants to chat. We talk about Celia Cruz and how she hasn't changed a hair or a vocal note in forty years. She's been fiftyish, it seems, since the Spanish-American War.

Then we get to talking about Lou Reed. It's funny how his fans can sniff each other out. We agree that his sexually ambiguous days—when he wore white face and black nail polish—were his best. It's hard to believe that Lou came out of a suburban home on Long Island and went to college in upstate New York. He should have been a lawyer or an accountant or somebody's father by now. I wonder if his mother thinks he's dangerous.

The cashier, Franco, puts on the *Take No Prisoners* album. I was at the Bottom Line the night they recorded it. How many lifetimes ago was that? I think about all that great early punk and the raucous paintings I used to do.

Shit, I'm only twenty-one years old. How can I be nostalgic for my youth?

Midterms are in a week and I can't seem to concentrate on anything. The only thing that helps is my bass. I've taught myself to play the thing these last two years and I'm not half bad. There's a group at Columbia that meets Sunday afternoons to jam on this punky fake jazz everyone's into. When things are cooking, me and my bass just move the whole damn floor.

Still, I feel something's dried up inside me, something a strong wind could blow out of me for good. That scares me. I guess I'm not so sure what I should be fighting for anymore. Without confines, I'm damn near reasonable. That's something I never wanted to become.

Franco and I commiserate about how St. Mark's Place is a zoo these days with the bridge-and-tunnel crowd wearing fuchsia mohawks and safety pins through their cheeks. Everybody wants to be part of the freak show for a day. Anything halfway interesting gets co-opted, mainstreamed. We'll all be doing car commercials soon.

It used to be you could see the Ramones in the East Village for five bucks. Nowadays you have to pay $12.50 to see them with five thousand bellowing skinheads who don't even let you hear the music. Count me out.

I enter a *botánica* on upper Park Avenue. I've passed the place before but I've never gone inside. Today, it seems, there's nowhere else for me to go. Dried snakeskins and *ouanga* bags hang from the walls. Painted wooden saints with severe mouths stand alongside plastic plug-in Virgins with sixty-watt bulbs. Iridescent oils are displayed with amulets, talismans, incense. There are sweet-smelling soaps and bottled bathwater, love perfumes and potions promising money and luck. Apothecary jars labeled in childish block letters are filled with pungent spices.

I'm not religious but I get the feeling that it's the simplest rituals, the ones that are integrated with the earth and its seasons, that are the most profound. It makes more sense to me than the more abstract forms of worship.

The owner of the shop is an elderly man who wears a white tunic and cotton fez. For a young woman with cropped hair, he prescribes a statuette of La Virgen de la Caridad del Cobre, a yellow candle, and five special oils: *amor* (love), *sígueme* (follow me), *yo puedo y tú no* (I can and you can't), *ven conmigo* (come with me), and *dominante* (dominant).

"Carve his name on the candle five times and anoint it with these oils," he instructs. "Do you have a picture of your intended?"

The woman nods.

"*Bueno*, put it on a dessert plate and coat it with honey. Then arrange five fishhooks on the picture and light the candle. Rest assured, he will be yours in two Sundays."

I envy this woman's passion, her determination to get what she knows is hers. I felt that way once, when I ran away to Miami. But I never made it to Cuba to see Abuela Celia. After that, I felt like my destiny was not my own, that men who had nothing to do with me had the power to rupture my dreams, to separate me from my grandmother.

I examine the beaded necklaces near the register. Most have five strands and come in two colors. I select a red-and-white one and place it over my head. I lift an ebony staff carved with the head of a woman balancing a double-edged ax.

"Ah, a daughter of Changó," the elderly man says and places a hand on my shoulder.

I say nothing but I notice that his eyes are the same almond color as his skin, that they're centuries older than his face.

"You must finish what you began," he says.

I rub the beads in my left hand and feel a warm current drifting up my arm, across my shoulders, down between my breasts.

"When?" I ask him.

"The moon after next."

I watch as he moves through the store. His back is long and straight, as if his ancestors were royal palms. He gathers herbs from various jars, then reaches for a white votive candle and a bottle of holy water.

"Begin with a bitter bath," he says, lining up the ingredients on the counter. "Bathe with these herbs for nine consecutive nights. Add the holy water and a drop of ammonia, then light the candle. On the last day, you will know what to do."

I reach in my jeans to pay him but he holds up his palm.

"This is a gift from our father Changó."

I can't wait to get back to my room and fill up the bathtub so I take a shortcut through Morningside Park. I feel shielded by the herbs, by the man with the straight spine and starched cotton fez. An elm tree seems to shade the world with its aerial roots. It begins to rain and I pick up my pace. The herbs shift rhythmically in my sack like the seeds of a maraca.

I remember the nannies in Cuba with their leaves and rattling beads. They prayed over me, sprinkled cinnamon in my bath, massaged my stomach with olive oil. They covered me with squares of flannel in the dead heat of summer.

The nannies told my mother that I stole their shadows, that I made their hair fall out and drove their husbands to other women. But my mother didn't believe them. She fired the nannies without an extra day's pay.

One night there was a furious thunderstorm. Lightning hit the royal palm outside my window. From my crib, I heard it snap and fall. The fronds whined in the wind. The aviary shattered. The toucans and cockatoos circled in confusion before flying north.

My new nanny wasn't afraid. She told me that it was only the temperamental Changó, god of fire and lightning. Changó, she said, once asked a young lizard to take a gift to the lover of a rival god. The lizard put the present in its mouth and scurried to the lady's house but it tripped and fell, swallowing the precious trinket.

When Changó found out, he tracked down his inept accomplice to the foot of a palm tree. The terrified reptile, unable to speak, ran up the tree and hid among the fronds, the gift still lodged in its throat. Changó, who believed the lizard was mocking him, aimed a lightning bolt at the tree, intending to scorch the sorry creature dead.

Since then, Lucila explained, Changó often takes out his rage on innocent palm trees, and to this day the lizard's throat is swollen and mute with the god's gift.

Three boys surround me suddenly in the park, locking me between their bodies. Their eyes are like fireflies, hot and erased of memory. The rain beads in their hair. They can't be more than eleven years old.

The tallest one presses a blade to my throat. Its edge is a scar, another border to cross.

A boy with a high, square forehead grabs the sack with the dried herbs and throws my Beny Moré album like a Frisbee against the elm. It doesn't break and I'm reassured. I imagine picking up the record, feeling each groove with my fingertips.

The boys push me under the elm, where it's somehow still dry. They pull off my sweater and carefully unbutton my blouse. With the knife still at my throat, they take turns suckling my breasts. They're children, I tell myself, trying to contain my fear. Incredibly, I hear the five-note pounding of Lou Reed's "Street Hassle," that crazy cello with its low, dying voice.

I watch as the last boy pinches some of the herb and arranges it on a rectangle of paper in his palm. He shapes it into a narrow cylinder then rolls the paper, licking the edge with the delicacy of a preening cat.

"Who's got a match?" he demands and the boy with the square forehead offers him a flame from a red plastic lighter. The boy takes a deep breath and holds it in his lungs. Then he passes it to the others.

I press my back against the base of the elm and close my eyes. I can feel the pulsing of its great taproot, the howling cello in its trunk. I know the sun sears its branches to hot wires. I don't know how long I sit against the elm, but when I open my eyes, the boys are gone. I button my blouse, gather up my herbs and my album, and run back to the university.

In the library, nothing makes sense. The fluorescent lights transmit conversations from passing cars on Broadway. Someone's ordering a bucket of chicken wings on 103rd Street. The chairman of the linguistics department is fucking a graduate student named Betsy. Gandhi was a carnivore. He came of age in Samoa. He traversed a subcontinent in blue suede shoes. Maybe this is the truth.

I buy apples and bananas in the cafeteria and eat them furtively in my room. I'd prefer a cave, a desert, a more complete solitude.

I light my candle. The bath turns a clear green from the herbs. It has the sharp scent of an open field in spring. When I pour it on my hair, I feel a sticky cold like dry ice, then a soporific heat. I'm walking naked as a beam of light along brick paths and squares of grass, phosphorescent and clean.

At midnight, I awake and paint a large canvas ignited with reds and whites, each color betraying the other. I do this for eight more nights.

On the ninth day of my baths, I call my mother and tell her we're going to Cuba.

15. Talking to the Dead

Judith Ortiz Cofer

My grandfather is a *Mesa Blanca* spiritist. This means that he is able to communicate with the spirit world. And since almost everyone has a request or complaint to make from the *Other Side*, Papá once was a much sought-after man in our pueblo. His humble demeanor and gentle ways did much to enhance his popularity with the refined matrons who much preferred to consult him than the rowdy *santeros* who, according to Papá, made a living through spectacle and the devil's arts. *Santería*, like voodoo, has its roots in African blood rites, which its devotees practice with great fervor. *Espiritismo*, on the other hand, entered the island via the middle classes who had discovered it flourishing in Europe during the so-called "crisis of faith" of the late nineteenth century. Poets like Yeats belonged to societies whose members sought answers in the invisible world. Papá, a poet and musician himself when he was not building houses, had the gift of clairvoyance, or *facultades*, as they are called in spiritism. It is not a free gift, however: being a spiritist medium requires living through *pruebas*, or tests of one's abilities.

Papá's most difficult *prueba* must have been living in the same house with Mamá, a practical woman who believed only in what her senses recorded. If Papá's eyes were closed that meant that her lazy man was sleeping in the middle of the day again. His visionary states and his poetry writing were, I have heard, the primary reasons why Mamá had, early in their married life, decided that her husband should "wear the pants" in the family only in the literal sense of the expression. She considered him a "hopeless case," a label she attached to any family member whose drive and energy did not match her own. She never changed her mind about his poetry writing, which she believed was Papá's perdition, the thing that kept him from making a fortune, but she learned to respect his *facultades* after the one incident that she could not easily dismiss or explain.

Although Papá had been building a reputation for many years as an effective medium, his gifts had not changed his position in Mamá's household. He had, at a time determined by his wife, been banished to the back of the house to pursue his interests, and as for family politics, his position was one of quiet assent with his wife's wise decisions. He could have rebelled against this situation: in Puerto Rican society, the man is considered a small-letter god in his home. But, Papá, a gentle, scholarly man, preferred a laissez-faire approach. Mamá's ire could easily be avoided by keeping his books and his spiritist practice out of her sight. And he did make a decent living designing and building houses.

In his room at the back of the house he dreamt his dreams and interpreted them. There he also received the spiritually needy: the recent widows, the women who had lost children, and the old ones who had started making plans for the afterlife. The voices were kept low during these consultations. I know from having sat in the hallway outside his door as a child, listening as hard as I could for what I thought should be taking place—howlings of the possessed, furniture being thrown around by angry ghosts—ideas I had picked up from such movies as *Abbot and Costello Meet the Mummy,* and from misinterpreting the conversations of adults. But, Papá's seances were more like counseling sessions. Sometimes there were the sounds of a grown person sobbing—a frightening thing to a child—and then Papá's gentle, persuasive voice. Although most times I could not decipher the words, I recognized the tone of sympathy and support he was offering them. Two or more voices would at times join together in a chant. And the pungent odor of incense seeping through his closed door made my imagination quicken with visions of apparitions dancing above his table, waiting to speak through him to their loved ones. In a sort of trance myself, I would sometimes begin softly reciting an *Our Father,* responding automatically to the familiar experience of voices joined together in prayer and the church-smell of incense. What Papá performed in his room was a ceremony of healing. Whether he ever communicated with the dead I cannot say, but the spiritually wounded came to him and he tended to them and reassured them that death was not a permanent loss. He believed with all the passion of his poet's heart, and was able to convince others, that what awaits us all after the long day of our lives was a family reunion in God's extensive plantation. I believe he saw heaven as an island much like Puerto Rico, except without the inequities of backbreaking labor, loss and suffering which he could only justify to his followers as their prueba on this side of paradise.

Papá's greatest prueba came when his middle son, Hernán, disappeared. At the age of eighteen, Hernán had accepted a "free" ticket to the U.S. from a man recruiting laborers. It was a difficult time for the family, and reluctantly, Mamá had given Hernán permission to go. Papá, on the other hand, had uncharacteristically spoken out against the venture. He had had dreams, nightmares, in which he saw Hernán in prison, being tortured by hooded figures. Mamá dismissed his fears as fantasy-making, blaming Papá's premonitions on too much reading as usual. Hernán had been a wild teenager, and Mamá felt that it was time he became a working man. And so Hernán left the island, promising to write to his parents immediately, and was not heard from again for months.

Mamá went wild with worry. She imposed on friends and relatives, anyone who had a contact in the U.S., to join in the search for her son. She consulted with the police and with lawyers, and she even wrote to the governor, whose secretary wrote back that the recruiting of Puerto Rican laborers by mainland growers was being investigated by the authorities for the possibility of illegal practices. Mamá began to have nightmares herself in which she saw her son mistreated and worse. Papá stayed up with her during many of her desperate vigils. He said little, but kept his hands on his Bible, and would often seem to be speaking to himself in a trance. For once, Mamá did not ridicule him. She may have been too wrapped up in her despair. Then one night, Papá abruptly rose from his chair and rushed to his room where, with his carpenter's pencil, he began drawing something on the white cloth of his special table. Mamá followed him, thinking that her husband had gone mad with suffering for their child. But seeing the concentration on his face—it seemed to be lit with a light from within, she later told someone—she stood behind him for what seemed a long time. When he finished, he held a candle over the table and began explaining the picture as if to himself. "He is in a place far north. A place without a name. It is a place that can be found only by one who has been there. Here, there are growing things. Fruit, maybe. Sweet fruit. Not ready to be picked yet. There are lights in the distance. And a tall fence. Hernán sleeps here among the lights. He is dreaming of me tonight. He is lonely and afraid, but not sick or hurt."

Mamá began to see the things Papá described in the rough pencil lines on that tablecloth. Her mind turned into a map of memories, scraps of information, lines from letters she had received over the years, Christmas cards from strange places sent by a dozen nephews, or the sons of neighbors—young men for whom she had been a second mother—until she remembered this: a few years before Hernán's departure, Alicia's (Mamá's older sister) son, had also been "recruited" as a laborer. Like Hernán, he had not been informed as to exactly where he was going, only that it was in another Nueva York, not the city. Unlike her own son, her nephew had written home to say that he had been picking strawberries and did not like the job. Soon after, he had moved to a city near the farm where he had worked for a season. There he had married and settled down. Alicia would know the name of the place. But Papá had said it was a place without a name. Mamá decided to follow up on the only premonition she had ever allowed into her practical mind.

At that early hour, not quite dawn, the two of them set out for the country, where Alicia lived; Papá was armed with his Bible and the symbol of his calling: a mahogany stick he had carved into a wand. Every spiritist must make one and take it with him on house calls. It is hollow and sometimes filled with Holy Water in order to keep "evil influences" at a distance, but Papá had put a handful of dirt from his birthplace in his, perhaps because his calling as a medium was more than anything a poet's choice of missions: a need to accept mortality while struggling for permanence. Anyway, that earthfilled stick was the only weapon I ever knew Papá to carry. That morning he and his wife walked together in silence, a rare occurrence: to Mamá, long silences were a vacuum her nature abhorred. They came home with hope in the form of a telephone number that day.

After sending for the high school English teacher to interpret, they called the city of Buffalo, New York. Mamá's nephew told them that he would start looking for Hernán at the farm right away. He said, everyone just called it "the farm."

It turned out that Hernán was at the farm. The situation was very bad. The workers had been brought there by an unscrupulous farm worker who kept the men (most of them very young and unable to speak English) ignorant as to their exact whereabouts. They lived in tents while they waited for the fruit to be ready for picking. Though they were given provisions, the cost was deducted from their paychecks, so by the time they were paid, their salary was already owed to the grower. The workers were told that mail was not picked up there and it would have to be taken to the nearest city after the harvest. Though Hernán and many of the other men protested their situation and threatened to strike, they knew that they were virtual prisoners and would have to wait for an opportunity to escape.

Mamá's nephew had connections in Buffalo and was able to convince a social worker to accompany him to the farm where he found Hernán eager to lead the exodus. It was not as easy as that, though. Many days passed before an investigation was started which revealed the scheme behind the farm and many others like it based on the recruitment of young men under false pretenses. But Hernán had been found. And Mamá learned to respect, if not quite ever to publicly acknowledge, her husband's gift of clairvoyance.

She paid her tribute to him in her own way by embroidering a new cloth for his *mesa blanca* in a pattern based on his drawings of that night. She did it with white thread on white cloth, so that to see it one had to get very close to the design.

16. *Mestizaje* as a Locus of Theological Reflection (1983)

VIRGILIO ELIZONDO

The Hispanic Catholics of the United States have experienced a long history of neglect and oppression not only by society at large, but by the very church that is supposed to be our mother. We had somewhat been ministered to but we had never been invited to be active ministers in our own church. The church was so foreign to us that many felt that priests came only from Ireland or Spain, but it was unthinkable that we would become a priest or a religious.

Quite often we were scolded because we were not sure what the foreign missioners expected us to be as measured by the standards of the Catholicism in their place of origin. But hardly ever were we confirmed in our faith and helped to grow and develop in our pilgrimage of faith. Yet it was the deep faith and simple home practices of our *abuelitas* and *abuelitos* (grandparents) that sustained us in the faith and maintained us loyal to the Catholic tradition.

Church institutions had been so oppressive to us that when the Chicano movement started in the 1960s, the leaders often told priests and religious who tried to join them to get lost. They felt that the only way to help Hispanics get ahead was to get rid of Catholicism. It was painful to hear their insults, but as painful as their accusations were, we had to admit that they were true—if not totally, at least 95 percent of what they were saying against the church was correct. The church had kept us out and had by its silence approved the ongoing exploitation and oppression of Hispanics.

The Chicano movement gave inspiration to the Chicano clergy and later on to all the Hispanic clergy in this country. We began to organize and to work for change within our own church. It was quickly evident that it was not sufficient simply to use Spanish in the liturgy, create our own music, and get more people involved in the work of the church. Much more was needed. We needed both practical know-how so that we could make the structures of our society work in favor of our people and we needed to have a new knowledge about ourselves, our social situation, and our religious beliefs. Until now, others had been telling us who we were. Nobody had bothered to ask us "Who are you?" Until now, all kinds of experts had studied us, but no one had even sought to enter into conversation with us so that they

---

"Mestizaje as a Locus of Theological Reflection" by Virgilio Elizondo in *Beyond Borders: Writings of Virgilio Elizondo and Friends,* Timothy Matovina, ed.

might truly understand who we see ourselves to be. This was the very root of our oppression. We were not allowed to be who we were. We were never allowed to simply say: "I am."

It was at this moment of the struggle that we met Gustavo Gutiérrez and became aware of his method of doing theology. It was God-sent! He was conceptualizing and expressing perfectly what we felt had to be done but had no idea of how to do it or even that we were on the right track. From the documents of Vatican II and our own experience of exclusion, we pretty well sensed what had to be done, but it was not yet clear. Reading Gustavo's work was like turning on the light switch.

The first thing we learned from Gustavo was that theology is important and we cannot leave it to the theologians alone—and much less to theologians who are foreigners. Theology cannot be imported. Neither can it be developed in isolation from the believing and practicing community. It is a joint enterprise of the believing community, which is seeking the meaning of its faith and the direction of its journey of hope lived in the context of charity. Great theologies were coming out of other parts of the world, but no one could do our theologizing for us. We had both the privilege and the responsibility! What follows is an attempt to do our own interpretation of our Christian existence.

The Human Situation of Mexican Americans

The ancestors of today's Mexican Americans have been living in the presentday United States since the early 1600s. Our group did not cross the border to come to the United States; rather the United States expanded its borders and we found ourselves to be a part of the United States. Since the early beginnings, many generations have crossed the Rio Grande to come over to the other side of family lands. Yet we have always been treated as foreigners in our own countryside—exiles who never felt at home. The Mexican Americans are a people twice conquered, twice colonized, and twice mestisized. This is our socio-historical reality!

Mestizaje: *Undefined Identity and Consequent Margination*

Mestizaje is simply the mixture of human groups of different makeup determining the color and shape of the eyes, skin pigmentation, and makeup of the bone structure. It is the most common phenomenon in the evolution of the human species. Scientists state that there are few, if any, truly "pure" human groups left in the world and they are the weakest, because their genetic pool has been gradually drained. Through mixture, new human groups emerge and the genetic makeup is strengthened. Biologically speaking, *mestizaje* appears to be quite easy and natural, but culturally it is usually feared and threatening. It is so feared that laws and taboos try to prevent it from taking place, for it appears as the ultimate threat to the survival of the species itself.

Mestizaje could certainly come in various ways, but it is a fact of history that massive *mestizaje* giving rise to a new people usually takes place through conquest and colonization. This has certainly been the case of the Mexican and the Mexican American *mestizaje*.

The first one came through the Spanish conquest of Mexico beginning in 1519, and the second one started with the Anglo-American invasion of the Mexican northwest beginning in the 1830s. The French biologist Ruffie states that, since the birth of Europe thirty-five thousand years ago when the invading Cro-Magnons mated with the native Neanderthals, no other event of similar magnitude had taken place until the birth of European Mexico some five hundred years ago. I would add that a similar event of equal magnitude is presently taking place in the southwest of the United States—an area larger than Western Europe and populated by several million persons.

Conquest comes through military force and is motivated by economic reasons. Yet, once it has taken place, conquest is totalitarian. It imposes not only the institutions of the powerful, but also a new worldview in conflict with the existing one. This imposition disrupts the worldview of the conquered in such a way that nothing makes sense anymore. In many ways, the ideas, the logic, the wisdom, the art, the customs, the language, and even the religion of the powerful are forced into the life of the conquered. Although the conquered try to resist, the ways and worldview of the powerful begin to penetrate their minds so that, even if political and economic independence come about, the native culture can never simply return to its pre-conquest ways.

Yet there is not only the obvious violence of the physical conquest, but the deeper violence of the disruption and attempts to destroy the conquered's inner worldview, which gives cohesion and meaning to existence. The conquered's fundamental core religious symbols provide the ultimate root of the group's identity because they mediate the absolute. They are the final tangible expressions of the absolute. There is nothing beyond them that can put us in contact with God. They are the ultimate justification of the worldview of the group and the force that cements all the elements of the life of the group into a cohesive, meaningful, and tangible world order. When such symbols are discredited or destroyed, nothing makes sense anymore. The worldview moves from order to chaos, from significant mystery to meaningless confusion.

Hence, the ushering in of new religious symbols, especially when they are symbols of the dominant group, are in effect the ultimate conquest. In a nonviolent way, missioners were the agents of a deeper violence. They attempted to destroy that which even the physical violence of the conquerors could not touch—the soul of the native people. In spite of the missionary's conscious opposition to the cruel and bloody ways of the conquistador, the nonviolent introduction of religious symbols of the Spanish immigrant in effect affirmed and justified the way of the powerful, and discredited and tried to destroy the way of the powerless. This same process has taken place with the predominantly Irish-German clergy and religious who have ministered to Mexican American Catholics.

The most devastating thing about the conquest is that it established a relationship so concrete and so permanent that it took on the nature of a metaphysical reality. In many ways, it determines the behavior and the characteristics of the members of each group. It even influences theological reflection as the members of the conquistador group will appeal to scripture and theology to explain and legitimate the relationship. In his classic book *The Righteous Empire*, Martin Marty gives an excellent exposition of how theology and biblical studies can be used to legitimize oppression. The powerful now establish their own version of truth as objective truth for everyone and impose it through their various means of power.

The image of the conquistador as "superior" and of the conquered as "inferior" will be imposed and interiorized by all the media of communications: dress, food, manners, language, modes of thinking, art, music, bodily gestures, mannerisms, entertainment, and all the institutions of society, such as the family, economics, school system, politics, and church, and most of all the religious imagery and mythology. It is now the gods of the powerful who preside over the new world order. The totalitarian image that colonizing Europe established and implanted in the colonized peoples as the universal model for everyone continues to have a determining influence around the world. This "normative image" of Western civilization continues to be reinforced and projected through television and movies, books, periodicals, universities, and the European/United States-controlled religions. Only the white Western way appears as the truly human way of life; all others continue to be relegated to an inferior status. This is not necessarily a conscious effort, but it takes place all the time.

Yet, in spite of the difficult situation of inequality, the very seeds for the destruction of this dichotomy of colonizer-superior vs. colonized-inferior are physically implanted by the conquistador himself. Through his very bodily intercourse with the women of the conquered group, a new biological-cultural race is born, a race that will be both conquistador and conquered, superior and inferior, at one and the same time: he or she will be a real blood sister/brother of both, without being exclusively either. Furthermore, because the mother is the fundamental transmitter of deep cultural traits, it is the culture of the conquered that will gradually triumph over the culture of the conquistador in providing the dominant and deepest personality characteristics of the new group.

Mestizos are born out of two histories and in them begins a new history. The symbolic and mental structures of both histories begin to intermingle so that out of the new story which begins in the *mestizo* new meanings, myths, and symbols will equally emerge. They will be meaningful to the *mestizo* as the firstborn of a new creation, but will remain incomprehensible to persons who try to understand them through the meanings, mythologies, and symbols of either of the previous histories alone. Yet from birth to maturity, there is a long period of painful search.

The deepest suffering of the *mestizo* comes from what we might call an "unfinished" identity or, better yet, an undefined one. One of the core needs of human beings is the existential knowledge that regardless of who I am socially or morally, I am. The knowledge of fundamental belonging—that is, to be French, American, Mexican, English—is in the present world order one of the deepest needs of persons. When this need is met, it is not even thought about as a need; but when it is missing, it is so confusing and painful that we find it difficult to even conceptualize it or speak about it. We strive "to be like" but we are not sure just which one we should be like. As Mexican Americans, we strive to find our belonging in Mexico or in the United States—only to discover that we are considered foreign by both. Our Spanish is too Anglicized for the Mexicans and our English is too Mexicanized for the Anglos.

In the case of Mexico, it was the *mestizo* image of Our Lady of Guadalupe that provided the beginning of the new socio-cultural synthesis. It was not merely an apparition, but the perfect synthesis of the religious iconography of the Iberian peoples with that of native Mexicans into one coherent image. This marks the cultural birth of a new people. Both the parents and the child now have one common symbol of ultimate belonging. For the first time, they can begin to say "we are." As the physical birth of Mexicans had come through conquest, cultural birth came through the new image. It is only after the apparition that those who had wanted to die now wanted to live and to celebrate life. In and through Our Lady, new meanings, myths, and symbols will begin to emerge that will be truly representative and characteristic of Mexico.

Struggles for Accepting and Belonging

In the first stages of the struggle to belong, the *mestizo* will try desperately to become like the dominant group, for only its members appear to be fully civilized and human. This struggle includes every aspect of life, because the whole world structure of the dominant will have been assimilated and made normative for human existence. It equally involves a violent rejection of the way of the conquered, because that now appears to be inferior. Only the scholars of the dominant group will appear as credible, only their universities as prestigious, their language as civilized, their medical practices as scientific, and their religion as true religion. The dominated will sometimes attempt to keep some of their original folklore, but, in every other way, they try to become like the dominant.

Some of the well-intentioned and kind members of the dominant group will help the brighter and more promising ones (according to their own standard of judgment) to better themselves by "becoming like us." They will privilege them with scholarships to the best universities in Europe or the United States and help them to learn the European or American way of life and language.

Some of the marginated will make it into the world of the dominant society, only to discover that they will never be allowed to belong fully, and furthermore that down deep inside they are still somewhat "other." Yet it is this very pain of not being able to belong fully that also marks the beginning of a new search.

In the first stages of the search, the ones who choose not to join the struggle to become like the dominant ones will tend to reject the world of the dominant in a total way: absolutely nothing good can come of it. They will not only reject it but will hate it passionately. The only way to treat the dominant ones is to get rid of them. They are the ones who are guilty not only of the individual sin of homicide, but of the collective sin of ethnocide.

Throughout all these struggles, there is something radically new beginning to emerge. Even though the seeds are planted from the very beginning and biologically this new life begins from the very start, it will take time for cultural identity to emerge as a distinct identity of its own. This new identity does not try to become like someone else, but it struggles to form its own unique individuality. It accepts from both parent cultures without seeking to be a replica of either. It is like the maturing child who no longer tries to be like the mother or like the father, nor to simply reject both of them, but is simply himself or herself. Through the pains and frustrations of trying to be what we are not, the uniqueness of our own proper identity begins to emerge. It is an exciting moment of the process and usually the most creative state in the life of the group.

It is at this moment that the quest to know ourselves begins to emerge in a serious way. In the beginning, knowledge of ourselves will be confused because we see ourselves through a type of double image—that is, through the eyes of the two parent groups. As the group develops, its own proper image will begin to emerge and it will be easier to study ourselves more critically. It is this new and more clearly defined self-image of who we are as Mexican Americans that is presently beginning to take shape. As usual, it is the poets, the artists, and the musicians who are beginning to point and to sing and to suggest the new identity. It is now the critical thinkers who are coming in and beginning to deepen, conceptualize, verbalize, and communicate the reality of our identity. And it is only now that for the first time we begin to ask ourselves about our Christian identity, about our church, and about our religion. What does it really mean? Who are we as Mexican American Christians?

The Human Situation: Divisions and Collective Self-Protection

When one looks at the history of humanity, wars, divisions, and family fights appear more natural than do peace, unity, and harmony. This is evident from the global level down to the family cell. It appears more natural for brothers and sisters to fight one another than to love one another. We struggle to protect ourselves against each other and to conquer others before they conquer us. We prepare for peace by preparing for war. Only violent means appear to help us control or curb violence. Might makes right because power establishes its views as objective truth so as to justify its own position of privilege. The survival of the fittest appears to be the first law of individuals and of society—the survival of the powerful at the cost of the weak.

From this struggle for survival at the cost of others, certain anthropologico-sociological characteristics and behavioral laws appear. The members of the dominant group in power see themselves as pure, superior, dignified, well-developed, beautiful, and civilized. They see themselves as the model for all others. They see their natural greatness as the source of their great achievements. Even the least among them consider themselves superior to the best of the dominated group.

On the other hand, they look upon the conquered and colonized as impure, inferior, undignified, underdeveloped, ugly, uncivilized, conservative, backward. Their ways are considered childish and their wisdom is looked upon as superstition. Because might is subconsciously assumed to be right, everything about the weak is considered to be wrong and unworthy of being considered human. The conquered are told that they must forget their backward ways if they are to advance and become human. Acculturation to the ways of the dominant, in every respect whatsoever, is equated with human development and liberation.

Even the best among the dominant group find it very difficult to truly accept the other as other: to enjoy their foods, learn from their wisdom, speak their language, dress in their styles, appreciate their art and their music, interpret life through their philosophies, live in their ways, even worship through their forms of cult. Even though many go out, even heroically, to be of service to the poor and the oppressed, and really love them, there is still an inner fear and rejection of their otherness. The way of the powerful as the normative human way for all persons is so deeply ingrained that it takes a dying to oneself to break through the cultural enslavements that keep the dominant from appreciating the inner beauty, the values, the worth, and the dignity of the ways of the conquered.

Because of the image imposed upon them about themselves, some of the conquered will begin to think of themselves as inferior and good for nothing. This develops a type of domesticated, happy-go-lucky, subservient attitude in relation to the dominant. It is a very dehumanizing existence, but the powerless have no choice—either conform to the status assigned by the powerful or be eliminated physically. Law and order work in favor of the rich against the poor. Whereas the rich tend to be considered innocent until proven guilty, the poor are usually considered guilty until proven innocent. They are blamed for all the problems of society and are considered to be the source of all evil and crime. Thus, the very victims of the institutionalized violence of power are labeled by the establishment as the causes of this violence! The powerful can define the image and status of the oppressed as "guilty of all evil" and force them to live accordingly. The poor and the oppressed thus serve as scapegoats for the crimes of the establishment, which can continue to think of itself as pure and immaculate. However, as long as the traditions of the oppressed continue, especially their deepest religious traditions, they may be forced to live as dirt, but they cannot be forced to perceive themselves as such. Through their traditions, perfectly understood by them but incomprehensible to foreigners, they continue to perceive themselves as they truly are: free human beings with full human dignity who, although dominated through external powers, nevertheless remain free and independent in the innermost core of their being.

The in-group will defend tradition, law, and order because its members are the privileged ones of the establishment. National and personal security will be among the top priorities of this group as it strives to maintain the status quo. For the powerful, tradition protects their position of privilege; for the powerless, their own traditions are the ultimate rejection of the status quo of the dominant—their bodies might be dominated but not their souls.

Tradition functions in a diametrically opposed way for the powerful and for the powerless. For the powerless, tradition is the affirmation of inner freedom, independence, and self-worth. It is the power for the radical transformation of the existing order. For the moment, it might appear as a tranquilizer, but we should not underestimate its power in keeping a people alive as a people. As long as their traditions are alive, they are assured of life and ultimate liberation. If their traditions disappear, they will no longer have to work for integral liberation because they will have ceased to exist as a people.

In attempting to analyze the dynamics between the oppressor in-group and the oppressed out-group, three constants seem to function as anthropological laws of human behavior.

First, when one studies the human story across the ages, the tendency of group inclusion/exclusion—that is, to protect our own by keeping others out—appears to be one of the most consistent and fundamental anthropological laws of nature. Dominant groups will struggle to curtail outside influences in a multiplicity of ways, and weaker or dominated ones will likewise fear and resist any type of intrusion. The purity of the group must be maintained. Human barriers of race, class, language, family name, education, economic status, social position, and religion are regularly used as signals to distinguish "our own" from "the others."

The second tendency that appears as an anthropological law of nature is: others can be used and enjoyed, but a social distance must be maintained. Deep friendships might develop and even strong love relationships, but the social barriers are so deeply interiorized and assimilated that they are very difficult to do away with. There are not just laws that keep peoples apart, but also sustain the relationship of superior-inferior that is established, projected, transmitted, assimilated, and even sacralized by religion. This keeps persons from truly appreciating each other as fully equal and from seeing the true human dignity of one another. Even the best among the dominant group tend to see and treat the others as inferior and "different." We can even do good things for the lesser others, but they remain lesser. They can be exploited legitimately, because the culture and the laws of the dominant sanction the superior-inferior relationship. This gives the "master" the right and the obligation to use and "protect" the lesser ones.

This law of social distance is probably the hardest one to break through, because it is not only enforced by external laws and the economic-political mechanisms of the land, it is also interiorized in a number of ways. For example, in ordinary commercials we see blacks waiting on whites, but I have never seen a commercial with a white serving a black. Blacks, but never racially mixed families, appear in commercials. Brown skins do not even appear at all. Social barriers of separability are drilled into a people through all the media of communication and education. Even religious education material and religious images in our churches exhibit a definite racial preference, thus indirectly telling the others that they cannot be reflected in the sacred.

Finally, the third constant that appears as an anthropological law of nature is: anyone who threatens to destroy or annul the barriers of separation will be an outcast—an impure untouchable who must be eliminated.

As should be evident by now, *mestizaje* is feared by established groups because it is the deepest threat to all the humanly made barriers of separation that consecrate oppression and exploitation. It is a threat to the security of ultimate human belonging—that is, to the inherited national/cultural identity that clearly and ultimately defines who I am to myself and to the world. It is even a deeper threat to established societies because the *mestizo* cannot be named with clarity and precision. So much is in the mystery of a name! I am comfortable when I can name you for, in many ways, it indicates that I am somewhat in control of the situation. I may not like what I know, but at least I have the comfort of knowing what it is. But there is a nervousness when I do not know who you are—your name and your cultural nationality are so important, for they tell me who you are personally and fundamentally. They give me your immediate and ultimate human identity.

Because of their hyphenated identity, *mestizos* cannot be named adequately by either group's categories of analysis. They do not fit into the single-history set of norms for testing and identifying persons. This is threatening to both groups—we can name them and even study them, but they cannot name us or even figure out how to really study us. It is threatening for anyone to be in the presence of one who knows us very well, even in our innermost being, but we do not know who they are. To be an outside-insider, as the *mestizo* is, is to have both intimacy and objective distance at one and the same time. Insofar as we are in Mexico, we are outside the United States; but insofar as we are in the United States, we are distant from Mexico. As such we can see and appreciate the aspects of both, aspects which neither sees of themselves or each other. In this very in-out existence lies the potential for our creativity: to pool the cultural genes and the chromosomes of both so as to create a new being!

The potential for newness will not be actualized automatically. The *mestizo* can simply become like one of the parent groups and continue to do unto others as they have done unto us. However, they can equally, although with more hidden difficulties than anyone suspects, choose to live out the radical meaning of their new being. This is exciting but difficult because, even though the dominant way may be rejected totally and explicitly, subconsciously the oppressed will strive to become like the oppressor, for they have already assimilated many of the dominant group's characteristics. Will the group simply obtain power and acceptance by reverting to the ways of the parent group or will they initiate new life? That is the key question.

As a Mexican American Christian, I am convinced that the full potential of *mestizaje* will be actualized only in and through the way of the Lord, which brings order out of chaos and new life out of death. It is in the Lord's way that the salvific and liberating role of our *mestizo* humanity finds its ultimate identity, meaning, direction, and challenge.

The Concrete Historical Meaning of God's Saving Way

The Human Identity of the Savior

The racial-cultural identity of a person is the very first and immediate revelation of who one is. We all have stereotype prejudices about certain colors, accents, languages, features, regions, and religions. There is a natural tendency to categorize persons according to our stereotypes of them and to prejudge them as to their human worth and potential even before they have said or done anything. Looks are all-important and they are the first revelation, according to the standards of the world, of the person's worth and dignity. Persons from the outer regions of any country are usually looked down upon as rustics, whereas those from urban centers look upon themselves as sophisticated.

What was the racial-cultural identity of Jesus? What did others think of when they first saw or heard of him, before they even heard him speak or saw his actions? These are all-important questions, for we know from the New Testament itself that it is in the human face and heart of Jesus that God has been self-revealed to us. It is through the full humanity of Jesus that God has allowed us to see God in a human way.

There is no doubt that, during his lifetime, Jesus was regularly known as a Galilean, that most of his disciples were from Galilee, and that most of the things we remember best of his activity took place in Galilee. There is no doubt that Galilee plays a key role in the life and mission of Jesus as presented in the Gospels.

The full human signification of the *kenosis* of the Son of God becomes evident when we look at the image of Galilee in Jesus'time. First of all, if it had not been for Jesus, Galilee would probably remain an unknown region of the world. Jerusalem, Greece, and Rome were all important with or without Jesus, but not Galilee. It was an outer region, far from the center of Judaism in Jerusalem of Judea and a crossroads of the great caravan routes of the world. It was a region of mixed peoples and languages. In Galilee the Jews were looked down upon and despised by the others as they were in the rest of the world. They were considered to be stubborn, backward, superstitious, clannish, and all the negative stereotypes one could think of. Furthermore, the Jews of Judea looked down upon the Galilean Jews, for they considered them ignorant of the law and the rules of the temple, contaminated in many ways by their daily contacts with pagans, and not capable of speaking correct Greek, for their language was being corrupted by admixture with the other languages of the region. In short, their own Jewish relatives regarded them as inferior and impure. Because of their mixture with others, they were marginated by their own people. There were no doubts about the cultural *mestizaje* that was taking place and, knowing the ordinary situation of human beings, a certain amount of biological *mestizaje* was equally taking place. Culturally and linguistically speaking, Jesus was certainly a *mestizo* between Judaism and the other cultures that flourished throughout Galilee. And we know from the early Jewish charges that tried to discredit Jesus that he was even accused of being the bastard son of a Roman soldier named Pantera, which could also be a colloquial term simply meaning "a Roman," which could have made of him a biological *mestizo* as well. I am, of course, in no way denying or even questioning that Jesus was conceived by the Holy Spirit. What I am saying is that in his human appearance, as viewed by those who knew him only in a worldly way and not through the eyes of faith, he certainly appeared to be of mixed origins. The New Testament itself gives clear evidence that nothing good was expected to come out of Galilee.

The point of bringing out all this is to appreciate the human beginnings of God's mission. God becomes not just a human being, but the marginated, shamed, and rejected of the world. He comes to initiate a new human unity, but the all-important starting point is among the most segregated and impure of the world. Among those whom the world has thrown out, God will begin the way to final unity. It is among those whom the world labels as "impure" that a new criterion for real purity will emerge.

Although the world expected nothing good to come out of Galilee, God chose it to be the starting point of God's human presence among us. The principle behind the cultural image of the Galilean identity is that God chooses what the world rejects. What is marginal to the world is central to God. It is through those whom the world has made nothing that God will reduce to nothing the power and wisdom of the world. It is through the poor and non-persons of the world that God continues to reveal God's face and heart in a human way and among them—the Galilees and Galileans of today—salvation continues to begin for all the peoples of the world.

The Cultural Function of His Mission

The mission of Jesus is not some sort of esoteric or aesthetic truth. He comes to live out and proclaim the supreme truth about humanity, which will have immediate and long-term implications in everyday life and in the history of humanity. Those who hear his word and are converted to his way will see themselves and will equally see all others in a radically new way. This new image of self and others will allow everyone to relate with each other as never before.

Because of his concrete human identity, Jesus had personally suffered the pains of margination and dehumanizing insults. He was concerned with the pains of hunger, sickness, bad reputation, rejection, shame, class struggles, loneliness, and all the real sufferings of humanity. His concern was not abstract, but real and immediate. He spoke with the Samaritan woman, ate with the rich, the tax collectors, and sinners alike. He did not feel repelled by the leper; he enjoyed the company of women and little children. Jesus was truly at home with everyone and it is evident that everyone felt at home with him. This is nowhere more evident than in his ability to enjoy himself in table fellowship with everyone without exception.

Out of the cultural suffering of rejection, Jesus offers a new understanding of the kingdom. He did not come to restore the kingdom of David for the Jewish people but to initiate the reign of God who is the Father of everyone. The innermost identity of Jesus was his life of intimacy with God-Father. It is this living relationship with the absolute that cuts through and relativizes all human images of importance or non-importance, be they dignified or undignified. When we know the ultimate origins of a person—that he is really the son of the king—the superficial appearances are no longer important. It is the ultimate origins and name of a person that give us his or her true worth. It is precisely this intimacy with God-Father which is the basis of the innermost identity of Jesus. It is not the labels that the world places on persons that count, but one's own innermost identity and image of oneself as reflective of the likeness of God.

By discovering that God is our Father we begin to see everything in a new way. No longer will I see others as superior or inferior to me, but as brothers and sisters of the same Father. In this realization is the basis for a totally new value system for humanity. In fidelity to God, Jesus refuses to conform to any human law or tradition that will dehumanize and make appear as inferior any human being whatsoever. The truth of Jesus will upset humankind's criteria of judgment. Because one is, one is a child of God. But precisely because everyone can now belong, those who have set up and guarded the multiple barriers of separation will not only refuse the invitation but will discredit the new way and try to prevent it from coming into existence. This allows them to enjoy the privileges of being "in" at the cost of keeping the so-called inferior ones "out."

But it is not sufficient to invite the rejected into the kingdom. It is not sufficient to tell the exploited and marginated of society that they are truly free human beings who are equal to all others. One must go to the roots of the human mechanisms, both to the external and the internal structures of society, to make known the segregating and dehumanizing evil that has been institutionalized and is now hidden in the various structures of the group. Jesus makes known that he must go to Jerusalem, where the sufferings of his people are highlighted. Truth in the service of love must bring out clearly the evil hidden in human structures, evil which passes as good. Such confusion allows the evils of power to appear as the good of society, while the sufferings of the marginated appear as the cause of all evil. Criminals appear as good; victims appear as criminals. This is the ongoing confusion of Babel, which continues to mask and confuse both the evil and the good of the world.

Jesus appears in the New Testament as the aggressive prophet of nonviolent love who refuses to endorse the violence of the structures and remains faithful to the tradition of the

God of his people, of the God who sees the suffering, who hears the cries of affliction, and who wills to save. He questions the human traditions that oppress or destroy a people. Jesus must go to Jerusalem, because that is the center of institutionalized power. When he arrives he goes to the very core of Judaism: the temple. In Jerusalem we see Jesus who does not hesitate to question the very legitimacy of the structures that were enslaving the masses of the people. The house of the God of compassion and justice had become the place that now legitimized and covered up the evil ways of the establishment. The same story is found in all human institutions. We need institutions in order to live in an orderly and peaceful way. Yet, all institutions have the tendency to become self-serving to the benefit of those in control. They are set up to serve persons, but persons end up serving them. It is this very tendency to absolutize that must be confronted and made known.

As institutions, customs, and traditions become absolutized, they function as the idols of the group. Whether we call them God or not, they function as the real gods of the group. To question them is the same as questioning God. And when we challenge them, we will be accused of blasphemy. Yet to the degree that these ways dehumanize or reject any human being, they must be questioned in the name of God. But Jesus does not confront the power of the world with a power of the same order. He does not give in to the ways of humanity. He confronts the power of the world and human violence with a power of an entirely different order: the power of unlimited love which will not engage in violence to eliminate violence.

The nonviolent way of Jesus worked in a diametrically opposed way to the nonviolent way of the missioners of the power countries. First of all, he begins by assuming the way, the language, and the worldview of Galileans—the non-persons of the world. The all-powerful God, in becoming a Galilean, converts to become the marginated, the rejected, and the non-person of the world. Second, he not only denounces the accepted practices of the powerful, as good missioners often do, but, unlike the average traditional missioner, he even denounces and desacralizes their ultimate authority as enshrined in their religious symbols, for it is the religious symbols of the powerful that ultimately legitimize their way as God's way. Third, the radical difference between the missionary activity of Jesus and that of missioners who are culturally and nationally members of the powerful countries is apparent in the response of officials.

Official Judaism condemned Jesus and got rid of him. His accusers disowned him to the Romans because he questioned their ultimate authority and the ultimate legitimacy of their structures. The officials of mission-sending countries support and reinforce the missionary endeavor because it in effect affirms and perpetuates the legitimacy of their own world order. In supporting the missions, they affirm their own ultimate authority and the divine legitimacy of their ways. Let me be clear on this point: this is not necessarily done in an intentional or malicious way. In fact, I would say that quite often it is done with the best of intentions; however, the final result remains the same. The Spanish missioners did not hesitate to chastise openly and consistently the crimes and abuses of the conquest; however, they legitimized the way of the conquerors by affirming their ultimate symbol as superior and true in relation to the captured peoples' symbols of ultimate reality.

The way of Jesus to Jerusalem and the cross is the challenging task of those who are on the margins of society. Their temptation will always be to become simply the powerful themselves, as even the disciples wanted to do. But the challenge is to be willing to die so that a new way will truly be ushered in. The authorities kill Jesus but they cannot destroy him. He remains faithful to his way to the very end. He came to reject every type of human rejection and, even when all appear to have rejected him, even his God, he rejects no one. He dies in perfect communion with his people and his God. He came to tear down barriers of separation and, no matter what humans tried to do to stop him, they were not able to break him down. As he lived his life in communion with everyone—so he died. All had rejected him, but he rejects no one.

God's love in and through Jesus triumphs over all the divisive hatreds and consequent violence of humanity. Jesus passes through death to life. In resurrecting him, God rejects the rejection of humanity, destroys all the charges of illegitimacy, and demolishes the idolized structures. In the resurrection, God ratified the entire way and message of Jesus. It is from the resurrection that the entire way of Jesus and every aspect of his life takes on a liberating and salvific signification.

It is in the resurrection that the new life initiated and offered to everyone by Jesus is now fully and definitively present. No human power will be able to destroy it or slow it down. Jesus is the firstborn of the new creation, and in his followers a new human group now begins. It is definitely a new human alternative now present in the history of humanity.

First of all, those who had nothing to offer now have the best thing to offer to everyone: new life. It is the rejected and marginated Galileans who receive the Spirit and, without ceasing to be Galileans, now see themselves in a new way as they begin to initiate the new humanity. Everyone is invited, but it is the very ones who had been excluded who now do the inviting. It is obvious from the history of the early church how quickly the new way spread to all peoples. It crossed all boundaries of separation. Without ceasing to be who they were culturally, people nevertheless saw themselves in such a new way that the ordinary human barriers were no longer obstacles to the new fellowship.

It is equally evident that the crossing of cultural boundaries was not easy, for each group had its own unsuspected idols, yet the miracle is that it took place. Cultural-national groups which had been totally separated, now can come together—no longer Jew or gentile, master or slave, male or female, but all one in Christ. They continued to be who they were, but they lived their nationality and religion in a radically new way. Their identity was affirmed but their exclusiveness was destroyed. This openness led them to discover new values and criteria of judgment: from competition to cooperation, from divisions to unity, from strangers to a common family, from a superior or inferior status to common friends and all children of the same Father.

The radical all-inclusive way of Christianity started among the rejected and lowly of society. This is the starting point. In the Spirit, they struggle to build new human alternatives so that others will not have to suffer what they have had to suffer. It is they who first hear the invitation to the new universal family of God, and it is the converted poor and suffering of the world who see themselves in a new way, who now go out and invite—by deeds and words—all others into the new society. God continues to begin where humanity would never suspect. Out of the Nazareths and Galilees of today, salvation continues to reach the entire world.

The God-Meaning of Our Mexican American Identity and Mission

"God chose those whom the world considers absurd to shame the wise." (1 Cor. 1:28)

It is in the light of our faith that we discover our ultimate identity as God's chosen people. It is in the very cultural identity of Jesus the Galilean and in his way from Galilee to Jerusalem that the real ultimate meaning of our own cultural identity and mission to society become clear.

For those who ordinarily have a good sense of belonging, the idea of being chosen is nothing special. But for one who has been consistently ignored or rejected, the idea of being noticed, accepted, and especially chosen is not only good news, but new life. For in being chosen, what was nothing now becomes something, and what was dead now comes to life. In the light of the Judeo-Christian tradition, our experience of rejection and margination is converted from human curse to the very sign of divine predilection. It is evident from the scriptures that God chooses the outcasts of the world not exclusively but definitely in a preferential way. Those whom the world ignores, God loves in a special way. But God does not choose the poor and the lowly just to keep them down and make them feel good in their misery. Such an election would be the very opposite of good news and it would truly be the opium to keep the poor quiet and domesticated. God chooses the poor and the marginated of the world to be the agents of the new creation.

The experience of being wanted as one is, of being needed and of being chosen, is a real and profound rebirth. Those who had been made to consider themselves as nothing or as inferior will now begin to appreciate the full stature of human beings. Out of the new self-image, new powers will be released, powers which have always been there but have not been able to surface. Through this experience, the sufferings of the past are healed though not forgotten, and they should not be forgotten. For it is precisely out of the condition of suffering that the people are chosen so as to initiate a new way of life where others will not have to suffer what the poor have suffered in the past. When people forget the experience of suffering, as has happened to many of our immigrant groups in this country, such as the Irish in Boston, then they simply inflict the same insults upon others that had previously been inflicted upon them. The greater the suffering and the more vivid the memory of it, the greater the challenge will be to initiate changes so as to eliminate the root causes of the evils which cause the suffering. It is the wounded healer, the one who has not forgotten the pain of wounds, who can be the greatest healer of society's illnesses.

It is in our very margination from the centers of the various establishments that we live the Galilean identity today. Because we are inside-outsiders, we appreciate more clearly the best of the traditions of both groups, while equally appreciating the worst from the situation of both. It is precisely in this double identity that we in effect have something of unique value to offer both. The very reasons for the margination are the bases of our liberating and salvific potential not only for ourselves but for the others as well. In a privileged way, God is present in the marginated, for distance from the powers of the world is closeness to God. It is consistently in the borderlands regions of human belonging that God begins the new creation. The established centers seek stability, but the borderlands regions can risk to be pioneers. It is the borderlands people who will be the trailblazers of the new societies. "The stone which the builders rejected has become the keystone of the structure. It is the Lord who did this and we find it marvelous to behold" (Matt. 21:42).

"I have chosen you to go and bear much fruit." (John 15:16)

God chooses people not just to make them feel good, but for a mission. "I have chosen you to go and bear much fruit" (John 15:16). To accept God's election is not empty privilege, but a challenging mission. It is a call to be prophetic both in deeds and in words. It is a call to live a new alternative in the world, to invite others into it, and to challenge with the power of truth the structures of the world that keep the new alternative from becoming a reality.

Our Mexican American Christian challenge in the world today is not to become like someone else—Mexicans or Americans—but to combine both into a new way. It is through the very mechanisms of forging a new and more cosmopolitan identity that new life begins to emerge. It must be worked at critically, persistently, and creatively, for the temptation will always be there to become simply one or the other of the previous models. The temptation will always be there to restore the kingdom rather than to usher in the kingdom of God. In our present powerlessness we may think that this is stupid but, in our faith, we know that we must take the risks and begin to initiate new ways of life that will eliminate some of the dehumanizing elements of the present one. We know that we will not eliminate them all, nor will this come about easily and without much effort, organization, and frustration, but nevertheless the efforts must be made to introduce new forms and new institutions that will continue some of the best of the past while eliminating some of the worst. We will not build the perfect society, but we must do our part to at least build a better one. We must begin with the grassroots, but we must equally go to the very roots of the problems.

This is our "divine must"! We, too, must harden our faces and go to Jerusalem. We must go to the established centers of power, whether political, economic, educational, or religious, to confront their sacred idols which prevent them from truly serving all the people. It is the idols of society which function in favor of the rich and the powerful, and against the poor and powerless. It is they which mask the hidden viciousness and manipulations of the wise of the world who find many ways of exploiting the poor and the simple of the world.

We really do not have a choice if we want to be disciples following Jesus on his way to the cross. It is this road from Galilee to Jerusalem which has to be continued if evil is to be destroyed, not with new forms of evil, but with the power of truth in the service of love. We have no choice but to speak the truth which brings to light clearly the evil of the world, knowing full well that the powers of darkness will not stop at anything in order to put out the light.

"Your grief will be turned to joy." (John 16:20)

It is in our fiestas that our legitimate identity and destiny are experienced. They are not just parties; in fact they are the very opposite. They are the joyful, spontaneous, and collective celebrations of what has already begun in us even if it is not recognized by others or verbalized even by ourselves. It is the celebration of the beginning of the ultimate eschatological identity where there will be differences but not division. It is the celebration of what has already begun in germ but is yet to be totally fulfilled. The fiesta is a foretaste and experience, even if for a brief moment, of the ultimate accomplishment. It is a result of who we are and a cause of what is yet to become. For just as it is true that the celebrations of the people can be used to drug the people and keep them in their misery, it is equally true that the fiestas can be used as rallying moments that not only give the people an experience of togetherness, but can also nourish the movements of liberation. In the fiestas, we rise above our daily living experiences of death to experience life beyond death. They are the moments of life that enable us to survive, come together, rally, and begin anew. The spirit not only to survive but to bring about a new existence can be enkindled in the fiestas so as to ignite the people to action.

Fiestas without prophetic action easily degenerate into empty parties, drunken brawls, or the opium to keep the people in their misery. But prophetic action without festive celebration is equally reduced to dehumanizing hardness. Prophecy is the basis of fiesta, but the fiesta is the spirit of prophecy. It is in the combination of the two that the tradition of faith is both kept alive and transmitted to newcomers. It is through the two of them that the God of history who acts on our behalf, on behalf of the poor and the lowly, continues to be present among us, bringing the project of history to completion.

Thus it is precisely through our fiestas that we are kept together as a people. It is through them that we have continued to maintain our identity and sense of belonging. They are the deepest celebrations of our existence—meaningful to those who belong and incomprehensible and folkloric to outsiders. They are the lifeline of our tradition and the life sources of our new existence.

17. Popular Religiosity, Spanish, and *Proyecto Histórico*—Elements of Latinas' Ethnicity

Ada María Isasi-Díaz

When the present is limiting—oppressive—one looks to the future to find a reason for living. Historically, religion has been used to encourage the poor and the oppressed to postpone hopes and expectations to "the next world." But liberation theologies turn the focus of the hopes and expectations of the poor and the oppressed from "the next world" to this world. For this reason liberation theologies are feared and opposed by those interested in maintaining the status quo.

In this chapter we will explore the hopes and expectations of Latinas grounded in our reality and aimed at historical fruition. It is the contention of *mujerista* theology that the *proyecto histórico*, historical project, of Latinas is one of the key elements in constructing our reality. We will then analyze popular religiosity and the role it plays in Latinas' struggle for survival, and how the Spanish language functions as part of Latinas' self-understanding and ethnic identification.

Latinas' Preferred Future: Our *Proyecto Histórico*

Mujerista theology uses the term *proyecto histórico* to refer to our liberation and the historical specifics needed to attain it. Though the plan is not a blueprint, it is "a historical project defined enough to force options."[1] It is a plan that deals with the structures of our churches, as well as with social, political, and economic institutions of society. The articulation of Latinas' *proyecto histórico* presented here is not only an explanation but also a strategy: it aims to help shape Latinas' understandings in our day-to-day struggle to survive, and our identity as a community. This articulation springs from our lived-experience and is a prediction of "our hopes and dreams toward survival,"[2] of our *lucha*—struggle.

Latinas' *proyecto histórico,* is based on an understanding of salvation and liberation as two aspects of one process. This is grounded in the belief that there is but one human history that has at its very heart the history of salvation. By "history of salvation" we refer to what we believe are divine actions—creation, incarnation, redemption—as well as our human responses to them, whether positive or negative. For us Latinas, salvation refers to having a relationship with God, a relationship that does not exist if we do not love our neighbor.

Our relationship with God affects all aspects of our lives, all human reality. As Latinas become increasingly aware of the injustices we suffer, we reject any concept of salvation that does not affect our present and future reality. For us, salvation occurs in history and is intrinsically connected to our liberation.[3]

For Latinas, liberation has to do with becoming agents of our own history, with having what one needs to live and to be able to strive towards human fulfillment. Liberation is the realization of our *proyecto histórico*, which we are always seeking to make a reality while accepting that its fullness will never be accomplished in history. Liberation is realized in concrete events which at the same time point to a more comprehensive and concrete realization.[4] For Latinas to talk about salvation, liberation, and the coming of the kin-dom of God are one and the same thing. Historical events are never clearly nor completely the fulfillment of the kin-dom of God, but they affect such fulfillment; they are "eschatological glimpses," part of the unfolding of the kin-dom which we do not make happen but which requires us to take responsibility for making justice a reality in our world.

The realization of the kin-dom of God—liberation—is related to our present reality. Our *proyecto histórico* is not divorced from the present but rather is rooted in it, giving meaning and value to our daily struggle for survival. The present reality of Latinas makes it clear that in order to accomplish what we are stuggling for, we need to understand fully which structures are oppressive, denounce them, and announce what it is that we are struggling for.[5] Our struggle for liberation has to start with an analysis of the root causes of our oppression. Such an analysis shows our oppression to be multifaceted—an intersection of ethnic prejudice or racism, sexism, and economic oppression—all of which are intrinsic elements of patriachal and hierarchical structures. Analysis of oppression must then lead to effective denunciation.

Denunciation as part of Latinas' *proyecto histórico* is a challenge to understand and deal with present reality in the name of the future. Such a challenge does not consist only in criticizing, reproaching, and attacking those who maintain the structures that oppress us. Denunciation also has to do with repudiating such structures—not aspiring to participate in them—and refusing to benefit from them.[6] Therefore, *mujerista* theology is not to be only a resource for social criticism from the perspective of Latinas but is also socio-critical at its point of departure.[7] This means that we insist on our preferred future from the very beginning and insist that our *proyecto histórico* grounds our theological task, which we understand to be a liberative praxis.

To denounce oppressive structures without having a sense of what we believe our future should be is irresponsible. For Latinas' denunciation of oppression to be effective, we must also announce, that is, proclaim what is not yet but what we are committed to bringing about. In this context, annunciation, like analysis and denunciation, is indeed a liberative praxis, an exercise that is intended to yield tangible results. Denunciation and annunciation have to contribute effectively to the creation of new structures that make possible the liberation of Latinas and of all humanity. To announce is an intrinsic part of our insistence on fullness of life against all odds and in spite of all obstacles. Such insistence is incarnated in the concrete daily struggle of Latinas, a struggle which makes tomorrow a possibility. Whether that tomorrow is for ourselves or for our children makes no difference to us. Our annunciation becomes reality in our struggle to find or create spaces for self-determination, a key factor in the struggle for liberation. The challenge to be agents of our own history is what pushes us on to do the analysis, denounce those who oppress us, and engage in building a future society with alternative values, no matter how foolish our efforts appear to those with power.[8]

Liberation is a single process that has three different aspects or levels[9] which must not be confused or identified in any simplistic way. Each one maintains its specificity; each is distinct but affects the other; none is ever present without the others. None of those aspects exists in isolation from the others.[10] These three aspects of liberation also serve as points of entry for Latinas into the struggle for liberation because they are concrete aspects of our *proyecto histórico*. We refer to these different aspects of liberation as *libertad, comunidad de fe*, and *justicia*: freedom, faith community, and justice.

Libertad has to do with acting as agents of our own history. This aspect of liberation involves the process of conscientization, with how we understand ourselves personally in view of our preferred future. *Libertad* has to do with a self-fulfillment that renounces any and all self-promotion while recognizing that commitment to the struggle and involvement in it are indeed self-realizing. *Comunidad de fe* is the aspect of liberation that makes us face sin, both personal and social sin. *Comunidad de fe* is both our goal (rejecting sin) and the community that makes rejecting sin possible. *Justicia* here refers to the political, economic, and social structures we struggle to build that will make oppression of anyone impossible. *Justicia* has to do with the understandings that guide us, challenge us, and enable us to survive daily.

Since these three aspects of liberation are interconnected and happen simultaneously, it is difficult to speak about them separately. We do so to distinguish each from the other, to explain and understand how they interrelate without confusing them. The specifics we discuss as part of each of these three elements are not to be understood as relating only to a single element. Each of the specifics has implications for and relates to all three elements.[11]

The first element we will consider is that of *libertad*. In Latinas' struggle for survival we must take great care not to oppose structural change to personal liberation. What is "personal" for us Latinas is neither individual nor necessarily private. For us the term "individual" carries a pejorative meaning, a sense of egocentrism and selfishness that we believe to be inherently bad since it works against what is of great value to us, our communities. Our sense of community keeps us from arrogating a sense of privacy to all aspects of the personal. Therefore, for us, *libertad* involves being aware of the role we play in our own oppression and in the struggle for liberation. It includes being conscious of the role we must play as agents of our own history. *Libertad* has to do with being self-determining, rejecting any and all forms of determinism, whether materialistic, economic, or psychological.[12] It has to do with recognizing that the internal aspiration for personal freedom is truly powerful, as both a motive and a goal of liberation.[13]

Libertad as an element of liberation for us Latinas happens, then, at the psychological and the social level. The two main obstacles to *libertad* among Latinas are apathy and fear.[14] As an oppressed group within the richest country in the world, Latinas view our liberation as such an immense task that a common response is apathy. We often think of our task as beyond accomplishment, and apathy appears as a protection against frustration. For those of us for whom the *proyecto histórico* becomes a motivational factor strong enough to enable us to shake off our apathy, our next struggle is with fear. Our fear is not mainly the fear of failing—fear of trying and not accomplishing what we set out to do—but rather the fear of being co-opted by the status quo.[15]

A central and powerful myth in the U.S.A. tells all those who come here, as well as everyone in the world, that, because this is the best of all societies, whether one accomplishes what one wants or not depends on the individual. It depends on whether one is ambitious enough, gets a good education (which the myth maintains is available to everyone), and is willing to work hard and sacrifice oneself.[16] This myth is promulgated constantly in the most pervasive way possible. It contributes significantly to the negative self-image of Latinas who cannot get ahead, not because we do not try hard, but because of socio-economic realities that militate against us in all areas of life. If a negative self-image is oppressive, the fact that this myth fills us with fear, often robbing us of even envisioning our *proyecto histórico*, is insidious.

In order to counteract apathy and fear, we have to continue to elaborate our vision of the future at the same time that we work to articulate the details of our *proyecto histórico*. Making our preferred future a reality needs much more than vague generalities. Latinas' *proyecto histórico* has to be specific enough for each of us to know how we are to participate in the struggle to make it a reality, and what our task will be when it becomes a reality. All Latinas must know what it is we are being asked to contribute. Our *proyecto histórico* must have concreteness and specificity. Only when we know the concrete details can we face our shortcomings and the tremendous obstacles that we find along the way. Knowing concrete details can also help us face and conquer the fear that an unknown future brings. We can mitigate our fear by insisting on particulars, by being precise, by concretizing our vision of the future. The more tangible our *proyecto histórico* becomes, the more realizable it will be, since once it moves from vision to implementable plan, we will be able to transfer to this task of building our preferred future all the skills we do have—those skills we use effectively to survive every day.

Our explanation of *comunidad de fe* as an element of liberation starts by recognizing that Latinas' relationship with the divine is a very intimate one. It is not only a matter of believing that God is with us in our daily struggle, but that we can and do relate to God the same way we relate to all our loved ones.[17] We argue with God, barter with God, get upset with God, are grateful and recompense God, use endearing terms for God. This intimate relationship with the divine is what is at the heart of our *comunidad de fe*. For Latinas, it makes no sense to say one believes in God if one does not relate to the divine on a daily basis.[18]

Because Latinas relate intimately to the divine, we know that sin hurts such a relationship. We know that sin, while personal, is not private, for it is something that affects our communities negatively. The reflections of grassroot Latinas about evil give a clear sense of their understanding of sin:

> Sin is not a matter of disobedience but of not being for others. Not going to church is not a sin. But not to care for the children of the community—that is a sin, a crime! And the women take direct responsibility for what they do or do not do. Though they have a certain sense of predestination, they do not blame anyone but themselves for what goes wrong, On the other hand, God is given credit for the good that they do, the good that occurs in their lives.[19]

The analysis that our *proyecto histórico* demands can help us deepen our understanding of how sin affects those around us by helping us to understand "structural sin" and the role it plays in our oppression. We need to recognize that there are structures that have been set up to maintain the privilege of a few at the expense of the many and that those structures are sinful. Our analysis of oppressive structures will help us understand that sin is "according to the Bible the ultimate cause of poverty, injustice, and the oppression in which [we] . . . live."[20]

To understand the structural implications of sin, Latinas need to actualize our sense of *comunidades de fe* by setting up communities which are praxis-oriented, which bring together personal support and community action, and which have as a central organizing principle our religious understandings and practices as well as our needs.[21]

We have to accept, however, that most of the time we will not be able to depend on church structures and personnel to help us develop our communities. Once again we are going to have to depend on ourselves and, perhaps, we will be able to find help in the few national Latina organizations that claim to be committed to the struggle for liberation. Our *comunidades de fe* must also find ways of relating to community organizations. Where there are no Latina community organizations, the *comunidades de fe* need to fulfill that function. We must resist the temptation to let our *comunidades de fe* become "support groups" that separate our lives into realms: the personal from the communal, the spiritual from the struggle for justice.

Our *comunidades de fe* must also be ecumenical. We must embrace the grassroot ecumenism practiced by many Latinas who relate to more than one denomination because of their need to avail themselves of help no matter what its source. For others of us, our ecumenicism has to do with our belief that the struggle for liberation—and not the fact that we belong to the same church—must be the common ground of our *comunidades de fe*. Our ecumenism must take into consideration and capitalize on our *religiosidad popular*, popular religiosity.

Finally, the *comunidades de fe* have to develop their own models of leadership, communal leadership that recognizes and uses effectively the gifts of Latinas. Characteristics emerging from our historical reality will make it possible for the *comunidades de fe* to contribute effectively to the building of our *proyecto histórico*.

The third element of liberation is *justicia*. Justice as a virtue does not refer only or mainly to attitudes but to a tangible way of acting and being; it involves not only personal conduct but also the way social institutions—the building blocks of societal structures—are organized, the way they operate, prioritize issues, and use resources. Justice is not only a matter of taking care of the basic needs of the members of society, nor is it a utilitarianism that insists on the greatest happiness for the majority of people.[22] Justice is not a matter of "to each according to one's needs," as Marxist principles proclaim.[23] For *mujerista* theologians justice is all of this and much more. Justice is a Christian requirement: one cannot call oneself a Christian and not struggle for justice.

Our understanding of justice is based on the lived-experience of Latinas, an experience that has as its core multifaceted oppression. In *mujerista* theology *justicia* is a matter of permitting and requiring each person to participate in the production of the goods needed to sustain and promote human life. It has to do with rights and with the participation of all

Latinas in all areas of life. Justice is indeed understood as the "common good." But striving for the "common good" can never be done at the expense of anyone. The "common good" is to be judged by the rights and participation of the poorest in society; it never places the rights of individuals against or over the rights and participation in society of others, particularly of the poor. It understands "welfare" in a holistic way and not just as limited to the physical necessities of life. In *mujerista* theology *justicia* is concretely expressed by being in effective solidarity with and having a preferential option for Latinas.[24]

Effective solidarity with Latinas is not a matter of agreeing with, being supportive of, or being inspired by our cause. Solidarity starts with recognizing the commonality of responsibilities and interests that all of us have despite differences of race or ethnicity, class, sex, sexual preference, age. Solidarity has to do with recognizing and affirming, valuing and defending a community of interests, feelings, purposes and actions with the poor and the oppressed. The two main, interdependent elements of solidarity are mutuality and praxis. Mutuality keeps solidarity from being a merely altruistic praxis by making clear that, if it is true that solidarity benefits the poor and the oppressed, it is also true that the salvation and liberation of the rich and the oppressors depend on it. Solidarity is truly praxis, because in order for a genuine community of interests, feelings, and purposes to exist between the oppressed and the oppressor, there must be a radical action on the part of the oppressors that leads to the undoing of oppression. Thus, for solidarity to be a praxis of mutuality, it has to struggle to be politically effective; it has to have as its objective radical structural change.[25]

Effective solidarity with Latinas demands a preferential option for the oppressed. This preferential option is not based on our moral superiority. It is based on the fact that Latinas' point of view,

> *pierced by suffering and attracted by hope, allows them, in their struggles, to conceive another reality. Because the poor suffer the weight of alienation, they can conceive a different project of hope and provide dynamism to a new way of organizing human life* for all.[26]

Solidarity with Latinas as oppressed people is a call to a fundamental moral option, an option that makes it possible and requires one to struggle for radical change of oppressive structures even when the specifics of what one is opting for are not known. As a matter of fact, only opting for a radical change of oppressive structures will allow the specifics of new societal structures to begin to appear.

The ability of Latinas to conceive "another reality" a different kind of social, political, and economic structure, is greatly hampered, as explained above, by the powerful U.S.A. myth regarding the possibility of success in this country for everyone. Poor and oppressed women in the shanty towns that surround Lima, Perú, for example, know very well that they will never be able to live—except as maids—in San Isidro, one of the rich neighborhoods in that city. Knowing that they cannot benefit from the present societal structures helps them to understand the need for radical change and to work for it. But it is not unusual to find Latinas living in the most oppressed conditions in the inner cities of the U.S.A. who think that if they work hard and sacrifice themselves, their children will benefit from the present order, and that they will eventually have the material goods and privileges this society claims to offer to all. I believe that this possibility, which becomes a reality for only the tiniest minority of Latinas and their children, hinders our ability to understand structural oppression. It keeps us from understanding that if we succeed in the present system, it will be because someone else takes our place at the bottom of the socio-economic-political ladder.

In order to overcome the temptation to leave behind oppression individually and at the expense of others, Latinas need to continue to set up strong community organizations. Such organizations are most important in constructing our own identity and strengthening our moral agency. Community organizations are fertile settings for supporting our liberative praxis. They provide spaces for us to gather our political will and power to help us question the present structures. Community organizations provide or help us to move into spaces that can bring together different political projects. These projects enable us to participate in the creation of a different kind of society—a participation that must be present if socio-economic transformation is to happen. Without community organizations that make it possible for us to analyze our reality and to explore alternatives, we will not be able to participate politically, socially, or economically at all levels of society; we will not be able to be agents of our own history, to make our *proyecto histórico* a reality.[27]

Our community organizing will be helped if those with privileges in this society are willing to stand in solidarity with us. To be in solidarity with Latinas is to use one's privileges to bring about radical change instead of spending time denying that one has privileges. For our part, Latinas must embrace the mutuality of solidarity; we have to be open to the positive role that those who become our friends by being in solidarity with us can play in our struggle for liberation. By culture and socialization Latinas are not separatists; we do not exclude others from our lives and from *la lucha*, nor do we struggle exclusively for ourselves. We extend this same sense of community to those who are in solidarity with us. They can enable us in our process of conscientization; they can help us see the deception behind the U.S.A. myth. They can assist us in getting rid of the oppressor within who at times makes us seek vengeance and disfigures our *proyecto bistórico* when we seek to exchange places with present-day oppressors.[28]

At present the unfolding of our *proyecto histórico* requires that Latinas organize to bring about an economic democracy in the U.S.A. that would transform an economy controlled by a few to the economy of a participatory community. Concretely, we must insist on a national commitment to full employment, an adequate minimum wage, redistribution of wealth through redistributive inheritance and wealth taxes, and comparable remuneration for comparable work regardless of sex, sexual preference, race, ethnicity, or age. Radical changes in the economics of the family that will encourage more "symmetrical marriages, allow a better balance between family and work for both men and women, and make parenting a less difficult and impoverishing act for single parents," the majority of whom are women, are a must.[29] We need a national health care plan with particular emphasis on preventive health care. Latinas call for a restructuring of the educational system so that our children and all those interested can study Latino culture and Spanish. We also call for a restructuring of the financing of public education so that its quality does not depend on the economics of those who live in the neighborhood served by a given school but is the responsibility of the whole community of that area, region, or state. Latinas must have access to political office to insure adequate representation of our community. Access to public means of communication including entertainment TV and movies is necessary so that the values of Latinas can begin to impact the culture of the nation at large.

Working for these changes in the U.S. system might not be considered radical enough. But we believe that these kinds of changes within the present system do strike at the

> *essential arrangements in the class-power-ideology structure. To respond to these . . . [demands] would necessitate such a fundamental change in the ownership, and use of domestic and international wealth as to undercut the ruling class's position in American society and in the world, a development of revolutionary rather than reformist dimensions.*[30]

These reforms demanded by Latinas significantly modify economic structures, gender, cultural relationships, and social and political institutions. Working for such changes also enhances our ability to build coalitions with other oppressed groups struggling for liberation. Thus we can have the numbers we need to be politically effective. Working for these changes strengthens our communities of struggle and makes our survival possible by enabling us to be self-defining and to strengthen our moral agency.[31]

Latinas' *proyecto histórico* is based on our lived-experience, which is mainly one of struggle against oppression. It has been argued that the subjectivity of lived-experience makes it impossible to consider it an adequate normative base. But the fact is that so-called adequate normative bases, such as different theories of justice, spring from the understandings of men, understandings that are based on and are influenced by *their* experiences. The liberative praxis of Latinas, having as its source our lived-experience, is an adequate base for moral norms and values because it enables our moral agency and empowers us to understand and define ourselves—to comprehend what our human existence is all about and what its goal is.[32]

Popular Religiosity as an Element of *Mujerista* Theology[33]

The starting point for a study of the popular religiosity of Latinas is our struggle to survive.[34] Popular religiosity for us is a means of self-identification and our insistence on it is part of the struggle to exist with our own characteristics and peculiarities. Popular religiosity allows religion to remain central to our culture in spite of the neglect we suffer as a people from most organized religions in this country.[35]

It should not be surprising that Latinas, as persons who are "vitally engaged in historical realities with specific times and places,"[36] and as persons who have to struggle for survival, are involved with and reflect on matters of ultimate concern. This reflection includes religious considerations that form "a system of symbols which acts to establish powerful, pervasive, and long-lasting moods and motivations . . . by formulating conceptions of a general order of existence and clothing these conceptions with such an aura of factuality that the moods and motivations seem uniquely realistic."[37]

Many of these powerful symbols arise from a certain kind of "official" Christian tradition. "Official" here refers to "those prescribed beliefs and norms of an institution promulgated and monitored by a group of religious specialists,"[38] the clergy and, in particular, the hierarchy of the church. Without question Christianity is the religion of Latinas—Catholicism being the specific form of Christianity which about 80 percent claim and pass on to our children. But the Christianity to which we relate, our way of relating with the divine and expressing such connection, is not "official" Christianity, nor does it necessarily have the church—either Catholic or Protestant—as its main point of reference. The Christianity of Latinas is of a very specific variety because of its history in the countries of our ethnic roots.

Christianity came to Latin America at the time of the *conquista*, the conquest. It came not only, or even primarily, in the form of organized religion, but as an intrinsic part of the conquering culture. Theology was indeed "the main discourse in the ideological production of the sixteenth century."[39] This is why the *conquistadores*, the conquerors, planted crosses to symbolize their taking possession of the land, and named the territories and the natives in the same way as species and persons are named or renamed in the Bible—to indicate having authority over them.[40] The *conquista* was not just a political conquest, but a conquest in which even the religious world of the conquered suffered total devastation. Christianity was not only imposed on the natives but also played a very important role as moral justifier in the whole process of the *conquista*.

When the Spanish world and the world of the indigenous people of what was to become the Americas met, a process of acculturation was set in motion during which the culture of the conqueror was imposed unilaterally on the conquered people. Real enculturation—"the process of making personal the traditional culture of the society," that is, the society of the *conquistadores*—did not take place because education was not made available to the vast majority of the population. Instead, what resulted was a "culturization" of Christianity; Christianity became culture. It has become a cultural expression in a continent in which the Spanish and the indigenous cultures have come together to give birth to a new culture.[41]

The Christianity that became and is an intrinsic part of Latino culture is one that uses the Bible in a very limited way, emphasizing instead the traditions and customs of the Spanish church.[42] Therefore, the Bible, biblical truth, and revelation are not repudiated by Latinas but, for the majority of Latinas, they are not central, they are not considered very important, they do not play a prominent role in our lives. Most of us seldom read the Bible and know instead popularized versions of biblical stories—versions Latinas create to make a point. One can consider these versions to be distortions, but for us they are "valid" interpretations, albeit imaginative ones, insofar as they contribute to the liberation of Latinas.[43]

The Christianity of Latinas also includes religious traditions brought to Latin America and the Caribbean by African slaves, and the Amerindian traditions bequeathed by the great Aztec, Maya, and Inca civilizations, as well as other Amerindian cultures, such as Taino, Siboney, Caribe, Araucano. The mingling of sixteenth-century Spanish Catholicism with religious understandings and beliefs of the African and Amerindian religions in these regions is what has given birth to Latino popular religiosity.[44]

Popular religiosity refers to the religious understandings and practices of the masses, in contrast to "official" Christianity or the Christianity of certain minorities that eschew popular religiosity. Popular religiosity is

> *the set of experiences, beliefs and rituals which more-or-less peripherical* [sic] *human groups create, assume and develop (within concrete socio-cultural and historical contexts, and as an answer to these contexts) and which to a greater or lesser degree distance themselves from what is recognized by the Church and the society within which they are situated, striving through rituals, experiences and beliefs to find an access to God and salvation which they feel they cannot find in what Church and society have regulated as normative.*[45]

Concretely we can say that the popular religiosity of Latinas has five general characteristics. First, it is a real religious subculture in the sense that it is a way of thinking and acting in their religious sphere not as individuals but as a group of persons. As a religious subculture, popular religiosity includes beliefs, attitudes, values, rituals, and so forth, that express the religiosity of Latinos. Second, insofar as rituals are concerned, central position is given to certain aspects of the Catholic tradition considered marginal, for example, "sacramentals."[46] Third, popular religiosity, as I have already begun to suggest, is syncretic for it invests Catholic religious practices with meaning from other religious traditions. Fourth, "official" religious practices are reinterpreted and given a different meaning. For example, Baptism and First Communion become rituals of passage; the Mass becomes a public ceremony used to solemnize the most important moments in the life of a person or a group of people. Fifth, all these behaviors are transmitted as part of the Latino culture in contrast to being personal options.[47]

In *mujerista* theology we see popular religiosity as an essential part of popular culture and, therefore, as a part of the identity of and central to the lived-experience of the people. It is an essential part of our deepest constitutive element.[48] In many ways popular religiosity is one of the most creative and original parts of our heritage and our culture, being a significant element in providing *fuerzas para la lucha*, strength for the struggle. In this sense popular religiosity is valuable not only culturally but also "in relation to its capacity for strengthening the political consciousness and mobilization of the people."[49]

Mujeristas take popular religiosity very seriously, then, finding it to be an essential source of our theology because it is operative in the lives of Latinas as a "system of values and ideas, and a complex of symbolic practices, discursive and non-discursive, enacted in ritual drama and materialized in visual images," relating us to the sacred, originated and maintained in a large measure by Latinas as poor and oppressed people.[50] But this does not exempt popular religiosity from being examined through the critical lens of the liberation of Latinas. As *mujerista* theologians we recognize that the popular religiosity of Latinas has its failings and ambiguities, as do other cultural forms of Catholicism and Christianity.[51] Using a liberative lens, *mujerista* theology recognizes that popular religiosity has elements that legitimize the oppression of Latinas. However, this does not lead us to minimize or dismiss it.

The evangelizing role that popular religiosity has had and continues to have among Latinas and within the Latino community is instrumental in the struggle for liberation because it is a major force in preserving the Latino community. "The historical neglect to which Latinos have been submitted in this country, by Church and society, added to the constant pressure to become 'anglicized,' would have long ago done away with Catholicism among Latinos and with Latino culture in general."[52] Instead, Latino Christianity and culture are alive today thanks to the evangelizing role of popular religiosity through which Latinas transmit the religious, cultural, and social values of our people. Moreover, it has provided common ground for the great variety of Latinos who live in the U.S.A., thus binding the different Latino communities together.[53]

For Latinas, popular religiosity also has another important role: it allows us to experience the sacred in our everyday lives. In many ways it makes it possible for us to live out religiosity as an intrinsic element of who we are and all that we do; it makes it possible to integrate the sacred and the secular. It is through the practices of popular religiosity that Latinas are aware of the sacred in the private as well as the public, in the personal as well as the social.[54]

"Official" churches, instead of seeing popular religiosity as a positive element,[55] either denounce it and work actively against it, or look for ways of purifying it, of "baptizing" it into Christianity—accepting only those elements that can be Christianized.[56] In *mujerista* theology we will not dismiss "the normative, graced, and even universal dimensions of the 'salvific' manifestations of non-Christian religions."[57] As *mujerista* theologians we are suspicious of an imperialistic approach that refuses to recognize and accept as true, good, and life-giving any and all religious understandings and practices that do not directly relate to a magisterial understanding and interpretation of the gospel, that do not have Christ as center, model, and norm.[58] We take exception to such refusal because it does violence to a valid understanding of Jesus as portrayed in Scripture: Jesus clearly indicated that his mission was not to point to himself, but rather to point the way to God.

This imperialistic attitude on the part of "official" churches, particularly vis-à-vis the Amerindian and African strands in popular religiosity, is anti-cultural, and in this case, anti-Latino. To insist on imposing the divinity of Jesus as the only true and relevant expression of the divine on people who because of cultural factors either believe differently or for whom such claim is irrelevant, shows a lack of respect for a people whose religion includes other claims, and whose religion is central to their culture.[59] Is this imperialistic attitude not one of the main reasons for the lack of pastoral care and inclusion of Latinos in the life of the church in the U.S.A.?

Latinas' Christianity is indeed a mixture, a fusion of different religious strands. In this regard it follows in the footsteps of "official" Christianity. For example, Christmas is celebrated at the time of the year when the Feast of the Unconquered Sun took place at Rome in the late third and early fourth centuries;[60] pagan buildings such as the Pantheon were turned into churches; civil offices and the garbs of different periods and cultures have become religious offices and liturgical garb; Greek philosophical concepts of substance are used by Catholics to talk about the Eucharist. Once this syncretism became official, however, it has been used as an orthodox norm which has excluded and continues to exclude other syncretisms.

But such an exclusion does not obliterate syncretism from the Latinas' *religiosidad popular*, popular religiosity. Is Our Lady of Guadalupe the Mother of Jesus, or is she Tonantzin, the Aztec goddess, Mother of the Gods on whose pilgrimage site, the hill of Tepeyac, Our Lady of Guadalupe appeared?[61] In their hearts, and often quite openly, Latinas with Caribbean roots who pray to St. Barbara are identifying her, directly or indirectly, with Chango, the Yoruban God of Thunder. The hierarchy's decision to declare the story of St. Barbara a legend and the improbability that such a person ever existed is irrelevant to them.

The history of Christianity shows that orthodox objections to syncretism have less to do with the purity of faith, and more with who has the right to determine what is to be considered normative and official. For the articulation of religious understandings, beliefs, and practices to be an act of liberation, it has to be an act of self-determination, not an attempt to comply with what the "official" church says, with what it considers to be orthodox. This is why *mujerista* theology does not shrink from claiming that the fusion of Christian, Amerindian, and African religious strands operative in the lives of Latinas may be good and life-giving.

Popular religiosity as a subculture pervades the lives of Latinas. Perhaps because of the precariousness of our lives, perhaps because our variety of Christianity is an intrinsic part of our culture, and because we are keenly aware of our culture since it is different from the dominant one, religion, religious thinking and practices, provide for us the moods and motivations operative in our day-to-day life. Questions of ultimate meaning, understandings of the divine and of ourselves and of our relationship to the divine are not matters for religion experts only. No, they are matters which preoccupy, touch, and affect everyone. "*Si Dios quiere*," God willing, is not an empty phrase for us. The belief that the divine cares about us and participates in our lives is something very real for us, something constantly taken into consideration. There is no doubt for us that what we are able to accomplish is due to much hard work; but it is also a fact that God has had something to do with it, and due credit is given to the divine by fulfilling promises at any physical or monetary cost.[62]

The day-to-day acknowledgment of the role the divine plays in our lives as well as a firm belief in the ongoing revelation of God in the midst of and through the community of faith is what leads us to claim the lived-experience of Latinas as the source of *mujerista* theology. This belief continues the long tradition very much present in the Hebrew Scriptures that God's revelation happens in and through the history of Israel's people. Salvation history *is* not something different from what actually happened to the Jewish people. Salvation history *is* precisely what happened to them; it has to do with how they interpreted what happened to them, with the role that God played in their struggles and accomplishments. Our claiming Latinas' lived-experience as the source of our theology is firmly rooted in this biblical understanding of the revelation of God. Knowing that as Latinas we have indeed been created in the image and likeness of God, trusting that our struggle to be faithful to our understandings of the divine make us worthy members of the Christian community of faith, we believe that God's revelation happens in the day-to-day living of Latinas.

Spanish: "The Language of the Angels"[63]

The Spanish language functions for Latinas not only as a means of communication but as a means of identification. Spanish has become "the incarnation and symbol" of our whole culture, making us feel that here in the U.S.A. we are one people, no matter what our country of origin is. The Spanish language identifies us by distinguishing us from the rest of society. It gives us a specificity that we need to be a certain kind of people within a culture not our own.[64]

White Americans are willing to accept Latinos who are "white enough" as one of them when we become sufficiently middle-class and sufficiently "Anglicized." Many African Americans are also ready to claim black Latinos. But Latinas in general consider ourselves neither white nor black:[65]

> *. . . for Hispanics the prime identifier is not color, but language, and so the Hispanic, whether black or white, tends to think that those who speak Spanish are 'his [sic] people' no matter what their color, while those who speak English (whether black or white) are 'the others'. For Hispanics the 'Anglo' is not the Anglo-Saxon, but the Anglophone.*[66]

The Spanish language for us Latinos here in the U.S.A. has become "the bearer of identity and values."[67] Our attachment to it is such that even those Latinos born and raised in the U.S.A. who understand a little Spanish and can speak only a few words insist on saying that they do know Spanish. Since the importance of Spanish for Latinas is not so much to be able to communicate but to be able to identify each other, grammatical and pronunciation correctness is totally secondary. For us Spanish is indeed a social construct and, therefore, we do not use Spanish to exclude from our communities those who know little Spanish or use it improperly.[68]

In a market study done in 1981 for the SIN National Spanish 'Television Network, 90 percent of Latinos claimed they knew at least enough Spanish to get by. Only 1 percent of Latinos said they knew only English. Twenty-three percent said they knew only Spanish, 20 percent said they knew Spanish and enough English to get by, 47 percent consider themselves bilingual, and 9 percent know English and enough Spanish to get by. Based on data gathered by the 1980 census and considering that any undercounting probably happened among undocumented Latinos who speak mostly Spanish, one can conclude that only in 10 percent of Latino homes is Spanish not used.[69]

The numbers of those who speak Spanish and use it at home go hand in hand with our sense of national allegiance: 88 percent consider themselves Latinos, 46 percent claiming they are Latino first, American second, and 42 percent saying that they are equally Latino and American. They also are in line with the 89-percent that either agree or strongly agree with the statement, "we should pass on to our children a sense of belonging to our religious and national tradition."[70]

The study also presented an open-ended question asking for the aspect of Latino culture and traditions that we feel is most important to preserve. Eighty one percent mentioned the

Spanish language as the most important—83 percent of Puerto Ricans, 77 percent of Mexicans, and 95 percent of Cubans.[71]

Yet maintaining usage of and fluidity in Spanish is no easy task for Latinas. In the U.S.A. the governing principle in this regard continues to be "one population—one language . . . [and it] has assumed overtones of moral, social, and psychological normalcy."[72] The recent successful attempts in several parts of the U.S.A. where Latinos are numerous to pass a law declaring English *the* official language make this obvious. At the same time this insistence on having an English-as-official-language law indicates that Spanish is used widely in certain states in the U.S.A. Laws will not stop Latinas from using Spanish, because it is a social construct that has enormous importance in maintaining our identity, and we will do everything in our power to continue to speak it and teach it to our children. We are aware that as an oppressed group we are not able to preserve the use of Spanish because we are "limited in being able to establish and control institutions of language monitoring, language ideologization [*sic*] and, most particularly, language use via the establishment and control of significant political and economic bases of . . . [our] own."[73] It is our hope, however, that the constant flow of new Spanish speaking people into the U.S.A. plus the frequent return to their country of origin of Latinos will help us preserve Spanish.

Latino Ethnicity: Social Construct

In these two first chapters I have analyzed the main elements of Latino ethnicity. Our ties with Latin America and the Spanish speaking Caribbean, *mestizaje*, our multilayered oppression and struggle for survival, popular religiosity, the insistence on speaking *español*, Spanish, and our *proyecto histórico*—all of these are pieces that together constitute and shape Latinas' ethnicity. It is the intersection and interplay of all of these elements that give us our pecularities and distinctiveness as Latina Women. In other words, the shared cultural norms, values, identities, and behaviors that form the core of our ethnicity are linked to these six elements we have explored.

At the same time we know that these cultural norms, values, identities, and behaviors are irreversibly impacted by the prejudice and discrimination to which we are subjected in this society.[74] This means that the oppression we suffer as Latinas has become an integral part of our ethnicity—of Latino ethnicity—and, therefore, it impacts every aspect of our lives as does our daily struggle to survive.

Notes

1. José Míguez Bonino, *Doing Theology in a Revolutionary Situation* (Philadelphia: Fortress Press, 1975), 38–39. Chap. 3 of this book is perhaps the most detailed description of the meaning of *proyecto histórico* by a Latin American liberation theologian. *Mujerista* theology appropriates this term critically according to our lived-experience.
2. Audrey Lorde, "Poems Are Not Luxuries," *Chrysalis* 3 (1977): 8.
3. See Gustavo Gutiérrez, *A Theology of Liberation*. (Maryknoll: Orbis Books, 1988), xxxix, 83–91. See also Gustavo Gutiérrez, *The Truth Shall Make You Free* (Maryknoll: Orbis Books, 1990), 14–16, 116–21.

4. Gutiérrez, *Theology of Liberation*, 94.

5. Using Paulo Freire, Gutiérrez sees the relationship of what he calls "utopia" to historical reality as appearing under two aspects: denunciation and annunciation. See Gutiérrez, *Theology of Liberation*, 136–40.

6. This is why we avoid using the terms "minority" or "marginalized." These labels communicate the way the dominant group sees us and not the way we see ourselves; they imply that what we want is to participate in present structures that are oppressive. We see ourselves as a group that has a significant contribution to make precisely because we demand radical change of oppressive structures.

7. See "Larry Rasmussen," *Christianity and Crisis*, 22 October 1990.

8. For the effectiveness of this understanding of struggling to build a preferred future see Renny Golden, *The Hour of the Poor, The Hour of Women* (New York: Crossroad, 1991).

9. We have appropriated Gutiérrez's understanding of the three levels or aspects of the process of liberation. The specifics of each of these aspects arise from our lived-experience as Latinas.

10. Gutiérrez refers to the "Chalcedonian Principle," and uses the Chalcedonian language regarding the two natures of the one person Jesus, in order to clarify the distinctiveness and intrinsic unity of the three aspects of liberation. In this, *mujerista* theology follows Gutiérrez quite closely. The distinctiveness of Latinas' struggle, however, will come in the "content" of each of the three aspects of the process of liberation. See Gutiérrez, *The Truth Shall Make You Free*, 120–24.

11. Following the venerable tradition refered to in Acts 1:26, we cast lots to decide the order in which we would deal with these three aspects of liberation! We know some will try to see in the order we use a certain priority of importance or relevance. That is indeed not our intention.

12. The only reason a *balsero*, a young man who escaped from Cuba in a makeshift raft, could give me for risking his life in such a way was the lack of *libertad* he experienced in Cuba. I assumed that for him, influenced by U.S.A. propaganda, *libertad* had to do with accessibility to consumer goods, with a better material life. But I was wrong. For him *libertad* had to do with self-determination, with wanting something different and being able to work towards making it a reality. Whether I agree or disagree with his assessment of the present Cuban situation, his understanding of *libertad* and his willingness to risk his life for it has helped me to understand what I and other Latinas mean by *libertad*.

13. Cf. Gutiérrez, *The Truth Shall Make You Free*, 132–34.

14. Since psychology is not my field of expertise, my attempt here is only to describe apathy and fear and to locate them in reference to the historical situation Latinas face.

15. This fear is compounded by the fact that seeing ourselves as different from the status quo is an intrinsic element of what it means for us to be Latina.

16. The best proof of this mindset is the name of the U.S.A. government program for Puerto Rico in the middle decades of this century: "Operation Bootstrap." The Puerto Ricans understood very clearly the American expression that was behind that title and they responded painfully and cleverly, "How do you expect us to lift ourselves by our bootstraps when we do not even have boots!"

17. I use the word "God" here not to refer to one divine being but rather as a collective noun that embraces God, the saints, dead ones whom we love, manifestations of the Virgin

(not always the same as manifestations of Mary, the mother of Jesus), Jesus (not very similar to the Jesus of the Gospels), Amerindian and African gods, and so forth.

18. To the accusation that this places us in the neo-orthodox ranks, we answer that Latinas have not been part of the "modern experiment"; that the kind of belief in the divine that for the enlightened, scientific mind signifies a lack of autonomous, critical, rational thought, is for us a concrete experience that we use as a key element in the struggle for liberation. See Christine Gudorf, "Liberation Theology's Use of Scripture—A Response to First World Critics," in *Interpretation—a Journal of Bible and Theology*. (January 1987): 12–13.
19. Ada María Isasi-Díaz and Yolanda Tarango, *Hispanic Women: Prophetic Voice in the Church* (Minneapolis: Fortress Press, 1992), 90.
20. Gutiérrez, *Theology of Liberation*, 24.
21. Though indeed we have much to learn from the Base Ecclesial Communities that are at the heart of the Latin American liberation struggle, our *comunidades de fe* have to develop their own characteristics based on our lived-experiences and needs. For a concise articulation of what Base Ecclesial Communities are and the role they play in Latin America, see Pablo Richard, "The Church of the Poor in the Decade of the 90s," *LADOC* XXI (Nov./Dec. 1990): 11–29.
22. See John Stuart Mill, *Utilitarianism* (New York: Bobbs-Merrill, 1957).
23. See also Acts 4:35.
24. For an excellent short analysis of six main justice theories see, Karen Lebacqz, *Six Theories of Justice* (Minneapolis: Augsburg, 1986).
25. For a more comprehensive analysis of the meaning of solidarity see Ada María Isasi-Díaz, Solidarity: Love of Neighbor in the 1980s," in *Lift Every Voice—Constructing Christian Theologies from the Underside*, ed. Susan Brooks Thistlethwaite and Mary Potter Engels (San Francisco: Harper and Row, 1990).
26. José Míguez Bonino, "Nuevas tendencias en teología," *Pasos* (1985): 22
27. Fernando Romero, "Sentido práctico y flexibilidad popular," *Páginas* 111 (Octubre 1991); 43. See also, Arthur F. McGovern, *Liberation Theology and Its Critics* (Maryknoll: Orbis Books, 1990), 177–212.
28. For an amplification of this theme see Isasi-Díaz, "Solidarity," 37.
29. Teresa L. Amott and Julie A. Matthaei, *Race, Gender & Work* (Boston: South End, 1991), 346–48.
30. Michael Parenti, *Power and the Powerless* (New York: St. Martin's, 1978), 226.
31. Romero, "Sentido práctico," 45–47.
32. Isasi-Díaz and Tarango, *Hispanic Women*, 77–80, 109–10; see below chap. 6
33. We set the basis for this section in chap. 3 of Isasi-Díaz and Tarango, *Hispanic Women.*
34. Though popular religiosity among Latinas is suffused with Catholic rituals and understandings, there begins to be a Protestant perspective regarding popular religiosity. See Tito Paredes, "Popular religiosity: A Protestant Perspective" *Missiology* XX, no. 2 (April 1992): 205–20; see also Juan Sepúlveda, "Pentecostalism as Popular Religiosity," *International Review of Mission* 78 (January 1989): 80–88.
35. Juan José Huitrado-Rizo, MCCJ, "Hispanic Popular Religiosity: The Expression of a People Coming to Life," *New Theology Review* 3, no. 4 (November 1990): 43–54.
36. Gutiérrez, *Theology of Liberation*, 13.

37. Clifford Geertz, *The Interpretation of Culture* (New York: Basic Books, 1973), 90.
38. Robert J. Schreiter, *Constructing Local Theologies* (Maryknoll: Orbis Books, 1985), 87–88.
39. Luis N. Rivera Pagán, *Evangelización y violencia—la conquista de América* (San Juan, Puerto Rico: Editorial Cemi, 1991), 1.
40. Ibid., 14–21. Rivera Pagán carefully explains how the discovery was accompanied by the juridical act of taking possession.
41. This definition of enculturation is found in Paulo Agirrebaltzategi, *Configuración eclesial de las culturas* (Bilbao, España: Universidad de Deusto, 1976), 82. The author explains the three terms acculturation, enculturation, and culturization on pp. 81–82. He indicates that what has become cultural expression is what is transcultural or transcendent. It also means the form in which culturally the Gospel message is realized in the Church. I use the term here in a narrower sense to mean simply that which has become a cultural expression.
42. Juan Luis Segundo, *The Liberation of Theology* (Maryknoll: Orbis Books, 1982), 185. Though it is true that an increasing number of Latinas are participating in denominations and churches that give great importance to the Bible, the majority of Latinas still relate to the Catholic church and do not use the Bible often. *Mujerista* theologians are concerned with the way the Bible is imposed on Latinas by some churches since it is done in a way that often threatens rather than enhances our moral agency.
43. The same is often true of sermons we hear on Sundays. Imaginative interpretations are not considered "good theology" when Latinas do it, but it is all right when priests and/or pastors do it.
44. Sixto J. García and Orlando Espín are doing very exciting work on developing a Hispanic American theology using popular religiosity as its key element. In 1987 and 1988 they gave workshops at the Catholic Theological Society of America Conferences. Only synopses of the papers they presented there have been published. See Orlando Espín and Sixto Garciá, "Hispanic-American Theology," *Catholic Theological Society of America Proceedings* 42 (1987): 114–19, and "The Sources of Hispanic Theology," *Catholic Theological Society of America Proceedings* 43 (1988): 122–25. In 1989 they gave a full presentation that has been published. See Garcia and Espín, "'Lilies of the Field'," *Catholic Theological Society of America Proceedings* 44 (1989): 70–90.
45. Espín and García, "Toward a Hispanic-American Theology," unpublished notes of workshop presented at *The Catholic Theological Society of America.* (1987): 6–7. All quotations from Espín and García's presentation at the CTSA conferences in 1987 and 1988 will be from unpublished notes the authors passed out which are much more complete than the published synopses.
46. Sacramentals in the Roman Catholic tradition are things or actions—candles, processions—used as reminders of God's effective presence in the world. The laity has access to the use of sacramentals without having to depend on the priests.
47. Manuel M. Marzal, "La religiosidad popular en el Perú" in *Panorama de la teología latinoamericana*, I, ed. Equipo Seladoc (Salamanca: Ediciones Sígueme, 1975), 28–29. These are adaptations of elements presented by Marzal that I have translated in such a way as to exclude the judgmental tone of his analysis, which I believe limits the value of popular religiosity.
48. See Segundo Galilea, "The Theology of Liberation and the Place of 'Folk Religion,'" in *What Is Religion: An Inquiry for Christian Theology.*, ed. Mircea Eliade and David W. Tracy, *Concilium* 136 (Edinburgh: T. & T. Clark, 1980), 43.

49. Ibid, 44.
50. Michael R. Candelaria, *Popular Religion and Liberation* (Albany: State Univ. of New York Press, 1990), 13.
51. Ibid., 43.
52. Espín and García, "Sources of Hispanic Theology," unpublished notes of workshop presented at the Catholic Theological Society of America (1988): 4.
53. García and Espín, 'Lilies of the Field,' 72.
54. María Pilar Aquino, *Nuestro Clamor par La Vida* (San Jose, Costa Rica: Editorial D.E.I., 1992), 218–22.
55. See Isasi-Díaz and Tarango, *Hispanic Women*, 67, where we indicate that popular religiosity could offer needed correctives to some of the religious understandings of "official" Christianity.
56. Ibid., 14–26. See also II Consulta Ecuménica de Pastoral Indígena, *Aporte de los pueblos indígenas de América Latina a la teología cristiana* (Quito, Ecuador, 1986). Espín and García, "Toward a Hispanic," 4. Jaime R. Vidal, "Popular Religion among the Hispanics in the General Area of the Archdiocese of Newark," in *Presencia Nueva* (Newark: Office of Research and Planning, Archdiocese of Newark 1988), 250–54.
57. Espín and García, "Toward a Hispanic-American Theology," 17. On this point Espín and García contradict themselves. In spite of the assertion they make here, they make only one reference to Amerindian and African religions and not in a very positive light. They place the Amerindian and African religious elements operative in popular religiosity in what they call a "second constellation" with which they seem to deal only insofar as it goes hand in hand with the "first constellation," which they call "popular catholicism." See pp. 4–6.
58. Tom F. Driver, *Christ in a Changing World* (New York: Crossroad, 1981), 32–81.
59. See Isasi-Díaz and Tarango, *Hispanic Women*, 13–55.
60. John F. Baldovin, S.J., "The Liturgical Year: Calendar for a Just Community," in *Liturgy and Spirituality in Context*, ed. Eleanor Bernstein, C.S.J. (Collegeville: The Liturgical Press, 1990), 104.
61. Compare the difference in interpretation and explanation of Guadalupe between Elizondo and Lafaye. See Virgilio Elizondo, *La morenita* (Liguori, MO: Liguori Publications, 1981), and J. Lafaye, *Quetzalcoatl et Guadalupe* (Paris: Gallimard, 1974).
62. One of my earliest memories has to do with fulfilling a promise my father had made to Our Lady of Charity, the title under which Mary is patroness of Cuba. During World War II my father tried to produce glucose from yucca starch. As a chemical engineer he knew that this could be done, but the process is an industrial secret and he had to start from scratch. To be sure he would succeed, he promised Our Lady of Charity a visit to her sanctuary by the whole family if she would help him, enlighten him in his research. He was able to get glucose from yucca starch, something needed and, therefore, profitable during the war. It was not until'a few years later that he was able to keep the promise. We traveled over twelve hours by car and then walked up the hill on the top of which the sanctuary sits. Thus we all honored the divine intervention in the life of my family. I was about seven years old at that time.
63. This is exactly what my grandmother always said!
64. A few years ago I arrived at the very southern tip of Manhattan for a 7 PM meeting. I could not find the building where we were to meet, so I decided to park my car and find someone

who could help me. Since there are no homes in that area, at that hour of the evening it is not unusual to see not a single soul. Finally I saw a man who was emptying trash cans in the back entrance of one of the huge office buildings. I approached him a little apprehensively and asked him for directions. Apologetically, he started in a very broken English to tell me he did not understand me. I stopped him by repeating the question in Spanish. His eyes lit up, he squared his shoulders, and told me he did not know where that building was. He then looked into my eyes and said, "*Venga aca, usted es cubana?*" (Listen here, are you Cuban?) When I told him I was, he became all the more helpful. Talking to me as you do to an old friend, he let me know that the doorman around the corner was also Cuban and that he surely knew the answer to my question. Without thinking much, because he spoke Spanish and was a Cuban, I put aside all the cautions I should have been taking and asked him if he thought my car was safe there. "*No hay problema, no hay problema*" (No problem, no problem). I smiled broadly, thanked him, and went to get directions from the Cuban doorman, whom I was sure would help me because I was his *compatriota* (compatriot), and he did!

65. I am not claiming that there is not racism in our culture, and certainly in our countries of origin, skin color, though dealt with in a different way from the way it is operative in the U.S.A., plays a role in societal stratification.

66. Vidal, "Popular Religion among the Hispanics," 257.

67. Ibid.

68. See Eldin Villafañe, "The Socio-Cultural Matrix of Intergenerational Dynamics: An Agenda for the 90s," *Apuntes* Year 12, no.1 (Spring 1992): 13–20.

69. Justo Gonzdlez, *The Theological Education of Hispanics* (New York: The Fund for Theological Education, 1988), 12. Notice that there is a difference between "knowing" Spanish (the question investigated by the SIN National Spanish Television Network), and "using" Spanish in the home (the focus of the 1980 U.S.A. Census study used by Gonzdlez).

70. *Spanish USA—A Study of the Hispanic Market in the United States*, by Yankelovich, Skelly & White, Inc. (New York: Yankelovich, Skelly & White, 1981), 7, 16.

71. The same table in this study gives a quick handle on what Latinos consider the most valuable elements of our culture which we wish to preserve. Here they are in descending order of importance: care of and respect for elders, music, religion, family/commitment to family, art/literature, food and beverages, love for life/know how to enjoy life, happy people, holidays/celebrations.

72. Joshua A. Fishman, "Language Maintenance," in *Harvard Encyclopedia of Ethnic Groups*, ed. Stephan Thernstrom (Cambridge, MA: The Belknap Press of Harvard Univ. Press, 1980), 631.

73. Ibid., 636.

74. Nelson and Tienda, "The Structuring of Hispanic Ethnicity: Historical and Contemporary Perspectives," in *Ethnicity and Race in the U.S.A.—Toward the Twenty-First Century*, ed. Richard D. Alba (London: Henley Routledge & Kegan Paul, 1985), 53.

Index

CPSIA information can be obtained
at www.ICGtesting.com
Printed in the USA
LVHW03s1217190718
584144LV00003B/7/P

9 781465 277503